Mentor Linguistics

멘토영어학
기출분석

LSI 영어연구소 앤드류 채 편저

교원임용시험 전공영어 대비

PREFACE

어떤 종류의 시험이든 기출문제를 토대로 시험을 준비하는 것은 꼭 필요한 과정 중의 하나이다.

특히 임용시험과 같이 방대한 양을 공부해야 하는 시험일수록 시험 전에 기출분석을 하는 것은 공부의 방향성을 설정할 수 있고 방대한 양을 좁혀서 공부할 수 있게 해준다.

하지만 어떤 주제가 몇 번 출제되었는지 정도의 단순한 접근은 영어학 시험을 준비하는 데 있어서 크게 도움이 되지 않는다. 반복적으로 출제되는 주제가 있다면 그 반복되는 주제의 핵심 개념은 무엇이며 출제자가 수험자에게 무엇을 요구하는지를 파악해야 한다.

이러한 분석이 용이하도록 이 책은 2002~2023학년도까지 출제된 문제를 주제별로 묶고, 각 주제 안에서는 출제된 문제를 연도 순서로 배열해 같은 주제에 대한 출제 방향성의 변화를 좀 더 쉽게 파악할 수 있게 하였다. 각 Chapter는 다음과 같은 3단계 방식으로 구성되었다.

Unit 01 Preview & Review

각 Chapter의 Preview & Review는 기출문제와 관련된 내용만을 간추려서 정리했다. 영어학 준비가 다소 부족한 수험생은 각 Chapter의 Preview & Review를 먼저 가볍게 읽은 후 문제를 풀어보고 중요 개념을 다시 정리하는 방식으로 공부한다. 언어학에 기초가 있는 수험생이라면 Unit 02의 문제를 먼저 풀어본 후 필요한 부분만 선택적으로 Preview & Review를 확인하는 것도 좋은 방법일 것이다.

Preview & Review는 해당 분야의 전반적인 내용을 요약한 것이므로 그 분야의 전체 내용이나 내용의 흐름을 파악하는 데 도움이 될 것이다.

Unit 02 Questions

2013년 12월 임용시험부터 서답형 방식으로 문제 유형이 바뀌었다. 그 이전에 출제된 문제들은 서답형 문제로 변형하지 않고 예전 출제 원형을 그대로 유지했다. 과거 출제 방식과 현재 출제 방식의 유사점/차이점 파악이 앞으로 출제될 문제의 방향성을 예측하는 데 도움이 되기 때문이다. 문제의 형식이 어떻게 변화되었는지를 파악하고, 주로 어떠한 내용이 문제로 주어졌는지도 파악하기를 바란다. 기출문제를 풀어봄으로써 어떻게 시험에 대비해야 할지에 대한 계획이 더욱 구체적이고 명확해질 것이다.

Answer Key

2013년 이전의 기출문제 중 우리말로 답을 적게 되어 있는 문제도 현재 출제 방식에 대한 연습을 위해 영어로 답안을 제시했다. 답안을 보지 않고 본인 스스로 먼저 답안을 작성한 후에 Answer Key에 제시된 답안과 비교하면서 답안 서술 방식을 익히기 바란다. 제시된 답안은 하나의 sample이며 guideline일 뿐이다. 본인이 작성한 답안과 제시된 모범답안을 비교한 후 서술형 답안 작성 시 빠지면 안 되는 핵심 내용이 무엇인지를 파악하고 스스로 다시 수정 답안을 작성해 보는 방식을 권한다.

기출문제를 풀 때 항상 염두에 둘 것은 출제자의 의도 파악이다. 문제를 풀 때 문제의 direction을 잘 읽고 출제자가 묻고 있는 내용에 대해서만 답안을 작성하는 훈련을 하길 바란다. 주어진 지문의 내용을 정확하게 파악하고 문제에 적확한 내용을 문제가 요구하는 형식으로 답안을 작성해야 감점 없이 점수를 받을 수 있다.

꿈을 이루기 위해 열심히 도전하는 여러분에게 이 책이 조금이라도 도움이 되기를 바란다.

2023년 4월

앤드류채

CONTENTS

Syntax

CONTENTS

MEN
TOR

Mentor Linguistics

멘토영어학
기출분석

Part 01

Syntax

MEN
TOR

Mentor Linguistics

멘토영어학
기출분석

Preview & Review

01 Raising and Control Constructions

1.1. Constructions and Labels

A primary motivation for the attention given to Raising and Control in generative syntax is the striking similarity of the constructions in English. This is obvious in the data in (1) and (2), which illustrate **Raising-to-Subject** and **Subject Control**.

(1) Barnett seemed to understand the formula.
(2) Barnett tried to understand the formula.

The surface strings in (1) and (2) are identical: an intransitive matrix clause with an infinitival complement, NP-V-to-VP. The sole surface difference is the choice of the matrix verb, *seem* vs. *try*. However, as will be seen in the following section, there are fundamental differences between the two sentences that center on the subject of the matrix clause. In the Raising construction in (1), the subject *Barnett* is semantically linked only to the embedded verb *understand*, while in (2) it is semantically linked to both the matrix verb *try* and the embedded verb. For this reason, the subject in (2) is said to "control" the reference of the subject of the embedded clause and the construction has come to be referred to as "Subject Control."

Parallel data are found with transitive matrix verbs where the locus of these differences is the immediately postverbal NP.

(3) Barnett believed the doctor to have examined Tilman.
(4) Barnett persuaded the doctor to examine Tilman.

Again, the surface strings are (virtually) identical, but there are fundamental differences in the characteristics of the NPs immediately following the matrix verbs. In (3), *the doctor* is semantically linked only with the embedded verb *examine*, while in (4) *the doctor* is semantically linked to both the matrix verb *persuade* and the embedded verb. The construction in (3) is referred to as Raising-to-Object and that in (4) as Object Control. Additionally, there are constructions such as (5) that parallel the surface strings (3) and (4).

(5) Barnett promised the doctor to examine Tilman.

In (5), the subject *Barnett* but not the object *the doctor* is semantically linked to the embedded predicate, and the sentence, like (2), is a case of Subject Control.

Whether or not the structures in (1-5) are **Raising or Control depend on properties of the matrix verb**, that is, the Raising and Control that are examined here are lexically governed. Now, we first turn to diagnostics for distinguishing the two constructions.

1.2. Empirical Distinctions Between Raising and Control

Despite the superficial similarities in word order and morphology, raising and control constructions differ in a variety of ways, many of them related to meaning. This section outlines the traditional arguments for distinguishing Raising and Control.

1.2.1. Thematic roles

Raising and control structures have distinct thematic structures; that is, the roles of the participants in the state of affairs described in the sentence are distinct. In the case of intransitive verbs, the matrix subject appears to have a role only in the action of the complement. Note that (1) is truth-conditionally equivalent to (6).

(6) It seemed that Barnett understood the formula.

In (6), *Barnett* is assigned the thematic role of "experiencer" as the subject of *understand*. *It*, on the other hand, as a pleonastic (or semantically empty) element, receives no thematic role, showing that the predicate *seem* need not assign a thematic role to its subject. The thematic structure of (1) is identical to (6). *Barnett* is understood to be an experiencer, but has no other thematic role assigned. Conversely, in (2), *Barnett* appears to have two roles in the sentence, one as experiencer of *understand* and one as agent of *try*. The control verb *try*, unlike the raising verb *seem*, assigns a thematic role to its subject. Thus, intransitive raising and control verbs have different thematic structures.

Transitive raising and control verbs exhibit a similar difference, with the difference residing in the postverbal argument. In (4), *Barnett persuaded the doctor to examine Tilman*, *the doctor* plays two roles in the sentence: one as the agent of the embedded verb *examine* (i.e., the examiner) and the other as the object of persuasion (i.e., the persuadee) of the verb *persuade*. In (3), *Barnett believed the doctor to have examined Tilman*, *the doctor* plays a single role, that of agent or examiner. That is, (3) is truth-conditionally equivalent to (7).

(7) Barnett believed that the doctor had examined Tilman.

In (7), as in (3), *believe* has two thematic roles to assign: agent to its subject and theme to the clausal complement. Thus, transitive raising and control predicates have distinct thematic structures, just as intransitives do.

1.2.2. Embedded passive

Raising and control structures can be distinguished by their behavior when the complement clause is passive. For raising predicates such as *seem*, a sentence with a passive complement is synonymous with the same sentence with an active complement. This is illustrated in (8).

(8) a. Barnett seemed to have read the book.
    b. The book seemed to have been read by Barnett.

With an intransitive control verb, the sentences with embedded passive are not synonymous with the active, and, in fact, an embedded passive is not always possible.

(9) a. The doctor tried to examine Tilman.

b. Tilman tried to be examined by the doctor.

(10) a. Barnett tried to read the book.

b. #The book tried to be read by Barnett.

The sentences in (9) are not synonymous. In (9a), it is the doctor who attempts the examination; however, the attempt may fail for some reason, be it Tilman's refusal to be examined or some other circumstance. On the other hand, in (9b), it is Tilman who makes the attempt, but may be unsuccessful due to the doctor's refusal or some other circumstance. (10) shows that the passive is not possible when the object of the embedded clause is an inanimate entity such as a book. This relates to the thematic structure of *try*, which assigns the agent role to its subject, and so in the normal state of affairs requires a sentient, volitional entity as subject.

The same situation is encountered with transitive raising and control predicates. With raising predicates, sentences with embedded passive and active are truth-conditionally equivalent; so, (11) and (3) are synonymous.

(11) Barnett believed Tilman to have been examined by the doctor.

In both (3) and (11), Barnett's belief is that the doctor examined Tilman. In contrast, with a matrix control predicate, the embedded passive and active are not synonymous. The state of affairs expressed in (12) is not the same as that expressed in (4).

(12) Barnett persuaded Tilman to be examined by the doctor.

In (12), Barnett must persuade Tilman of the need for the examination, while in (4), it is the doctor that must be persuaded. The synonymy or nonsynonymy of sentences with active and passive complements thus provides a second diagnostic for distinguishing Raising and Control.

1.2.3. Selectional restrictions

Another diagnostic distinguishing raising and control constructions is available from selectional restrictions imposed by embedded predicates. For semantic reasons, many predicates require that one argument or another have particular properties. This is illustrated in (13).

(13) a. The rock is granite.

    b. #The rock understands the important issues of the day.

(13a) is a perfectly well-formed sentence; the predicate *be granite* selects for a subject that can in fact be granite. (13b), on the other hand, is pragmatically odd; the predicate *understand* requires that its subject be sentient. Since rocks do not have this property, (13b), while syntactically well-formed, is semantically ill-formed.

The influence of the selectional restrictions of predicates of complement clauses provides a diagnostic for distinguishing Raising from Control. The data in (14, 15) illustrate.

(14) a. The rock seems to be granite.

    b. #The rock seems to understand the important issues of the day.

(15) a. #The rock tried to be granite.

    b. #The rock tried to understand the important issues of the day.

Looking first at (14), we see that (14a) is perfectly well-formed, while (14b) is semantically odd. The data precisely parallel the situation in (13). In (14a), the embedded predicate is *be granite*, and *the rock* can be the subject of the entire sentence, while in (14b), the embedded predicate is *understand*, and having *the rock* as subject of *seem* is semantically ill-formed. Thus, it is possible to account for the judgments in (14) on the basis of the semantics of the embedded predicate. With the control predicate *try*, the situation changes. Both sentences in (15) are semantically ill-formed, the embedded predicate having no influence over the judgments of acceptability. In fact, the oddness in (15a) and (15b) results from the semantic requirements of *try*; *try* assigns the agent role to its subject, which requires an entity capable of volition. The sentences in (15) are ill-formed precisely because rocks violate this selectional restriction. Raising constructions can thus be distinguished from control constructions on the basis of whether or not the selectional restrictions of the **embedded** predicate can determine the semantic well-formedness of the sentence.

The sentences in (16) and (17) show that the situation is similar with transitive raising and control predicates. With raising predicates such as *believe*, when the selectional restrictions of the embedded predicate are satisfied, the sentence is well-formed (16a), but when they are violated, the sentence is semantically ill-formed (16b). As (17) shows, with control verbs such as *persuade* the situation changes. Despite the fact that the selectional restrictions of the embedded predicate are satisfied in (17a), this sentence is as semantically ill-formed as (17b). The reason is that *persuade* requires a sentient object, an object that is capable of being persuaded; *the rock* satisfies this requirement in neither (17a) nor (17b).

(16) a. Barnett believed the rock to be granite.

    b. #Barnett believed the rock to understand the issues of the day.

(17) a. #Barnett persuaded the rock to be granite.

    b. #Barnett persuaded the rock to understand the issues of the day.

1.2.4. Pleonastic subjects

A further diagnostic where this is relevant involves the *it* of meteorological expressions and existential *there*. While either can be the subject of an intransitive raising predicate such as *seem* (18), neither is possible with control predicates (19).

(18) a. It seemed to be raining.

    b. There seems to be a unicorn in the garden.

(19) a. *It tried to be raining.

    b. *There tried to be a unicorn in the garden.

Since pleonastic elements are semantically empty, they can be assigned no thematic role. Therefore, they are not possible subjects for verbs such as *try*, which assign thematic roles to their subjects, in this case agent, and the sentences in (19) are ungrammatical. Conversely, as was seen above, intransitive raising verbs do not assign a thematic role to their subjects and so pleonastic elements are semantically allowable subjects. As the sentences in (18) show, as long as the pleonastic subjects are sanctioned by the predicates of the embedded clause, they are possible subjects of intransitive raising predicates.

Again, parallel data are found with transitive raising and control predicates.

(20) a. Barnett believed it to have rained.

b. Barnett believed there to be a unicorn in the garden.

(21) a. *Barnett persuaded it to rain.

b. *Barnett persuaded there to be a unicorn in the garden.

Raising predicates such as *believe* accept meteorological *it* or existential *there* as postverbal NPs (20), while control predicates such as *persuade* do not (21). Again, the ungrammaticality of the sentences in (21) is attributable to the fact that *persuade* has a thematic role to assign to its object, and this role cannot be assigned to semantically empty elements such as *it* and *there*.

1.2.5. Idiom chunks

A final diagnostic for distinguishing raising from control constructions comes from the behavior of idiomatic expressions. In (22), *the cat* can take on a special meaning.

(22) The cat is out of the bag.

The sentence in (22) is ambiguous. When interpreted literally it describes a situation in which a particular feline is not in a particular container, and *the cat* denotes that feline. As an idiom, (22) means that a one-time secret is no longer a secret, and *the cat* denotes that secret. Clearly this is an unusual meaning of *the cat* and is only possible when *the cat* occurs in this particular idiomatic expression.

As (23) and (24) show, the possibility of idiomatic interpretations distinguishes Raising from Control.

(23) a. The cat seemed to be out of the bag.

    b. ?The cat tried to be out of the bag.

(24) a. Tina believed the cat to be out of the bag by now.

    b. ?Tina persuaded the cat to be out of the bag.

With raising predicates, expressions can retain their idiomatic interpretation: (23a) and (24a) can still be interpreted as describing situations in which *the cat* can refer to a secret. On the contrary, with control predicates, the idiomatic interpretation is no longer possible: in (23b) and (24b) *the cat* can only be interpreted as referring to a particular feline.

02 Tough Movement Sentences

The object of an infinitive clause in an extraposition pattern sentence like that shown in (30a) may be moved out of its clause into the position occupied by *it,* to produce a sentence that has an identical meaning as shown in (30b), The rule that does this is called *tough movement.*

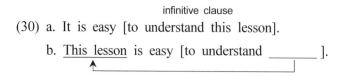

(30) a. It is easy [to understand this lesson].

   b. This lesson is easy [to understand _____].

Although the infinitive clause in (30) has no overt subject, *tough* movement also operates on infinitive clauses with subjects, as illustrated in (31).

(31) a. It's easy for John to understand this lesson.

   b. This lesson is easy for John to understand.

Moreover, the object that is moved into main clause subject position can be the object of a preposition in the infinitive clause, as in (32).

(32) a. It's a real **pleasure** to work with John.

   b. John is a real **pleasure** to work with.

Tough movement cannot be applied to all extraposition pattern sentences with infinitive clauses. For *tough* movement to apply, the main clause must have *be,* or a similar verb, followed by either

- an ***ease/difficulty adjective*** such as *dangerous, difficult, easy, fun, hard, impossible, pleasant, simple, tough, or wonderful,* or
- an **NP** that has a similar "ease/difficulty" meaning, for example, *a chore, a cinch, a joy, a pain, a piece of cake, a pleasure, a snap.*

Applying *tough* movement to sentences in which *be* is followed by an adjective or NP that is not a member of the ease/difficulty set results in ungrammatical sentences, as illustrated in (33) and (34).

(33) a. It is <u>possible</u> to see the director.

     b. *The director is <u>possible</u> to see.

(34) a. It is a real <u>honor</u> to work with Professor Hobson.

     b. *Professor Hobson is a real <u>honor</u> to work with.

03 Hollow To-infinitivals: As Complement to Predicative Adjectives and Nouns

Consider the sentences below:

[5] i _Max_ is **impossible** to live with _____.

    ii _The assignment_ was an absolute **pain** to do _____.

A sample of adjectives and nouns (or nominals) licensing this construction is given in:

[6] i (a)

awkward	bad	boring	convenient	cumbersome
dangerous	depressing	desirable	difficult	dreadful
easy	embarrassing	essential	exciting	expensive
fashionable	fine	good	hard	ideal
impossible	instructive	interesting	nice	odd
painful	pleasant	safe	simple	tedious
ticklish	tough	tricky	useful	wonderful

   (b)

bastard	bitch	breeze	cinch	delight
devil	doddle	dream	embarrassment	joy
nightmare	pain	piece of cake	pig	pleasure

  ii

available	beautiful	fit	free	frosty
homely	pretty	ready	soft	suitable

The adjectives and nouns in [6i] have to do mainly with **the ease or difficulty of the situation described in the infinitival clause or with one's emotional attitude to it**. Note that _impossible_ belongs in the class but _possible_ does not: _That claim is impossible_ / _*possible to substantiate_. PPs with similar meanings are also occasionally found: _The temptation was beyond his capacity to resist_. A number of nouns used in this construction (including, for example, the first four cited in [ib]) belong to colloquial style. The adjectives in [ii] are semantically and syntactically less homogeneous. Some are collocationally quite restricted: _The air was frosty to breathe; They were pretty to look at; Silk was soft to touch._

The main difference between [6i] and [6ii], however, is that the former also license ordinary *to*-infinitivals as subject or extraposed subject:

[7] i) a. *His speech* was embarrassing / an embarrassment [to listen to _____].
b. It was embarrassing / an embarrassment [to listen to his speech].

ii) a. *The document* is now ready [for you to sign _____].
b. *It is now ready [for you to sign the document].

04 Control Theory

Let us start by defining some terminology. This terminology is subtly similar to that of the binding theory, but it is different. If PRO gets its meaning from another DP, then PRO is said to be **controlled**. This is identical to the notion coreferent and very similar to the notion **bound** (we will make this distinction clearer below). The DP that serves as PRO's antecedent is called its controller.

We are going to contrast two different kinds of PRO. The first kind is called **arbitrary PRO** (or **PROarb**). The meaning of this pronoun is essentially "someone":

(1) [PRO$_{arb}$ to find a new mate], go to a dating service.

Arbitrary PRO is not controlled by anything. Arbitrary PRO is a bit like an R-expression or a pronoun, in that it can get its meaning from outside the sentence.

Non-arbitrary PRO (henceforth simply PRO) also comes in two varieties. On one hand we have what is called **obligatory control**. Consider the sentence in (2). Here, PRO must refer to *Jean*. It can't refer to anyone else:

(2) Jean$_i$ tried PRO$_{i/*j}$ to behave.

There are other circumstances where PRO does not have to be (but can be) controlled. This is called **optional control**, and is seen in (3):

(3) Robert$_i$ knows that it is essential [PRO$_{i/j}$ to be well-behaved].

PRO here can mean two different things. It can either refer to *Robert* or it can have an arbitrary PRO$_{arb}$ reading (indicated in (3) with the subscript$_j$). You can see this by looking at the binding of the following two extensions of this sentence:

(4) a. Robert$_i$ knows that it is essential [PRO$_i$ to be good on his$_i$ birthday].

    b. Robert$_i$ knows that it is essential [PRO$_j$ to be good on one's$_j$ birthday].

(4a) has the controlled meaning (as seen by the binding of *his*); (4b) has the arbitrary reading (as seen by the presence of one's).

With this in mind let's return to the central question of this section. Is PRO an anaphor, a pronoun, or an R-expression? We can dismiss the R-expression option right out of hand. R-expressions must always be free. PRO is only sometimes free (=not controlled). This makes it seem more like a pronoun; pronouns can be either free or bound. The data in (3) seems to support this – PRO is behaving very much like a pronoun. Compare (3) to the pronoun in (5).

(5) Robert$_i$ knows it is essential [that he$_{i/j}$ is well-behaved].

You'll notice that the indexing on (5), which has a pronoun, is identical to the indexing on PRO in (3). We might hypothesize then that PRO is a pronoun. This can't be right, however. Recall that we also have situations where PRO must be bound (=controlled) as in the obligatory control sentence *Jean$_i$ tried PRO$_{i/*j}$ to behave*. This makes PRO look like an anaphor, since anaphors are obligatorily bound. Williams (1980) suggests that in obligatory control constructions PRO must be c-commanded by its controller, just as an anaphor must be c-commanded by its antecedent. However, as should be obvious, this can't be right either. First, as noted above, we have situations where PRO is free (as in (1)); anaphors can never be free. Second, if we take the binding theory, PRO and its controller *Jean* are in different binding domains, violating Principle A. We thus have a conundrum: PRO doesn't seem to be an R-expression, a pronoun, or an anaphor. It seems to be a beast of an altogether different color.

Since the distribution of PRO does not lend itself to the binding theory, an entirely different module of the grammar has been proposed to account for PRO. This is called **control theory**. Control theory is the bane of professional theoreticians and students alike. It is, quite simply, the least elegant part of syntactic theory. We'll have a brief look at it here, but will come to no satisfying conclusions.

First let's observe that some parts of control are sensitive to syntactic structure. Consider what can control PRO in (6):

(6) [Jean$_i$'s father]$_j$ is reluctant PRO$_{j/*i}$ to leave.

If you draw the tree for (6), you'll see that while the whole DP *Jean's father* c-commands PRO, *Jean* by itself does not. The fact that *Jean* cannot control PRO strongly suggests that there is a c-command requirement on obligatory control, as argued by Williams (1980). This said, the structure of the sentence doesn't seem to be the only thing that comes into play with control. Compare now a subject control sentence to an object control one:

(7) a. Robert$_i$ is reluctant [PRO$_i$ to behave].   *subject control*
    b. Susan$_j$ ordered Robert$_i$ [PRO$_{i/*j}$ to behave].   *object control*

In both these sentences PRO must be controlled by *Robert*. PRO in (7b) cannot refer to *Susan*. This would seem to suggest that the closest DP that c-commands PRO must control it. In (7a), *Robert* is the only possible controller, so it controls PRO. In (7b), there are two possible controllers: *Susan* and *Robert*. But only *Robert*, which is structurally closer to PRO, can control it. This hypothesis works well in most cases, but the following example shows it must be wrong:

(8) Jean$_i$ promised Susan$_j$ [PRO$_{i/*j}$ to behave].   *subject control*

In this sentence it is *Jean* doing the behaving, not *Susan*. PRO must be controlled by *Jean*, even though *Susan* is structurally closer. So structure doesn't seem to be the only thing determining which DP does the controlling.

One hypothesis is that the particular main clause predicate determines which DP does the controlling. That is, the theta grid specifies what kind of control is involved. There are various ways we could encode this. One is to mark a particular theta role as the controller:

(9) a) *is reluctant*

Experiencer	Proposition
DP *controller*	CP

b) *persuade*

Agent	Theme	Proposition
DP	DP *controller*	CP

c) *promise*

Agent	Theme	Proposition
DP *controller*	DP	CP

In this view of things, control is a thematic property. But a very careful look at the data shows that this can't be the whole story either. The sentences in (10) all use the verb *beg*, which is traditionally viewed as an object control verb, as seen by the pair of sentences in (10a) and (10b), where the (10b) sentence shows an embedded tense clause paraphrase:

(10) a. Louis begged Kate$_i$ [PRO$_i$ to leave her job].

    b. Louis begged Kate that she leave her job.

    c. Louis$_i$ begged Kate [PRO$_i$ to be allowed [PRO$_i$ to shave himself]].

    d. Louis$_i$ begged Kate that he be allowed to shave himself.

Sentences (10c) and (10d), however, show subject control. The PROs in (10c) must be controlled by the subject *Louis*. The difference between the (10a) and the (10b) sentences seems to be in the nature of the embedded clause. This is mysterious at best. Examples like these might be used to argue that control is not entirely syntactic or thematic, but may also rely on our knowledge of the way the world works. This kind of knowledge, often referred to as pragmatic knowledge, lies outside the syntactic system we're developing.

Unit 02 Questions

Answer Key p.484

01 형용사 impossible이 술어일 때 구문을 아래와 같이 전환할 수 있다. 이와 같은 통사적 특성을 지닌 형용사 3개를 <보기>에서 찾아 쓰시오. [3점]

2005년 전국 16번

> To play this sonata on the violin is impossible.
> → It is impossible to play this sonata on the violin.
> → This sonata is impossible to play on the violin.

┤ 보기 ├

boring	eager	likely	merry
obvious	pleasant	sorry	tough

_____

_____

_____

02 다음 예문을 보면 sure와 probable은 동일한 유형의 형용사로 보이지만 차이점이 있다. 그 차이점을 통사적 근거를 들어 우리말로 쓰시오. 2006년 전국 22번

It is sure that John will pass the test.

It is probable that John will pass the test.

03 Read the passage and follow the directions. 2007년 서울/인천 14번

Examples (1) and (2) show that the verb *believe* may take as its complement a finite clause, as in (1), or a non-finite clause, as in (2).

(1) John believes [that Bill is taller than him].
(2) John believes [Bill to be taller than him].

Complement-taking gets more complicated with the adjective *likely*. It can take a finite clause as its complement, as in (3). But, can it take a non-finite clause complement?

(3) It is likely [that Bill is taller than him].
(4) It is likely [Bill to be taller than him].
(5) Bill is likely [to be taller than him].

Since (4) is ungrammatical, we are tempted to say that the adjective cannot take a (A) _____ as its complement. We can't do so, however, because (5) is acceptable. Hence, let us say that *likely* can take a non-finite clause complement, but it cannot allow an NP like *Bill* to immediately follow it. Then, what about the verb *believe* in (2)? Well, we have to say that the verb allows an NP to immediately follow it.

At this point, let us think about the passive past participle of the verb *believe*. Compare (6) and (7) with (1) and (2), respectively.

(6) It is believed [that Bill is taller than him].
(7) It is believed [Bill to be taller than him].

It is interesting to see that it is not the case that both (6) and (7) are okay. ...

(1) Fill in the blank (A) with two words from the passage.

_____

(2) Write down the correct version of any ungrammatical sentence in (6) and (7), preserving their (non-)finiteness.

_____

(3) How can you characterize *believed* in (6) and (7) in comparison with *believes* in (1) and (2)? Complete the following sentence with words from the passage.

Believed in (6) and (7) _____

_____

04 Read <A> and <B> and follow the directions.

A

In English, there are nouns which allow the transformation of sentences like the example given in (1) into the examples in (2) and (3).

(1) To be with Margaret is a blessing.
→ (2) It is a blessing to be with Margaret.
→ (3) Margaret is a blessing to be with.

B

a. To teach Elizabeth is a pleasure.
b. To work with Mary is a tragedy.
c. To hear the news is a surprise.
d. To deal with the man is a problem.
e. To meet the Nobel Prize winner is an honor.

Choose all the sentences in <B> which can be transformed correctly into the two patterns as in (2) and (3) in <A>.

① a, c, d　　　② a, d　　　③ b, c, e

④ b, d　　　⑤ c, e

05 Read the following and answer the question. [2.5점]   2012년 21번

Sentence (1) seems to have the same structure as sentence (2).

(1) The researchers appeared to start their project.
(2) The researchers planned to start their project.

A close analysis, however, would show sentence (1) is different from sentence (2) in the source of the thematic role of the subject *the researchers*. The subject acquires its thematic role from the predicate of the complement clause *start* in sentence (1), but from the predicate of the main clause *planned* in sentence (2). Some of the sentences below show the same pattern of assigning a thematic role to the subject as sentence (1).

a. The manager preferred to please his staff.
b. The man was relieved to see his son safe.
c. The angry crowd is unlikely to leave the plaza.
d. The candidate was keen to resign and support his opponent.
e. The supervisors turned out to be under investigation.
f. The children were found to have rashes.

Which of the following lists all and only sentences which show the same pattern as sentence (1)?

① a, b   ② a, d, f   ③ b, c, d
④ c, e   ⑤ c, e, f

06 Read the passage in <A> and the sentences in <B>, and follow the directions. [4 points]

| A |

Not all intransitive verbs are of the same kind. Compare the two sentences in (1) and (2).

(1) An angel jumped on the hill.
(2) An angel appeared on the hill.

Although both of the above sentences are intransitive, they are not of the same kind. They have different syntactic and semantic properties. In (1), the subject originates in the specifier position external to the V-bar constituent, receiving an Agent role. Verbs like *jump* are known as unergative verbs. However, in (2), the superficial subject originates in the complement position within the immediate V-bar projection of the verb, receiving a Theme role. Then it moves to subject position. Verbs like *appear* are known as unaccusative verbs.

The two types of intransitive verbs can be distinguished by means of tests such as the following. Unaccusative verbs like *appear* allow a word order called *there* inversion, where the underlying complement remains in its original position after the verb. On the other hand, since the subject of unergative verbs like *jump* does not originate in the complement position of the verbs, it isn't allowed to appear in that position after the verbs with *there* inversion, as shown below.

(3) *There jumped an angel on the hill.
(4) There appeared an angel on the hill.

Note : * indicates that the sentence is ungrammatical.

┤ B ├

(i) Several people ate in the Korean restaurant.

(ii) Several customers shopped in the new shopping center.

(iii) Several students remained in the school library.

(iv) Several soldiers saluted in the military ceremony.

(v) Several complications arose in the medical experiment.

Identify the TWO sentences containing an unaccusative verb in <B>, and explain the reason by using the test described in <A>.

_____

_____

_____

_____

_____

07 Read the passages and follow the directions. [5 points]   2019년 B형 6번

┤ A ├

Despite their similarity on the surface, sentences in (1) are of different types, as suggested in their paraphrasing in (2). Sentences like (1a) are called 'Control' construction; the ones like (1b) 'Raising/ECM' construction. Unlike the latter, an empty pronominal NP PRO is postulated in control constructions.

(1) a. John persuaded Sue to obey her parents.

    b. John believed Sue to be obedient to her parents.

(2) a. John persuaded Sue that she should obey her parents.

    b. John believed that Sue was obedient to her parents.

In fact, there are two kinds of PRO. One is called 'arbitrary PRO,' whose meaning is basically "someone" as shown in (3a). Arbitrary PRO is like a referring expression or a pronoun in that it can get its meaning from outside the sentence. The other is 'non-arbitrary PRO,' which can be further distinguished into two varieties: 'obligatory control' and 'optional control.' The optional control is exemplified in (3b). PRO here can either refer back to *John* or it can have an arbitrary PRO_{arb} reading. The obligatory control is exemplified in (3c) and (3d): PRO in (3c) obligatorily refers back to the main clause Subject, hence called 'subject control,' while PRO in (3d) obligatorily refers back to the main clause Object, hence called 'object control.'

(3) a. [PRO_{arb} to go to college] is not essential for success in life.

    b. John$_i$ knows that it is essential [$PRO_{i/j}$ to be well-behaved].

    c. John$_i$ tried [$PRO_{i/*j}$ to behave].

    d. John persuaded Sue$_i$ [PRO_i to obey her parents].

Note : * indicates the ungrammaticality of the sentence.

B

(i) a. [PRO to improve himself], John should consider therapy.

   b. John is easy [PRO to talk to].

(ii) a. John motivated Sue to study harder.

   b. John reported Sue to be obnoxious.

   c. John threatened Sue$_i$ to leave her$_i$.

Based on the description in <A>, first, identify whether PRO in (ia) and (ib) is arbitrary or non-arbitrary, and for non-arbitrary PRO, whether it is obligatory control or optional control. Second, in (ii), identify control constructions only, and then state whether they are subject control or object control.

_____

_____

_____

_____

_____

MEMO

MEN
TOR

Mentor Linguistics

멘토영어학
기출분석

Chapter 02

Complements & Adjuncts

Unit 01 Preview & Review

01 Complements and Adjuncts

1.1. Complements and Adjuncts and Specifiers

Consider now the two prepositional phrases that are subconstituents of the following NP:

68) the book [PP of poems] [PP with the glossy cover]

Using the X-bar rules, we can generate the following tree for this NP :

69)

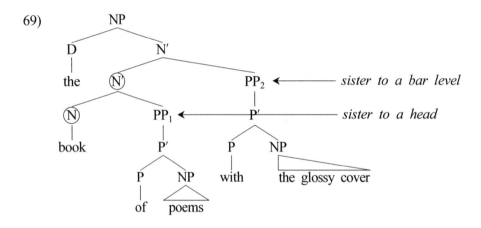

You'll note that the two PPs in this tree are at different levels in the tree. The lower PP_1 is a sister to the head N (book), whereas the higher PP_2 is a sister to the N′ dominating the head N and PP_1. You'll also notice that these two PPs were introduced by different rules. PP_1 is introduced by the rule:

70) X′ → X (WP)

and PP_2 is introduced by the higher level rule:

71) X′ → X′ (ZP)

An XP that is a sister to a head (N, V, A, or P) is called a **complement.** PP₁ is a complement. Complements roughly correspond to the notion "object" in traditional grammar. XPs that are sisters to single bar levels (N′, V′, A′, or P′) and are daughters of an X′ are called **adjuncts.** PP₂ is an adjunct. Adjuncts often have the feel of adverbials or obliques and are typically optional additional information.

72) *Adjunct* : An XP that is a sister to a single bar level (N′, V′, A′, or P′) and a daughter of a single bar level (N′, V′, A′, or P′).

73) *Complement* : An XP that is a sister to a head (N, V, A, P), and a daughter of a single bar level (N′, V′, A′, or P′).

The rules that introduce these two kinds of XPs get special names:

74) *Adjunct rule* : X′ → X′ (ZP)
75) *Complement rule* : X′ → X (WP)

A tree showing the structural difference between these is given below:

76)

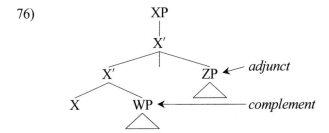

1.2. Complements and Adjuncts in NPs

Take NPs as a prototypical example. Consider the difference in meaning between the two NPs below:

77) the book of poems
78) the book with a red cover

Although both these examples seem to have, on the surface, parallel structures (a determiner, followed by a noun, followed by a prepositional phrase), in reality, they have quite different structures. The PP in (77) is a complement and has the following tree:

79)

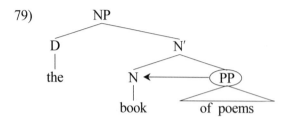

You'll note that the circled PP is a sister to N, so it is a complement. By contrast, the structure of (78) is:

80)

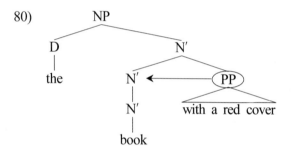

Here the PP *with a red cover* is a sister to N', so it is an adjunct. The difference between these two NPs is not one that you can hear. The difference between the two is in terms of the amount of structure in the tree. In (80), there is an extra N'. While this difference may at first seem abstract, it has important implications for the behavior of the two PPs. Consider first the meaning of our two NPs. In (77), the PP seems to complete (or complement) the meaning of the noun. It tells us what kind of book is being referred to. In (78), by contrast, the PP seems more optional and more loosely related to the NP. This is a highly subjective piece of evidence, but it corresponds to more syntactic and structural evidence too.

An easy heuristic (guiding principle) for distinguishing complements from adjunct PPs inside NPs, is by looking at what preposition they take. In English, almost always (although there are some exceptions) complement PPs take the preposition of. Adjuncts, by contrast, take other prepositions (such as from, at, to, with, under, on, etc.). This test isn't 100 percent reliable, but will allow you to eyeball PPs and tell whether they are complements or adjuncts for the vast majority of cases. With this in mind, let's look at some of the other behavioral distinctions between complements and adjuncts.

Think carefully about the two rules that introduce complements and adjuncts. There are several significant differences between them. These rules are repeated here for your convenience:

81) Adjunct rule : $X' \rightarrow X'$ (ZP)
82) Complement rule : $X' \rightarrow X$ (WP)

First observe that because the complement rule introduces the head (X), **the complement PP will always be adjacent to the head**. Or more particularly, **it will always be closer to the head than an adjunct PP will be**. This is seen in the following data:

83) the book   [of poems]   [with a red cover]
    head   *complement*   *adjunct*

84) *the book   [with a red cover]   [of poems]
    head   *adjunct*   *complement*

There is another property of the rules that manifests itself in the difference between adjuncts and complements. The adjunct rule, as passingly observed above, is an iterative rule. That is, within the rule itself, it shows the property of recursion: On the left-hand side of the rule there is an X' category, and on the right hand side there is another X'. This means that the rule can generate infinite strings of X' nodes, since you can apply the rule over and over again to its own output:

86)

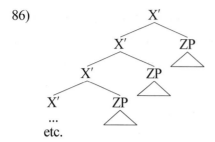

The complement rule does not have this property. On the left side of the rule there is an X′, but on the right there is only X. So the rule cannot apply iteratively. That is, it can only apply once within an XP. What this means for complements and adjuncts is that **you can have any number of adjuncts (87), but you can only ever have one complement (88):**

87) the book   [of poems]   [with a red cover]   [from Blackwell]   [by Robert Burns]
    head   *complement*   *adjunct*   *adjunct*   *adjunct*

88) *the book   [of poems]   [of fiction]   [with a red cover]
    head   *complement*   *complement*   *adjunct*

The tree for (87) is given below; you'll note that since there is only one N, there can only be one complement, but since there are multiple N′s, there can be as many adjuncts as desired.

89)

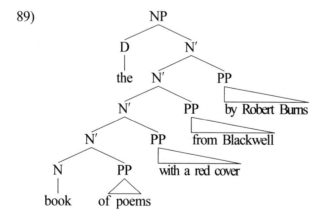

Related to the facts that the number of adjuncts is unlimited, but only one complement is allowed, and complements are always adjacent to the head, observe that **you can usually reorder adjuncts with respect to one another, but you can never reorder a complement with the adjuncts:**

90) a) the book of poems with a red cover from Blackwell by Robert Burns

    b) the book of poems from Blackwell with a red cover by Robert Burns

    c) the book of poems from Blackwell by Robert Burns with a red cover

    d) the book of poems by Robert Burns from Blackwell with a red cover

    e) the book of poems by Robert Burns with a red cover from Blackwell

    f) the book of poems with a red cover by Robert Burns from Blackwell

    g) *the book with a red cover of poems from Blackwell by Robert Burns

    h) *the book with a red cover from Blackwell of poems by Robert Burns

    i) *the book with a red cover from Blackwell by Robert Burns of poems (etc.)

Note that adjuncts and complements are constituents of different types. The definition of adjuncthood holds that adjuncts are sisters to X'. Since conjunction requires that **you conjoin elements of the same bar level, you could not, for example, conjoin an adjunct with a complement.** This would result in a contradiction: Something can't be both a sister to X' and X at the same time. Adjuncts can conjoin with other adjuncts (other sisters to X'), and complements can conjoin with other complements (other sisters to X), but complements cannot conjoin with adjuncts:

91) a) the book of poems with a red cover and with a blue spine

    b) the book of poems and of fiction from Blackwell

    c) *the book of poems and from Blackwell

There is one final difference between adjuncts and complements that we will examine here. Recall the test of *one*-replacement:

92) *One-replacement* : Replace an N' node with one.

This operation replaces an N′ node with the word one. Look at the tree in (93):

93)

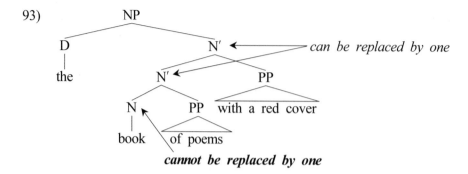

If you look closely at this tree you'll see that two possibilities for *one*-replacement exist. We can either target the highest N′, and get:

94) the one

or we can target the lower N′ and get:

95) the one with a red cover

But we cannot target the N head; it is not an N′. This means that *one* followed by a complement is ill-formed:

96) *the one of poems with a red cover

Since complements are sisters to X and not X′, they cannot stand next to the word *one*. Adjuncts, by definition, can.

1.3. Complements and Adjuncts in VPs, AdjPs, AdvPs and PPs

The distinction between complements and adjuncts is not limited to NPs; we find it holds in all the major syntactic categories. The best example is seen in VPs. The direct object of a verb is a complement of the verb. Prepositional and adverbial modifiers of verbs are adjuncts:

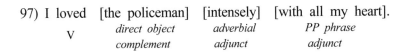

97) I loved   [the policeman]   [intensely]   [with all my heart].
    V   *direct object*   *adverbial*   *PP phrase*
                 complement   *adjunct*   *adjunct*

98)
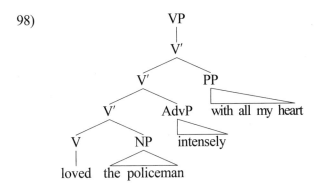

Direct objects must be adjacent to the verb, and there can only be one of them.

99) a) *I loved intensely the policeman with all my heart.
    b) *I loved the policeman the baker intensely with all my heart.

Did-so (did-too) replacement targets V′. Like *one*-replacement, this means that it can only apply before an adjunct and not before a complement:

100) Mika loved the policemen intensely and
    a) Susan did so half-heartedly.
    b) *Susan did so the baker.

This is classic adjunct/complement distinction. In general, complements of all categories (N, V, A, P, etc.) are the semantic objects of the head. Consider for example all the complements below:

101) a) John fears dogs. (verb)
    b) John is afraid of dogs. (adjective)
    c) John has a fear of dogs. (noun)

In all these sentences, *(of) dogs* is a complement.

The evidence for the adjunct/complement distinction in adjective phrases and prepositional phrases is considerably weaker than that of nouns and verbs. Adverbs that modify adjectives have an adjunct flair—they can be stacked and reordered. Other than this, however, the evidence for the distinction in PPs and AdjPs comes mainly as a parallel to the NPs and VPs. This may be less than satisfying, but is balanced by the formal simplicity of having the same system apply to all categories.

02 Complements vs. Adjuncts: Extraposition (Postposing)

It appears that PP Adjuncts can be extraposed from their Heads (i.e. separated from their Heads and moved to the end of their Clause) more freely than PP Complements: cf.

(83) (a) a student came to see me yesterday [with long hair]
    (b) *a student came to see me yesterday [of Physics]

It would seem that in some sense PP Complements are more 'inseparable' from their Heads than PP Adjuncts. Thus, we might posit that the more closely related a PP is to its Head, the less freely it can be extraposed. Complements are more resistant to being extraposed.

NOTE (163) (a) [A review of my latest book] has just appeared
    (b) [A review _____] has just appeared of my latest book

03 Complements vs. Adjuncts: Preposing

Given that Extraposition involves *Postposing,* the obvious question to ask is whether Complements and Adjuncts behave any differently with respect to *Preposing.* There is some evidence that this is indeed the case. It would seem that an NP which is the Object of a Preposition heading a *Complement* PP can be preposed more freely than an NP which is the Object of a Preposition heading an *Adjunct* PP: cf. the contrast below:

(85) (a) [*What branch of Physics*] are you a student of?
    (b) *[*What kind of hair*] are you a student with?

Thus, in (85) (a), the preposed bracketed NP is the Object of the Preposition *of,* and *of* introduces a Complement phrase, so that (85) (a) involves preposing an NP which is part of a Complement PP. But by contrast, the bracketed preposed NP in (85) (b) is the Object of the Preposition *with,* and *with* introduces an Adjunct, so that the ungrammaticality of (85) (b) suggests that an NP which is part of an Adjunct PP cannot be preposed. Thus, there is an obvious contrast insofar as the Object of a Complement Preposition can be preposed, but not the Object of an Adjunct Preposition.

04 Coordination

In an acceptable coordination the coordinates are syntactically similar. The examples given so far contrast with the ungrammatical combinations shown in [1], where the underlined elements are manifestly quite different in kind:

[1] i *We invited [the Smiths and because they can speak Italian].
    ii *She argued [persuasively or that their offer should be rejected].

In a large majority of the coordinate structures found in texts, the coordinates belong to the same CATEGORY. But coordinates do not have to be of the same category. Other examples are given in [2]:

[2] i He won't reveal [the nature of the threat or where it came from].   [NP + clause]

   ii I'll be back [next week or at the end of the month].   [NP + PP]

   iii He acted [selfishly and with no thought for the consequences].   [AdvP + PP]

   iv They rejected the [United States and British] objections.   [Nom + Adj]

The coordinates here belong to the categories shown on the right; *where it came from* in [i] is, more specifically, a subordinate interrogative clause, while *United States* in [iv] is a nominal, the name we use for the unit intermediate between noun and noun phrase.

FUNCTION is more important than category in determining the permissibility of coordination. What makes the coordinations in [2] acceptable despite the differences of category is that each coordinate could occur alone with the same function.

[3] i a. He won't reveal the nature of the threat.   b. He won't reveal where it came from.

   ii a. I'll be back next week.   b. I'll be back at the end of the month.

   iii a. He acted selfishly.   b. He acted with no thought for the consequences.

   iv a. They rejected the United States objections.   b. They rejected the British objections.

In each pair here the underlined element in [b] has the same function as that in [a]: complement of the verb in [i], time adjunct in [ii], manner adjunct in [iii], attributive modifier in [iv]. Contrast these examples with those in [4]:

[4] i *We're leaving [Rome and next week].   [NP + NP]

   ii *I ran [to the park and for health reasons].   [PP + PP]

Here the coordinates belong to the same category, but don't satisfy the requirement of functional likeness. Each could appear in place of the whole coordination, but the functions would be different:

[5] i a. We're leaving Rome.   b. We're leaving next week.

   ii a. I ran to the park.   b. I ran for health reasons.

- Example [ia] has *Rome* as direct object, but *next week* in [ib] is an adjunct of time.
- In example [iia], *to the park* is a goal complement, but *for health reasons* in [iib] is an adjunct of reason.

In [6] we state the likeness requirement a bit more precisely in the light of these observations.

[6] A coordination of *X* and *Y* is admissible at a given place in sentence structure if and only if each of *X* and *Y* is individually admissible at that place with the same function.

To see how this works, consider the examples given in [7]:

[7] i a. We invited [Kim and Pat].   b. She is [very young but a quick learner].
    ii a. We invited Kim.   b. She is very young.
   iii a. We invited Pat.   b. She is a quick learner.

- In the [a] set, let *X* be *Kim* and let *Y* be *Pat*: we can replace *Kim and Pat* by *Kim*, and we can replace it by *Pat*, without change of function, so the coordination is admissible.
- The same holds in the [b] examples, where the coordinates are of different categories: *very young* and *a quick learner* can both stand in place of the coordination with the same function (predicative complement), so again this is an admissible coordination.

But [4i-ii] are not permitted by condition [6]. Although we can replace the coordination by each of the coordinates *Rome* and *next week or to the park* and *for health reasons,* the functions are not the same, as explained in the discussion of [5]. So condition [6] is not satisfied in these cases.

A number of qualifications and refinements to [6] are needed to cover various additional facts, but [6] does represent the basic generalisation. And of course, [6] does not have any application to the combination of *X* and *Y* in a head + dependent construction.

A special case of the syntactic likeness requirement applies in various constructions such as relative clauses. Compare the following examples:

[8] i <u>They attended the dinner</u> but <u>they are not members</u>.
    ii The people [<u>who attended the dinner</u> but <u>who are not members</u>] owe $20.
    iii *The people [<u>who attended the dinner</u> but <u>they are not members</u>] owe $20.

In [i] we have a coordination of main clauses. If we embed this to make it a modifier in NP structure, we have to relativise BOTH clauses, not just one.

- In [ii] both coordinates are relative clauses (marked by *who*): *who attended the dinner* is a relative clause and so is *who are not members*. That makes the coordination admissible.
- In [iii], by contrast, just the first embedded clause is relativised: *who attended the dinner* is a relative clause but *they are not members* isn't, so the coordination is ungrammatical.

Relativisation is thus said to work across the board, i.e. to all coordinates. Example [8iii] clearly doesn't satisfy condition [6]: the second underlined clause cannot occur alone in this context (**The people *they are not members* owe $20* is ungrammatical), so the coordination of the two underlined clauses is inadmissible.

We find a sharp contrast here with head + dependent constructions:

[9] i <u>They attended the dinner</u> although <u>they are not members</u>.
    ii *The people [<u>who attended the dinner</u> although <u>who are not members</u>] owe $20.
    iii The people [<u>who attended the dinner</u> although <u>they are not members</u>] owe $20.

But in [8] is a coordinator. Although in [9] is not: it's a preposition with a content clause complement. When we relativise here, then, it is just the *attend* clause that is affected, as in [9iii] (the clause *they are not members* is the complement of a preposition inside the *attend* clause). Version [9ii] is ungrammatical, because the relative clause *who are not members* is complement of a preposition. This is not a permitted function for relative clauses.

05 Overview

5.1. Complements vs. Adjuncts

Complements	
Semantic(의미적 구분): 의미를 완성시키는 데 빠지면 안 되는 것	In general, complements of all categories (N, V, A, P, etc.) are the semantic objects of the head. a. John fears dogs.　　　　(verb) b. John is afraid of dogs.　　(adjective) c. John has a fear of dogs.　(noun)
Syntactic(통사적 구분) 문장 안에서 위치를 바꿀 수 없 는 것은 Complement이고 바 꿀 수 있는 것은 Adjunct	a. the book [of poems] <u>with a red cover</u> from Blackwell by Robert Burns b. the book [of poems] <u>from Blackwell</u> with a red cover by Robert Burns c. the book [of poems] <u>from Blackwell</u> <u>by Robert Burns</u> with a red cover
Complements in NPs (1): almost always (although there are some exceptions) complement PPs take the preposition of.	a. the destruction of the building b. the writer of the book c. the investigator of the murder d. the makers of cars
Complements in NPs (2): 명사구에서 핵 명사를 동사로 전환했을 때 그 동사가 보충어 가 뒤따를 것을 요구할 경우	a teacher of Syntax → teaches syntax an analysis of the sentence → analyze the sentence
Complements in NPs (3): 명사가 뒤에 특정 전치사를 요 구하는 경우	a. his insistence on the arrangement 　(cf. He insists on the arrangement.) b. their specialization in wines 　(cf. They specialize in wines.)

Adjuncts	
Arguments(논항 관련)	Adjuncts are never arguments (cf. complements는 논항이다)
Adjunct in a restricted sense	대체로 how, when, where, why의 대답으로 나올 수 있는 것들
Syntactic(통사 관련)	(1) Adjuncts는 주변적인 것 　a. John went <u>to a museum</u> <u>in Seoul</u>. 　b. <u>In Seoul</u>, John went to a museum. 　c. *<u>To a museum</u>, John went in Seoul. (2) Adjunct는 다른 표현으로 바꿀 수 있음

Unit 02 Questions

Answer Key p.485

01 Read the passage and follow the directions.

2006년 서울/인천 21~22번

Consider the underlined noun phrases below:

(1) a. Mr. Smith is <u>a teacher of children</u>.

   b. Mr. Smith is <u>a teacher from America</u>.

(2) Mr. Smith is <u>a teacher of children from America</u>.

The noun phrase in (2), which is a combination of (1a) and (1b), is ambiguous. The phrase *from America* modifies either the head *teacher* or the head *children*. Thus, the ambiguity results from the possible modification of either head by the phrase *from America*.

However, with the intended meaning 'Mr. Smith teaches children and he is from America,' sentence (3) is ungrammatical:

(3) *Mr. Smith is <u>a teacher from America of children</u>.

The notions of complement and adjunct can be used to explain the ungrammaticality of (3).

A complement is a phrase required by the head while an adjunct is its optional modifier; *from America* is an adjunct of the head *teacher* and *of children*, its complement. The noun phrase in (3) is ungrammatical since it does not satisfy the structural requirement that the _____(A)_____ should come closer to the head than the _____(B)_____ does.

---

(1) Fill in each blank with ONE word from the passage. [2점]

(A) _____

(B) _____

(2) The underlined verb phrase below is also ambiguous. Identify the modifier and its two modified heads in the underlined part. [3점]

> The student <u>read the book on the stool</u>.

• the modifier : _____

• the modified heads : _____

02 글 <A>를 읽고 <B>에서 비문법적인 문장을 찾아 기호를 쓰고 비문법적인 이유를 <A>에 나오는 용어를 이용하여 15단어 이내로 쓰시오. (단, 영어와 우리말 혼용 가능) [4점]

2008년 전국 15번

┤ A ├

X-bar theory is a very simple and general theory of phrase structure. Using only three rules, this theory accounts for the distinction between adjuncts, complements, and specifiers.

(1) a. Specifier rule : XP → (YP) X′

    b. Adjunct rule : X′ → X′ (ZP) or X′ → (ZP) X′

    c. Complement rule : X′ → X (WP)

X is a head, WP is a complement, ZP is an adjunct, and YP is a specifier. Let us think, here, about differences between the complement and adjunct rules. Because the complement rule introduces the head, the complement will always be adjacent to the head. Or more particularly, it will always be closer to the head than an adjunct. This is seen in the following tree:

(2)

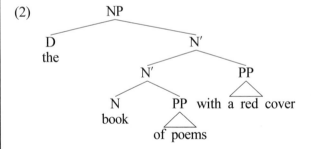

Since the adjunct rule takes an X′ level category and generates another X′ category, it will always be higher in the tree than the output of the complement rule. Since lines can't cross, this means that complements will always be lower in the tree than adjuncts, and will always be closer to the head than adjuncts.

┤ B ├

(a) It is very interesting and of great help.

(b) The flower moved of itself and with elegance.

(c) She likes the book of poems and from The MIT Press.

(d) I read the book of poems with a red cover and with a blue spine.

• 비문법적인 문장의 기호 : (   )

• 비문법적인 이유 : _____

_____

_____

03 Read <A> and <B> and follow the directions.

2009년 32번

| A |

A phrase consists of a head and non-head elements. Some non-head elements complete the meaning of the head. These elements are referred to as a complement. It is a general term to denote any element whose presence is required by the head. Although the presence of a complement is normally obligatory, that of an N can be omitted. There are also elements in a phrase which describe the head rather than complete it. These elements are modifiers (or adjuncts). They can be omitted without affecting grammaticality.

| B |

An example of error in popular views ⓐ <u>about the mind</u> appears in the idea of a faculty of observation. One often hears it said that we should train the observation ⓑ <u>of our students</u>; and it is imagined that by training them to observe certain things we are training them to observe anything and everything. Observation, however, relies on interest and knowledge. We have no reason to suppose that a botanist, trained in the observation ⓒ <u>of flowers</u>, will be more observant than us ⓓ <u>of the faces of the people he meets</u>. People are more likely to have their attention diverted ⓔ <u>by the objects of their special interests</u>. So training in the careful observation of the varied endings ⓕ <u>of Latin words</u>, or of the changes in chemical substances in experiments, will have no effect on the observation of pictures or the movements of the stars.

Based on <A>, choose all the complement PPs from the underlined parts in <B>.

① ⓐ, ⓑ, ⓒ   ② ⓐ, ⓒ, ⓓ   ③ ⓑ, ⓒ, ⓓ

④ ⓑ, ⓔ, ⓕ   ⑤ ⓓ, ⓔ, ⓕ

04 Read <A> and <B> and follow the directions.

2010년 36번

---| A |---

The phrase structure rules in (1) enable English speakers to understand and produce noun phrases of any length. However, there are syntactic restrictions on the way linguistic expressions are built up by the phrase structure rules.

(1) a. NP → (D) N$'$

    b. N$'$ → N$'$ PP

    c. N$'$ → N (PP)

    d. PP → P NP

(2) a. *a student in London of linguistics

    b. a philosopher with letters from friends

    c. a student with a paper on physics

    d. *a student of physics of chemistry

    e. a man with books in the store

('*' indicates that the expression is ungrammatical.)

---| B |---

a. In (2a), both PPs are sisters to N$'$.

b. In (2b), both PPs are sisters to N$'$.

c. In (2c), both PPs are sisters to N.

d. In (2d), both PPs are sisters to N$'$.

e. In (2e), both PPs are sisters to N$'$.

Choose all the statements in <B> that correctly describe the structural relations of PPs within the noun phrases in <A>.

① a, b   ② a, b, e   ③ a, d

④ b, e   ⑤ c, d, e

05 Read the passage in <A> and the sentences in <B>, and follow the directions. [5 points]

2016년 B형 6번

A

A PP modifier has distinct grammatical functions; it can be either a Complement exemplified by the underlined PP in (1a) or an Adjunct as in (1b).

(1) a. the specialist <u>in phonology</u>

    b. the specialist <u>at the stage</u>

Two types of syntactic arguments can be presented for the structural distinction between PP Complements and PP Adjuncts. First, they are strictly ordered when they both occur as postnominal modifiers, as the contrast in (2) shows.

(2) a. The specialist in phonology at the stage

    b. *The specialist at the stage in phonology

Another syntactic argument can be formulated in relation to Wh-movement, as shown in (3): NPs within PP Complements can be preposed, while NPs within PP Adjuncts cannot.

(3) a. What area of linguistics is he a specialist in?

    b. *Which place is he a specialist at?

Note : * indicates that the sentence is ungrammatical.

B
---

a. He is a contender <u>with a knee injury</u>.

b. He is a contender <u>for the PGA title</u>.

Based on the description in <A>, identify the grammatical function of the underlined PPs in <B>. Then provide two pairs of evidence for your identification, using BOTH sentences in <B>: a pair of NPs and a pair of wh-questions, with ungrammaticality marked with an asterisk (*) at the beginning of the evidence.

_____

_____

_____

_____

_____

06 Read the passage and follow the directions. [2점]   2021년 A형 3번

In the languages of the world, we have two different types of adposition: a preposition type (e.g., English) and a postposition type (e.g., Korean). With the preposition type, we find that a preposition head precedes its complement as in (1a). As for the postposition type, a postposition follows its complement as in (1b).

(1) a. Preposition   b. Postposition

However, some linguists argue that all languages uniformly have the preposition system and the seemingly postposition system is derived from the preposition type by movement as in (2).

(2)

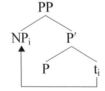

We can apply the analysis in (2) to the so-called particle structure.

(3) They left [PP [NP this part]i out ti].

In (3), NP *this part* moves from the _____ position of the head *out* to the specifier position.

Fill in the blank with the ONE most appropriate word from the passage.

MEMO

MEN
TOR

Mentor Linguistics
멘토영어학
기출분석

Chapter 03

Constituency

Unit 01 Preview & Review
Unit 02 Questions

Preview & Review

01 Constituency

1.1. Tests for Constituency in English

Let us begin by comparing (9a) with (9b), both of which end with the sequence V-P-NP. These two sentences are identical except for the last word. How then can we explain the contrast in (10)?

(9) a. John ran up a big hill.
   b. John ran up a big bill.

(10) a. Up a big hill John ran.
    b. *Up a big bill John ran.

What exactly is the difference? The phrase *run up* in (9b) is an example of a phrasal verb, or "verb-particle" construction. Phrasal verbs in English involve fixed combinations of a verb plus a prepositional particle. One way of identifying phrasal verbs is that the particle may occur either before or after the object NP, unlike normal prepositions which always precede their object. Note the contrast between the phrasal verb in (11) and the normal preposition phrase in (12):

(11) a. Peter <u>blew out</u> the candle.
    b. Peter <u>blew</u> the candle <u>out</u>.

(12) a. Peter *flew out* the window.
    b. *Peter *flew* the window *out*.

In fact, when the object of a phrasal verb is a pronoun, the particle must follow the object as in (13b). But with true PPs, the preposition always precedes its object, whether the object is a pronoun (as in 14a) or a full NP.

(13) a. I want to <u>look</u> <u>*over*</u> the contract before I sign.

b. Before I sign the contract, I want to <u>look</u> it <u>*over*</u>.

c. *?Before I sign the contract, I want to look *over* it.

(14) a. Since the gate was locked, John climbed *over* it.

b. *Since the gate was locked, John climbed it *over*.

There is often a semantic difference as well. A normal preposition is generally used in its basic, literal meaning, whereas the particle in a phrasal verb generally has a metaphorical or idiomatic meaning. For example, sentence (9b) *John ran up a big bill* does not mean that either John or the bill were literally moving up to a higher location, or that John was literally running. The meaning of the verb plus particle combination is often quite unpredictable, e.g., *put off* 'to offend'; *turn down* 'to reject'; *knock back* 'to reject' (Australian English).

However, for our present purposes we are most interested in looking for structural differences between (9a) and (9b). Specifically, we will use some familiar constituency tests to look for constituent boundaries within these V-P-NP strings.

1.1.1. Clefting

The two constructions illustrated in (15) and (16) are used to focus, or place special emphasis on, a constituent that conveys new information. In a cleft sentence (15) the focused constituent comes first, while in the Pseudo-Cleft construction (16), the focused constituent appears at the end of the sentence.

(15) **Cleft sentences :**

a. It was [your big brother] who built this house.

b. It is [her artificial smile] that I can't stand.

c. It was [for Mary] that John bought the flowers (not for Susan).

d. It was [just last week] that Mary offered me the job.

(16) **Pseudo-Clefts :**

    a. What I can't stand is [her artificial smile].

    b. What John said to Mary was [that he intended to run for parliament].

    c. What I like for breakfast is [fried noodles].

In both constructions, the material that occurs in the focused position must be a complete constituent, and only one constituent may appear in this position at a time.

(17) **Cleft sentences :**

    a. *It was [a book] [to Mary] that John gave.

    b. *It was [last week] [your brother] that I arrested.

    c. *It was [your big] who built this house brother.

(18) **Pseudo-Clefts :**

    a. *What John gave was [a book] [to Mary].

    b. *?What Bill stole was [my diary] [from my desk drawer].

    c. *What I can't stand smile is [her artificial].

As McCawley points out, the Pseudo-Cleft construction cannot generally be used to focus preposition phrases; but we can use clefting to test the structure of the sentences in (9). As (19) demonstrates, the sequence [P+NP] can be clefted in (9a), but not in (9b). This contrast suggests that the clefted material forms a constituent (a PP) in (9a), but not in (9b). Applying the same test to the sentences in (13) and (14), we again find that the sequence [P+NP] forms a constituent in the prepositional example (20a) but not in the phrasal verb example (20b).

(19) a. According to tradition, it was [up this hill] that Napoleon and his 500 soldiers ran.

    b. *According to the head waiter, it was [up this bill] that John ran.

(20) a. If my hypothesis is correct, it was [over this fence] that the prisoners climbed.

    b. *If my hypothesis is correct, it was [over this contract] that my lawyer looked.

1.1.2. Topicalization

In this construction, a constituent which normally follows the verb is moved to the front of the sentence, preceding the subject NP. Constituents of various categories can be topicalized, as illustrated in (21).

(21) a. [Your elder sister]$_{NP}$ I can't stand.

　　b. [That you sincerely wanted to help]$_{S'}$ I do not doubt.

　　c. [Out of his pocket]$_{PP}$ John pulled a crumpled $100 bill.

　　d. John arrived 15 minutes late, and [very sorry indeed]$_{AdjP}$ he appeared.

Only one constituent can be topicalized in any given clause, as shown in (22). Moreover, as the examples in (23) show, nothing less than a whole constituent (in this case an NP) can be topicalized. This means not only that the fronted elements must form a single constituent, but also that no "fragments" (i.e., words which do not form a constituent) can be left behind in post-verbal position.

(22) a. I gave that book to Mary last Christmas.

　　b. *[That book] [to Mary] I gave last Christmas.

　　c. *[Last Christmas] [that book] I gave to Mary.

　　d. *[Last Christmas] [to Mary] I gave that book.

(23) a. *[Your elder] I can't stand sister.

　　b. *[Elder sister] I can't stand your.

　　c. *[Sister] I can't stand your elder.

　　d. *[Your] I can't stand elder sister.

The examples in (10) involve the topicalization of a sequence [P+NP]. The fact that (10a) is grammatical indicates that the sequence forms a constituent in (9a), which we identified as a normal preposition phrase. The fact that (10b) is ungrammatical indicates that the sequence [P+NP] does not form a constituent in (9b), the phrasal verb example. The same result holds for examples (11)-(14): topicalization is impossible with the phrasal verb examples (24a and 25a), but fine for the normal preposition phrase (24b and 25b). Thus the topicalization patterns lead us to the same conclusion as the clefting data we examined in the previous section.

(24) a. *[Out the candle] Peter blew.

    b. [Out the window] Peter flew.

(25) a. *[Over the contract] John looked.

    b. [Over the gate] John climbed.

1.1.3. Sentence fragments

One type of utterance which may be less than a complete sentence is the "short form" answer to a content question. As the examples in (26) through (28) illustrate, these sentence fragments must normally form a single, complete constituent.

(26) A : What did you throw just now?

    B : *?A rock into the water.

(27) A : What did you buy at the flea market?

    B : An old Swedish wineskin. / *An old Swedish.

(28) A : Which sister gave you that florescent green necktie?

    B : My second sister. / *My second.

However, this test must be applied carefully, since there are various contexts in which an element which is normally obligatory can be omitted from a constituent. For example, in many languages adjectives can be used without any head noun to name classes of people, as in (29). Head nouns can also be omitted in certain other contexts, e.g., (30) and (31).

(29) a. [the good], [the bad], and [the ugly]

    b. [The rich] get richer and [the poor] get children.

(30) Would you like [white wine] or [red]?

(31) A : Which of these sentences sounds more natural to you?

    B : The second.

So the fact that a string of words can occur as **a sentence fragment does not always mean that the string forms a complete constituent.** But the converse appears to be true: if a given string cannot occur as a sentence fragment, that generally means that the string is not a constituent. With this qualification in mind, let us try to apply this test to our [P+NP] sequences.

As the following examples show, a normal PP can be used as a sentence fragment (32 and 34), but this does not work for the phrasal verb examples (33 and 35). This contrast provides additional evidence that the combination of preposition plus NP in the phrasal verb construction does not form a constituent.

(32) A : Where did John run?

  B : Up a big hill.

(33) A : (?)What did John run?

  B : *Up a big bill.

(34) A : Where did Peter fly?

  B : Out the window.

(35) A : What did Peter blow?

  B : *Out the candle.

1.1.4. Coordination

Coordination is often used to provide evidence about constituent boundaries, but, as with sentence fragments, this test needs to be used with caution. A general constraint on coordinate structures is that only constituents can be conjoined. This is illustrated in (36).

(36) a. [John's video camera] and [Mary's digital camera] were stolen by bandits.

  b. *[John's video] and [Mary's digital] camera were stolen by bandits.

However, the comments in the preceding section concerning elliptical constructions apply here as well. Sentence (30) above is an example of coordination involving one elliptical conjunct. So the fact that coordination is possible does not necessarily mean that both conjuncts are complete constituents. But it does seem safe to say that if a string cannot be conjoined, it is not a constituent.

This generalization can be used to test the constituent structure of phrasal verb constructions. True PPs can be freely conjoined, as illustrated in (37). But the combination of preposition plus NP in the phrasal verb construction cannot be conjoined, as illustrated in (38-39). This fact again indicates that the sequence of words does not form a constituent.

(37) a. Peter flew [out the window] and [across the river].

    b. John ran [up a big hill] and [through a grassy meadow].

(38) a. Peter blew out the candle and blew up the balloon.

    b. *Peter blew [out the candle] and [up the balloon].

(39) a. John turned off the lights and turned on the radio.

    b. *John turned [off the lights] and [on the radio].

Examples like (40) and (41) are sometimes cited as evidence for the claim that only constituents of the same category can be conjoined. Certainly this is the normal pattern; and virtually any category can be conjoined with itself, as illustrated in (42).

(40) a. John wrote [a letter] and [a postcard].   [NP with NP]

    b. John wrote [to Mary] and [to Fred].   [PP with PP]

    c. *John wrote [to Mary] and [a postcard].   [PP with NP]

(41) *Mary knows [the truth] and [that you are innocent].   [NP with S']

(42) a. My true love gave me [four calling birds] and [three French hens]. [NP with NP]

    b. I found ants [in the sugar bowl] and [under the bread box].   [PP with PP]

    c. You have a [very beautiful] but [slightly crazy] daughter.   [AdjP with AdjP]

    d. Mary knows [that the police made a mistake] and [that you are innocent]. [S′ with S′]

However, this preference for same-category coordination is not an absolute requirement. One of the best-known exceptions to the general pattern involves predicate complements with the copular verb *be*. Phrases which can function as complements to *be* can often be conjoined even if they belong to different syntactic categories:

(43) a. Gen. Lee was [a rebel to the core] and [proud of it].   [NP with AP]

    b. John hasn't returned my calls;

      he must be either [out of town] or [extremely busy].   [PP with AP]

    c. Mary is [a dedicated professional] and [under a binding contract];

      she will perform as scheduled.   [NP with PP]

In addition to the regular coordinate structures discussed thus far, English permits a second type of coordination called Shared Constituent Coordination or "Right Node Raising." This construction, which is only used in relatively formal speaking or writing, is illustrated in (44b) and (45b):

(44) a. John walked up the hill, and Mary ran up the hill.

    b. John walked, and Mary ran, [up the hill].

(45) a. The CIA admitted responsibility for the incident, but the KGB denied responsibility for the incident.

    b. The CIA admitted, but the KGB denied, [responsibility for the incident].

This construction actually involves the coordination of two truncated sentences, each of which would be completed by the same final phrase. This final, "shared" group of words must normally form a constituent, as shown by examples like (46):

(46) a. John handed bananas to the monkeys, but Peter threw bananas to the monkeys.

    b. ?*John handed, but Peter threw, [bananas to the monkeys].

As expected, we find that Right Node Raising is possible with normal PPs, as in (44), but not with the sequence of particle plus NP in the phrasal verb construction, as seen in (47) and (48):

(47) a. John crossed out the best answer, and Mary figured out the best answer.

    b. *John crossed, and Mary figured, [out the best answer].

(48) a. Peter picked up the telephone, and Wendy hung up the telephone.

    b. *Peter picked, and Wendy hung, [up the telephone].

1.1.5. Adverb placement

Contrast the distribution of *probably* with *violently* in the following examples:

(64) a. *Probably* Morris will disagree with your theory.

    b. Morris *probably* will disagree with your theory.

    c. Morris will *probably* disagree with your theory.

    d. *Morris will disagree *probably* with your theory.

    e. *Morris will disagree with *probably* your theory.

    f. *Morris will disagree with your *probably* theory.

    g. Morris will disagree with your theory *probably*.

(65) a. *_Violently_ Morris will disagree with your theory.

    b. *Morris *violently* will disagree with your theory.

    c. Morris will *violently* disagree with your theory.

    d. Morris will disagree *violently* with your theory.

    e. *Morris will disagree with *violently* your theory.

    f. *Morris will disagree with your *violently* theory.

    g. Morris will disagree with your theory *violently*.

At first glance the distribution of these adverbs seems quite complex, and it may not be clear how to explain the differences between the two. But constituent structure does seem to be relevant. For example, neither adverb can come between the modifier *your* and its head noun *theory* (as in the [f] sentences), or between the preposition *with* and its object NP (as in the [e] sentences). In other words, **no adverb can occur inside the NP or PP constituents**.

Now, if we assume that the main verb and its PP complement (*disagree with your theory*) form a VP constituent, then we can make a further generalization about the data: the adverb *probably* never occurs inside the VP, while the adverb *violently* can never be separated from the VP. To be more precise, let us assume (for the moment) that the basic sentence has the phrase structure shown in (66). Then we can account for all the data in (64) and (65) with two simple statements: **(i) *probably* must be an immediate daughter of the S node; and (ii) *violently* must be an immediate daughter of the VP node.**

(66)

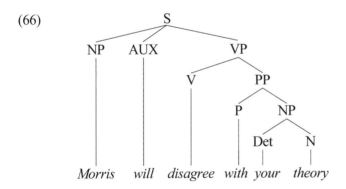

Adverbs of one type (which we will call sentence adverbs) must be daughters of S, while those of another type (VP adverbs) must be daughters of VP.

Adverbs which describe the speaker's evaluation of the proposition (e.g., *fortunately, tragically, surprisingly,* etc.), epistemic comments relating to truth or probability (e.g., *certainly, obviously, possibly, definitely,* etc.), and certain time and place expressions modify the sentence as a whole. They are elements of S, and so do not normally occur within the VP. Adverbs of manner (e.g., *completely, carefully, quickly,* etc.) are generally elements of the VP; but they can sometimes be topicalized, or fronted, to the beginning of the sentence. The position of both types of adverbs can be influenced by a wide variety of semantic and pragmatic factors. And some adverbs do not seem to fit neatly into either type.

NOTE We noted that certain adverbs (e.g., *violently*) must be immediate daughters of the VP node. But nothing in this statement explains why (67b) should be ungrammatical. The contrast between that example and the grammatical (67a, c) is due to an independent principle of English grammar which states that nothing can separate a verb from its direct object.

(67) a. Morris will *violently* attack your theory.

b. *Morris will attack *violently* your theory.

c. Morris will attack your theory *violently*.

02 Structural Differences Between Prepositional Verb and Phrasal Verb

Having outlined our structural diagnostics, let's see how we might apply them to help us determine the constituent structure of the following pair of sentences:

(124) (a) Drunks would get off the bus

(b) Drunks would put off the customers

Now at first sight, the two sentences in (124) might appear to be parallel in structure. And yet, what I'm going to suggest here is that the two sentences have very different constituent structures.

(125) (a)

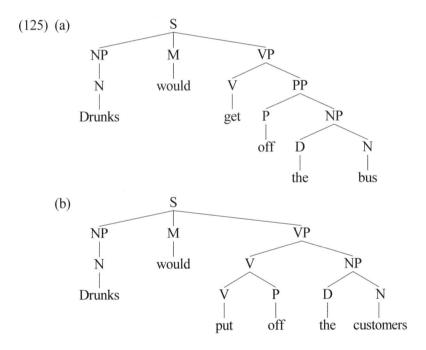

The essential difference between the two structures is that in (125) (a) the Preposition *off* 'goes with' the following Noun Phrase [*the bus*] to form the Prepositional Phrase [*off the bus*]; whereas in (125) (b), the Preposition *off* 'goes with' the Verb *put* to form the complex 'Phrasal Verb' [*put off*] Thus, in traditional terms, we might say that *get* in (125) (a) is a **Prepositional Verb** (because it is a Verb which takes a Prepositional Phrase after it), whereas *put* in (125) (b) is a **Phrasal Verb** because the sequence [*put off*] seems to form some kind of 'compound verb'.

Let's now turn to further **syntactic evidence** in support of claiming that Prepositional and Phrasal Verbs have different structures.

2.1. Movement Test

Only full phrases can undergo movement. In this connection, it is interesting to note that in *get off* structures like (125) (a), the whole sequence [*off the bus*] can be preposed for emphasis: cf.

(141) Every afternoon, the big red bus would stop in front of the village clock, and [*off the bus*] would get Δ a dear old lady carrying a shopping bag

Since only full phrases can undergo movement, it follows that the italicised sequence in (141) must be a full phrase; and since it contains the head Preposition *off,* it clearly must be a Prepositional Phrase. By contrast, note that the sequence *off the customers* can't be preposed in (125) (b): cf.

(142) *The manager suspects that drunks would put off the customers,

  and *off the customers* they certainly would put Δ

Why should this be? The answer suggested here is that only full phrases can be preposed in this way, and—as we see from the tree diagram in (125) (b) above—**the sequence *off the customers* isn't a phrase**: in fact, **it isn't even a constituent.**

2.2. Sentence-fragment Test

The sequence [*off the bus*] can serve as a sentence-fragment in (125) (a):

(143) speaker A : Did he get off the train?
  speaker B : No, *off the bus*

Since **only full phrases can serve as sentence-fragments**, this confirms the PP status of the italicised sequence. By contrast, the string *off the customers* in (125) (b) cannot function as a sentence-fragment, as (144) below illustrates:

Part

01

(144) speaker A : Would drunks [put off] the waitresses?

speaker B : *No, *off the customers*

Why can't *off the customers* function as a sentence-fragment? The answer suggested by analysis (125) (b) is that the italicised sequence in (144) is not even a constituent, let alone a Phrase (and recall that only full Phrases can function as sentence-fragments). So, our sentence-fragment test lends further support to analysis (125).

2.3. The Distribution of Adverbial Phrases

Recall that we drew a distinction between **S-Adverbials** (which occur in positions where they are attached to an S node), and **VP-Adverbials** (which occur in positions where they are attached to a VP node). The class of VP-Adverbials includes expressions such as *quickly, slowly, completely,* etc. Now, since **VP-Adverbials can occur internally within VPs**, then we should expect that such an Adverbial could be positioned in between the Verb *get* and the Prepositional Phrase [*off the bus*] in (125) (a); and (145) below shows that this is indeed the case:

(145) Drunks would get *slowly* off the bus

By contrast, it is not possible to position a VP-Adverbial between *put* and *off* in (125) (b), as we see from the ungrammatically of (146) below:

(146) *Drunks would [put *completely* off] the customers

(147) (a)

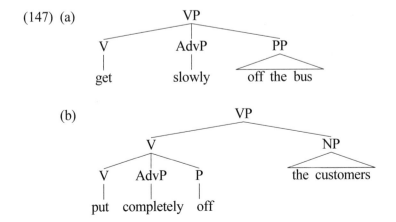

What's wrong with (147) (b) is that here we have a VP-Adverbial attached to a V node, not to a VP node.

2.4. Coordination Test

Given our assumption that [*off the bus*] is a PP constituent in (125) (a), we should expect that it can be coordinated with another PP of the same type: and as (148) below shows, this is indeed the case:

(148) Drunks would get [*off the bus*] and [*on the train*]

But given our assumption that the sequence *off the customers* is not a constituent of any type in (125) (b), we should expect that it cannot be coordinated with another similar sequence: and this is exactly the right prediction, as the ungrammaticality of (149) below illustrates:

(149) *Drunks would put *off the customers* and *off the waitresses*

Thus, **Ordinary Coordination** facts support the analysis we proposed in (125).

But what about the **Shared Constituent Coordination** test? Given our assumption that the sequence [*off the bus*] in (125) (a) is a PP constituent, we should expect that it can function as the 'shared constituent' in sentences involving Shared Constituent Coordination: and we see from (150) below that this is indeed the case:

(150) Drunks would get — and junkies would fall — *off the bus*

By contrast, the sequence *off the customers* cannot be used in the same way in (125) (b) : cf.

(151) *Drunks would put — and junkies would also put — *off the customers*

2.5. Ellipsis Test (Gapping)

One such type is known as **gapping**, because it has the effect of leaving a 'gap' in the middle of some Phrase or Clause. For example, the second occurrence of the Verb *bought* can be gapped in this way in a sentence such as:

(152) John bought an apple, and Mary Δ a pear

When a Verb is gapped, any Modal preceding it can also be gapped along with the Verb, even if the two do not form a continuous sequence, as in (153) below:

(153) Could John close the window, and ~~could~~ Mary ~~close~~ the door?

The exact conditions determining what kind of constituent can and cannot undergo gapping in a given sentence are extremely complex, and need not be of concern to us here. What is of more immediate interest to us here is the fact that the Verb *get* can be gapped along with the Modal *would* in structures such as (125) (a), resulting in sentences such as:

(154) Drunks would get off the bus, and junkies ~~would get~~ off the train

However, what is even more interesting is that we cannot gap the Verb *put* along with the Modal *would* in structures like (125) (b), as illustrated by the ungrammaticality of:

(155) *Drunks would put off the customers, and junkies ~~would put~~ off the waitresses

By contrast, we can gap the whole expression *put off* along with *would*: cf.

(156) Drunks would put off the customers, and junkies ~~would put off~~ the waitresses

2.6. Pronominalisation

Simple Coordination facts tell us that they must be Noun Phrases, since they can be coordinated with other Noun Phrases: cf.

(157) (a) Drunks would get off [*the bus*] and [*the train*]

     (b) Drunks would put off [*the customers*] and [*the waitresses*]

Now, if they are Noun Phrases, we should obviously expect that they can be replaced by an appropriate pro-NP constituent such as *it* or *them*. And yet, while this is true of the object of a Prepositional Verb like *get off*: cf.

(158) The trouble with the bus was that drunks would want to get off *it* every few miles, to exercise their natural bodily functions

it is not true of Phrasal Verbs such as *put off*: cf.

(159) *What worries me about the customers is whether drunks would put off *them*

So, it would seem that Prepositional Verbs can take pronominal Objects, but Phrasal Verbs require non-pronominal Objects. Why this should be is not entirely clear.

In actual fact, our claim that Phrasal Verbs don't take pronominal objects is something of an oversimplification, as (160) below illustrates:

(160) (a) *Drunks would put off *them*

     (b) Drunks would put *them* off

We see in (160) that a Phrasal Verb like *put off* can indeed take a pronominal object, but only when the Preposition is positioned at the end of the sentence. Moreover, it isn't just a pronominal object which can appear between *put* and *off*: as (161) below indicates, an ordinary nominal NP can also appear in this position:

(161) Drunks would put [*the customers*] off

By contrast, a Prepositional Verb like *get off* does not permit the Preposition to be moved to the end of the VP in this way: cf.

(162) *Drunks would get the bus *off*

Thus, whereas a Phrasal Verb allows its accompanying Preposition to be positioned either before or after a Noun Phrase Object (though when the Object is pronominal, the Preposition must be positioned after the Object), a Prepositional Verb only allows the Preposition to be positioned *before* the NP Object.

The obvious question to ask at this point is what is the structure of a sentence such as (161), in which the Preposition is positioned at the end of the VP. We shall argue here that (161) has the structure (163) below:

(163)

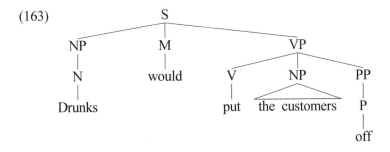

It seems clear that *off* must be a constituent of the VP here, since it can be preposed along with the other constituents of VP for emphasis: cf.

(164) The manager said that drunks would put the customers off, and

   [*put the customers off*] they certainly would

Questions

Answer Key p.486

01 <A>를 읽고, 구성 성분 테스트(constituent test)를 이용하여 <B>에 주어진 문장의 밑줄 친 부분이 구성 성분(constituent)이 될 수 있는지 없는지를 우리말로 밝히시오. [4점]

2006년 전국 7번

┤ A ├

Consider the sentences below.

(1) John will meet his employer at the castle.

(2) a. At the castle, John will meet his employer.
   b. His employer, John will meet at the castle.
   c. Meet his employer at the castle, John will (indeed).

(3) a. *Employer at the, John will meet his castle.
   b. *Meet his, John will employer at the castle.

In each of the sentences in (2) a group of words has been moved to the beginning of the sentence, since it forms a syntactic unit called *a constituent*. On the other hand, in (3), the preposed words do not form constituents. That is why they are ungrammatical. Only a constituent can be preposed.

+ B +

① The people can move <u>the sculpture into the museum</u>.

② The people can see <u>the sculpture from the museum</u>.

① _____

   _____

   _____

② _____

   _____

   _____

02 Read <A> and <B> and follow the directions. 2009년 27번

---| A |---

The pronouns *one* and *it* are used to refer to nominal expressions. However, they are not only semantically but also syntactically different. Thus, students may misuse them unless they understand their usage. This means that teachers need to have a good knowledge of the principles governing pronominal usage in order to teach their students how to use the pronouns correctly. In relation to their syntactic characteristics, *one* can replace an N′ (not an N) while *it* can replace an NP.

---| B |---

A : I bought a book in this bookstore yesterday.

B : What kind of book did you get?

A : It's a book of poems with a pink cover by Wordsworth.

B : Is it interesting?

A : Yes, very interesting. Why don't you buy a poetry book too?

B : Yes, I'd like to. But I'd like to buy a modern ⓐ one by a different author.

A : Which ⓑ one?

B : I'd like to get a book of poetry by T. S. Eliot.

A : How about that ⓒ one over there?

B : Do you mean the ⓓ one of poetry with a yellow cover? The book on the top shelf?

A : Yes, ⓔ one with a green-colored spine just next to the poetry book by Frost.

Choose all the INCORRECT uses of one in <B> based on <A>.

① ⓐ, ⓑ   ② ⓐ, ⓒ   ③ ⓑ, ⓒ

④ ⓒ, ⓓ   ⑤ ⓓ, ⓔ

03 Read the passage in <A> and the sentences in <B>, and follow the directions. [4 points]   2014년 A형 4번

A

   A constituent is a string of one or more words that syntactically and semantically behaves as a unit. The constituency of a string of words can be verified by a number of constituency tests, two of which are *movement* and *substitution*.

B

(1) Can you confirm your receipt of my application for membership?

(2) Call the reviewers of Bill's new book in a week.

(3) The music festival was crowded with young composers of jazz from Asia.

(4) Tina bears a striking resemblance to her mother.

Choose all the sentences where the underlined part qualifies as a constituent and identify the syntactic category of each constituent. Then explain how *movement* and/or *substitution* can be applied to verify the constituency of each string of words.

_____

_____

_____

_____

_____

04 Read the passage and follow the directions. [4 points] 2019년 A형 9번

┤ A ├

Clausal modifiers of NPs which function as the Subject or the Object can move to the end of the sentence, which is called 'extraposition,' as shown in (1) and (2), respectively. The extraposed CP can be adjoined to VP or TP.

(1) a. A man [who has red hair] just came in.
   b. A man just came in [who has red hair].

(2) a. John won't turn a friend [who needs help] away.
   b. John won't turn a friend away [who needs help].

Let's take a closer examination of the extraposition of the CP from the Object position in (2b). As confirmed in (3), VP preposing can be further applied to (2b) and the resulting sentence is grammatical. This suggests that the extraposed CP from the Object position is adjoined to VP, since only phrasal constituents can move.

(3) John said that he wouldn't turn a friend away who needs help, and [turn a friend away who needs help] he won't.

The whole process can be represented as in (4): from the structure in (4a) the clausal modifier CP adjoined to VP in (4b) and the resulting VP constituent moved to the front of the sentence in (4c).

(4) a. [$_{TP}$ John won't [$_{VP}$ turn [$_{NP}$ a friend [$_{CP}$ who needs help]] away]]
   b. [$_{TP}$ John won't [$_{VP}$ [$_{VP}$ turn a friend t$_i$ away] [$_{CP}$ who needs help]$_i$]]
   c. [[$_{VP}$ [$_{VP}$ turn a friend away][$_{CP}$ who needs help]]$_j$ [$_{TP}$ John won't t$_j$]]

From the brief observation, it can be proposed that an extraposed CP is adjoined to the first phrasal constituent containing the NP out of which it is extraposed.

┤ B ├

(i) Few people who knew him$_i$ would work with John$_i$.

(ii) Few people would work with John$_i$ who knew him$_i$.

(iii) Work with John$_i$ who knew him$_i$ few people would.

Based on the proposal in <A>, first identify in <B> what syntactic category the extraposed CP in (ii), derived from (i), is adjoined to. Second, state whether the preposing in (iii), derived from (ii), is grammatical or not, and then explain why.

_____

_____

_____

_____

_____

05 Read the passage and follow the directions. [2점]

There is an intriguing phenomenon in English in which two semantically related constituents are separated, as shown below.

(1) a. All the students will work hard.

    b. The students will all work hard.

In both (1a) and (1b), the quantifier *all* modifies the subject *the students*. What is interesting is that in sentence (1b), the quantifier positioned after the subject forms a discontinuous constituent with no major change in meaning.

This fact can be straightforwardly accounted for if it is assumed that the entire constituent *all* the students is base-generated in the _____ position of VP. As illustrated in (2a), *all the students* undergoes movement to the surface subject position. By contrast, in (2b), just part of the constituent, *the students*, moves to the subject position, leaving *all* behind in its base position, marked as [*all* t_i].

(2) a. [$_{TP}$ [all the students]$_i$ will [$_{VP}$ t_i work hard]]

    b.

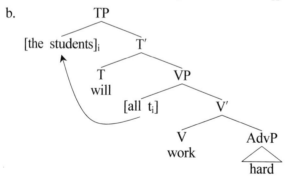

This account is based upon 'VP-internal subject hypothesis,' which states that a subject is base-generated in the _____ position of VP and in turn moves to the _____ position of Tense Phrase (TP).

Fill in the three blanks with the ONE most appropriate word. Use the SAME word for all the blanks.

06 **Read the passage and follow the directions.** [4 points]

┤ A ├

To account for some syntactic phenomena in English, we can resort to phrasal categories such as VP, TP, CP, and so on. First, let us assume that only constituents which belong to the same phrasal category can be coordinated. For example, NP can conjoin with another NP, but not with AP.

(1) a. The student or the teacher
   b. *The student or very pretty

The same restriction also holds true with clausal structures. The bracketed structures in (2a) and (2b) are clearly different, since they cannot be coordinated by the conjunction *or*, as shown in (2c).

(2) a. We didn't intend [you to hurt him].
   b. We didn't intend [for him to hurt you].
   c. *We didn't intend [you to hurt him] or [for him to hurt you].

So, based on the phrasal category and the assumption about coordination, we can explain the ungrammaticality of the sentences such as (2c).

   Second, the restriction on *wh*-cleft sentences can also be attributed to phrasal categories.

(3) What I'll do is [$_{VP}$ postpone the meeting].

VP can be in the focus position (the position after *be* verb) of *wh*-cleft sentences like (3). Consider further the following examples.

(4) a. Bill promised [$_{CP}$ Ø PRO to behave himself].
   b. What Bill promised was [$_{CP}$ Ø PRO to behave himself].

(5) a. They believe [$_{TP}$ him to be innocent].
   b. *What they believe is [$_{TP}$ him to be innocent].

The verb *promise* in (4a) is known to take a CP (Complementizer Phrase) complement which is headed by a null complementizer Ø, and we find that CP can be in the focus position, as shown in (4b). Meanwhile, in (5a), the verb *believe* requires a TP (Tense Phrase) complement, and from the ungrammaticality of (5b), it is clear that TP cannot be in the focus position of a *wh*-cleft sentence. Thus, based on the types of phrasal categories, we can explain the restriction on *wh*-cleft sentences.

Note : '*' indicates the ungrammaticality of the sentence.
Note : 'PRO' is a null pronoun which represents the understood subject of some infinitive clauses.

B

(i) She argued persuasively or that their offer should be rejected.
(ii) They offered us a choice of red wine, white wine, or beer.
(iii) What he claims is that he was insulted.
(iv) What we hadn't intended was you to get hurt.

Based on <A>, choose ONE ungrammatical sentence between (i) and (ii) in <B> and ONE grammatical sentence between (iii) and (iv) in <B>. Then, explain why the chosen sentences are ungrammatical or grammatical on the basis of the description in <A>.

07 Read the passage and follow the directions. [4 points]

2022년 A형 7번

───────────────┤ A ├───────────────

Coordination is possible when two constituents share the same type of syntactic function. As shown in (1a), a complement can be conjoined by another complement. If it is combined with an adjunct, however, ungrammaticality results as in (1b).

(1) a. We won't reveal [Complement the nature of the threat] or [Complement where it came from].

   b. *I went [Complement to the park] and [Adjunct for health reason].

The syntactic function of dependents (i.e., complements or adjuncts) influences *one*-replacement of nouns, too. Note, for example, that a noun *prince* can be replaced by one in (2a), but not in (2b). The difference lies in what syntactic function the PP serves in each example. The noun is modified by an adjunct in (2a), but by a complement in (2b).

(2) a. The prince from Denmark and the one from Japan met each other yesterday.

   b. *The prince of Denmark and the one of Japan met each other yesterday.

It is possible for dependents of nouns to appear in a pre-nominal position, which triggers structural ambiguity. For instance, *Korean* in 'the Korean professor' can be interpreted as either complement or adjunct: the professor teaching the Korean language and the professor from Korea, respectively.

Note : '*' indicates the ungrammaticality of the sentence.

───────────────┤ B ├───────────────

(i) The man who entered the room was the linguistics and Korean professor.
(ii) Mina is not the Japanese professor but the Korean one.

Based on <A>, identify in <B> whether *Korean* in (i) and (ii) should be interpreted as language, nationality, or both. Write your answers in the correct order. Then, explain your answers on the basis of the description in <A>.

_____

_____

_____

_____

_____

08 **Read the passage and follow the directions.** [2 points]   2022년 B형 2번

The tense-affix, such as *-ed* or *-s*, forms an independent head (T) that is separated from a verb in the underlying structure, as shown in (1) and (2). The T-affix needs to attach to a verb in the surface structure via so-called 'Head Movement.' To be specific, T lowers onto lexical verbs, and auxiliary verbs *be/have* raise to T.

(1) a. Joe finished the cake.

    b. [$_{TP}$ Joe T -ed [$_{VP}$ finish the cake]]

(2) a. Joe was listening to music.

    b. [$_{TP}$ Joe T -ed [$_{VP}$ be listening to music]]

Let us now observe the data in (3) and (4) that involve so-called 'Verb Phrase ellipsis (VP-ellipsis).' VP-ellipsis is assumed to be licensed when the verb phrase in the second conjunct is isomorphic to that of its corresponding antecedent. For example, the VP of the second conjunct in (3a) is identical to the one in the first conjunct, and deletion of the VP is possible in (3b). The same holds of (4b). However, an interesting difference is observed; namely, dummy *do* is required in the second conjunct in (3), but prohibited in (4).

(3) a. Joe didn't finish the cake, but Mary finished the cake.

    b. Joe didn't finish the cake, but Mary did <finish the cake>.

    c. *Joe didn't finish the cake, but Mary <finish the cake>.

(4) a. Kim wasn't listening to him, but Sue was listening to him.

    b. Kim wasn't listening to him, but Sue was <listening to him>.

    c. *Kim wasn't listening to him, but Sue did <listening to him>.

Note 1: '*' indicates the ungrammaticality of the sentence.
Note 2: Strikethrough inside angled brackets indicates deletion.

Fill in the blanks ① and ② in the correct order with the TWO syntactic operations from the passage.

> To derive (3b) and (4b) and prevent the derivation of (3c) and (4c), a certain order of syntactic operations must take place. For (3b), ____①____ must take place prior to ____②____, but for (4b), ____②____ must take place prior to ____①____.

09 **Read the passage and follow the directions.** [4 points]   2022년 B형 5번

---| A |---

Subjacency is a syntactic constraint that restricts movement to be local; namely, movement should cross over only one bounding node (i.e., TP, NP, or CP). Crossing over more than one bounding node in one cycle of movement would result in ungrammaticality. Let us consider the example in (1a), whose derivation is presented in (1b).

(1) a. *What did Sue hear the rumor that Bill broke?
    b. *What did [TP Sue hear [NP the rumor [CP t_{WH}' that [TP Bill broke t_{WH}]]]]?

The *wh*-phrase in (1) involves two cycles of *wh*-movement. In the first cycle, the *wh*-phrase raises from the complement of *broke* to the specifier of CP in the embedded clause, from which it raises to the matrix specifier position of CP in the second cycle. It is crucial to note that the second cycle crosses over three bounding nodes. This is a violation of Subjacency and ungrammaticality results. Now consider a grammatical sentence in (2), which involves one cycle of *wh*-movement crossing over two TPs, hence apparently violating Subjacency.

(2) Which book does [TP John seem [TP to like t_{WH}]]?

To explain the grammaticality of the example in (2), an additional condition in (3) should be imposed for one of the TPs not to be counted as a bounding node.

(3) Complements of a verb are not bounding nodes.

Bearing the above description in mind, let us reconsider sentence (1). When *what* undergoes the second cycle of *wh*-movement in (1), it crosses over two bounding nodes. This is because the _____ phrase is no longer a bounding node.

Note : '*' indicates the ungrammaticality of the sentence.

┤ B ├

(i) Which actress did you think that John had a strong influence on t_{WH}?

(ii) Which actress did a picture of t_{WH} scare the entire population?

(iii) Which actress did John believe t_{WH} spoiled the whole movie?

Fill in the blank in <A> with a part of speech. Then, based on <A>, identify ONE ungrammatical sentence in <B>, and explain how the sentence violates Subjacency by specifying the bounding nodes that the *wh*-phrase crosses over.

_____

_____

_____

_____

_____

10 Read the passage in <A> and the examples in <B>, and follow the directions. [4 points]

2023년 A형 7번

────── ┤ A ├ ──────

A sentence sometimes allows for more than one reading when a modifier has more than one option to take. For instance, in (1) the PP *in France* may modify a verb to derive the meaning of "I went to France where a seminar on language took place," or a noun to derive the meaning of "The seminar was about language in France."

(1) I went to a seminar on language in France.

In syntax, branches are not allowed to cross in tree structure, which is also known as the No Crossing Branches (NCB) constraint. Observe that sentence (2a) is ruled out, and its ungrammaticality is attributed to a violation of the NCB constraint, as shown in (2b).

(2) a. *The baby might be afraid in the park of new people.

b.

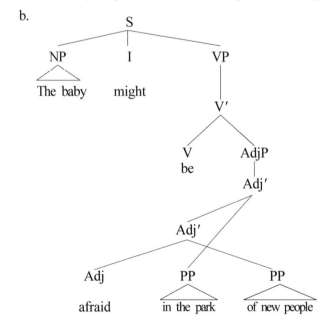

Note : '*' indicates the ungrammaticality of the sentence.

B

(3) The man is talking to the woman with a tablet on the desk.

    a. The man is on the desk, and the woman owns a tablet.

    b. The woman is on the desk, and the man owns a tablet.

    c. The woman owns a tablet, and the tablet is on the desk.

(4) a. He should not surely break his promise.

    b. He should surely not break his promise.

    c. He surely should not break his promise.

Note 1 : Assume that *surely* is a sentence adverb adjoining to the S node.

Note 2 : Assume that *not* merges at SpecVP in tree diagrams.

Based on <A>, first, identify the ONE structurally unavailable reading in (3) in <B> and identify the ONE ungrammatical sentence in (4) in <B>, both of which violate the NCB constraint. Second, explain how the sentence you chose in (4) violates the NCB constraint.

_____

_____

_____

_____

_____

11 Read the passages in <A> and <B>, and follow the directions. [2 points]

2023년 B형 2번

─┤ A ├─

Traditionally the parts of speech such as adjective, adverb, noun, preposition, or verb have been defined under semantic criteria. For example, nouns are defined as words that denote people, things, animals, and places. In many cases, the traditional definition works well as *teachers, tables, cats,* and *schools* are all categorized as nouns. However, there are many other cases in which the definition does not work. For instance, *sincerity, love,* and *destruction* are all nouns but they denote a personality trait, an emotional state, and a process, respectively.

As an alternative, syntacticians categorize the parts of speech under distributional criteria. They group words that can fit in the syntactic context and then name the category. In the distributional context in (1), for example, words such as *dog, child, analysis,* or *love* can fill in the blank, but other words like *in, eliminate,* or *sadly* can't; in other words, no part of speech other than a noun can occur in the blank.

(1) His _____ is great.

Bearing the description above in mind, consider the following examples in (2) - (5) that show the distributions of *there* and *fast.*

(2) a. They repaired the car right there.
    b. *They repaired the car right fast.
    c. They repaired the car right in that building.
(3) a. They repaired the car very fast.
    b. *They repaired the car very there.
    c. They repaired the car fast enough.
    d. *They repaired the car there enough.
(4) a. The people there are very cheerful.
    b. *The people fast are very cheerful.
    c. The people at work are very cheerful.

(5) a. The place he drove his car to is in the center.

   b. *The place he drove his car to is fast.

   c. The place he drove his car to is there.

Note : '*' indicates the ungrammaticality of the sentence.

| B |

Under distributional criteria, we can draw a conclusion that *there* should be counted as a(n) ① _____ functioning as the head of its own phrase and *fast* as a(n) ② _____ functioning as the head of its own phrase.

Fill in the blanks ① and ② in <B> each with ONE word from <A>, in the correct order.

MEN
TOR

Mentor Linguistics

멘토영어학
기출분석

Chapter 04

Verb Complements

Preview & Review

01 Verb Complements

1.1. Believe Type: *believe* + NP + *to*-infinitive

1.1.1. Meaning

The number and type of arguments that a particular predicate needs is clearly determined to a large extent by the meaning of the predicate in question.

(5) Ed believes the story.

In (5) the meaning of *believe*, a two-place predicate, is such that it requires somebody who does the believing (a Subject) as well as a specification of what is being believed (a Direct Object).

(6) Ed believes that the story is false.

In (5) it takes two NP arguments, whereas in (6) it takes an NP Subject and a clausal DO. Notice that both the NP *the story* in (5) and the clause *that the story is false* in (6) are DOs which carry the thematic roles of Patient and Proposition, respectively. It is worth stressing again the fact that for some element to act as an argument of some predicate it must bear a thematic relation to that predicate.

(7) Ed believes the story to be false.

We might wonder how many further arguments *believe* has in this sentence. There are a number of possible analyses we can assign to (7). One common analysis involves taking the NP *the story* to be a DO, and the clause *to be false* to be a further Complement.

One reason for taking *the story* to be a DO is that when we passivise (7) it is this NP that is fronted:

(8) <u>The story</u> is believed _____ to be false by Ed.

Furthermore, if we have a pronominal NP following *believe*, it must take accusative case:

(9) Ed believes him to be a traitor.

If something intervenes between the verb and the pronoun, for example a complementiser, as in (10), then the pronoun receives subjective case.

(10) Ed believes that he is a traitor.

Not only are the arguments in favour of an analysis of *the story* as a DO in (7) not wholly convincing, they lead to a serious problem: if *believe* indeed takes this NP as its DO, we would expect there to be a thematic relationship between *believe* and *the story,* such that *believe* assigns the thematic role of Patient to *the story,* exactly as in (5). With respect to its meaning, this entails that 'Ed believes the story'. Clearly, this is not what (7) means. Quite the contrary: (7) expresses Ed's incredulity with regard to the story in question. This suggests that the story is not a DO argument of *believe,* but the Subject of the string *the story to be false.* We conclude that **the string** *the story to be false* **is a clausal Object of** *believe.*

1.1.2. Dummy elements and idiom chunks

Dummy elements are lexical elements without semantic content, i.e. they are meaningless. English has two such elements, namely nonreferential *it* and existential *there.*

(11) *It* is raining.
(12) *It* is cold.
(13) *There* are a number of solutions to this problem.
(14) *There* has been an increase in crime in America.

Because they are meaningless, there can be no thematic relationship between them and the associated predicate. Put differently, no thematic role is assigned to them, and for that reason they cannot act as arguments. Nonreferential *it* and existential *there* (also called *expletive* or *pleonastic* elements) **always occur in the Subject position** and should be distinguished from referential *it* and locative *there*.

(15) I don't like his pipe. *It* stinks.
(16) Los Angeles? I have no desire to go *there*.

We turn now to idioms and idiom chunks.

(17) The coast is clear.
(18) The fat is in the fire.

In these examples *the coast* and *the fat* are Subject idiom chunks. These NPs cannot be replaced by different NPs without the particular meanings associated with the full expressions being lost.

Dummy elements and Subject idiom chunks can be used to show that the NP in *believe* + NP + *to*-infinitive structures like (7) cannot be analysed as a DO.

(19) Ed believes *it* always to be raining in London.
(20) Ed believes *there* to be a traitor in the company.

Dummy elements must occur in the Subject position and they cannot be analysed as DOs, because an element must have a thematic relationship with a preceding main verb for it to occur in the DO slot. We therefore analyse them as Subjects of subordinate clauses.

We can pursue a similar line of reasoning for Subject idiom chunks.

(21) Ed believes [*the coast* to be clear].
(22) Ed believes [*the fat* to be in the fire].

We conclude that the idiom chunks *the coast* and *the fat* function as Subject in the subordinate clauses *the coast to be clear* and *the fat to be in the fire.*

1.1.3. Passivisation

There is an additional argument we can use to show that the NP in *believe* + NP + *to*-infinitive constructions is not a DO. Consider the following data:

(23) Ed believes the jury to have given the wrong verdict.
(24) Ed believes the wrong verdict to have been given by the jury.

Ed holds a belief in the content of a proposition, namely the proposition that the jury has given the wrong verdict. In other words, there exists no thematic relationship between *believe* and the NPs *the jury* in (23) and *the wrong verdict* in (24). These phrases cannot therefore function as the DO of *believe.*

With regard to (23) and (24) the generalisation we can now make is that if we can passivise the postverbal portion in any verb + NP + to-infinitive construction without a resulting change in meaning, then the postverbal NP is not a DO, but the Subject of a subordinate clause. (23) and (24) are bracketed as follows:

(25) Ed believes [the jury to have given the wrong verdict].
(26) Ed believes [the wrong verdict to have been given by the jury].

Incidentally, do not confuse the passive in (24) with an alternative passive version of (23), namely (27):

(27) The jury is believed to have given the wrong verdict by Ed.

Here the *main* clause, rather than the subordinate clause, has been passivised.

1.2. Persuade Type: *persuade* + NP + *to*-infinitive

1.2.1. Meaning

Take a look at the following sentence:

(28) Ed persuaded Brian to interview Melanie.

Unlike in the *believe* + NP + *to*-infinitive construction, notice that there is a thematic relationship between the verb *persuade* and the NP that follows it: in (28) the individual Brian undergoes Ed's act of persuasion, and the NP *Brian* can therefore be said to function as DO.

1.2.2. Dummy elements and idiom chunks

Now, if the postverbal NP in the *persuade* + NP + *to*-infinitive construction is indeed a DO, it should not be possible for this position to be occupied by dummy elements, because these can only occur in a Subject position.

(29) *Ed persuaded it to be hot in the room.
(30) *Ed persuaded there to be a party.

Idiom chunks also cannot occupy the position following *persuade:*

(31) *Ed persuaded the coast to be clear.
(32) *Ed persuaded the fat to be in the fire.

1.2.3. Passivisation

What about the passivisation test? Consider the following pair of sentences:

(33) Ed persuaded Brian to interview Melanie. (= (28))
(34) Ed persuaded Melanie to be interviewed by Brian.

Unlike in the case of the *believe* + NP + *to*-infinitive construction, we can establish a thematic relationship between the verb and the postverbal NPs here, i.e. between *persuade* and *Brian* in (33), and between *persuade* and *Melanie* in (34). Put differently, Ed persuaded an individual in both cases, not a proposition. We therefore conclude that the NP in the *persuade* + NP + *to*-infinitive construction functions as DO. In addition, we indicate the fact that the main clause DO and the Subject of the Complement clause are coreferential (i.e. share the same referent) by using a subscript letter 'i'. The representation for (28) is then as in (35):

(35) Ed persuaded Brain$_i$ [Ø$_i$ to interview Melanie]

1.3. Want Type: *want* + NP + *to*-infinitive

1.3.1. Meaning

Like *believe* and *persuade,* the verb *want* can also occur in the verb + NP + to-infinitive construction. Here is an example:

(36) Kate wants Ralph to get out of her life.

What is it that Kate wants? Clearly, what she wants is a situation, and situations are described by propositions, in this case 'that Ralph gets out of her life'. In other words, the thematic relationship in (36) holds between *want* and its Subject *Kate,* and between *want* and the string *Ralph to get out of her life.* The latter is a nonfinite clause which takes *Ralph* as its Subject, and functions as a Direct Object.

1.3.2. Dummy elements and idiom chunks

Consider (37) and (38):

(37) Kate wanted <u>it</u> to rain on Ralph's birthday.
(38) Ralph wanted <u>there</u> to be a ceasefire between him and Kate.

We must analyse *it* and *there* as the subjects of subordinate clauses. The same conclusion can be drawn from sentences that contain idiom chunks:

(39) Kate wants <u>the coast</u> to be clear, in order for her to escape from Ralph.
(40) Kate doesn't want <u>the fat</u> to be in the fire, because of some stupid action of Ralph's.

1.3.3. Passivisation

We find that if we passive the entire postverbal string of a *want* + NP + *to*-infinitive construction the meaning of the overall sentence remains constant:

(41) Kate wanted Janet to poison Ralph.
(42) Kate wanted Ralph to be poisoned by Janet.

We conclude that there is no thematic relationship between *want* and the NPs that follow it, namely *Janet* in (41) and *Ralph* in (42).

It seems, then, that our earlier supposition that *want* is like *believe* is warranted. However, this is only partially the case. The similarity between *believe* and *want* is that both verbs take a clausal postverbal argument in the verb + NP + *to*-infinitive pattern. The difference is that in the case of *believe,* but not in the case of *want,* the main clause can also be passivised:

(43) Ed believes the jury to have given the wrong verdict. (= (23))
(44) The jury is believed to have given the wrong verdict by Ed. (= (27))
(45) Kate wanted Janet to poison Ralph. (= (41))
(46) *Janet was wanted to poison Ralph by Kate.

This is a general difference between *believe* and *want,* which also shows up when these verbs take simple DOs in the form of a noun phrase:

(47) Ed believed the wild allegations.
(48) The wild allegations were believed by Ed.
(49) Ed wanted a new CD player.
(50) ?*A new CD player was wanted by Ed.

1.4. Summary

(51) Ed believes the story to be false.

(52) Ed persuaded Brian to interview Melanie.

(53) Kate wants Ralph to get out of her life.

Believe class : consider, expect, intend, know, suppose, understand

Persuade class : advise, convince, notify

Want class : demand, hate, hope, love, prefer, wish

NOTE This list is not exhaustive, and some of these verbs can also appear in other patterns.

Unit 02 Questions

Answer Key p.489

01 다음을 읽고 지시에 따라 답하시오. [4점]

2007년 전국 16번

Consider the sentences:

① Max believed that there was a rose in the garden.

② Max believed Mary to have chocolate.

① and ② show that the verb *believe* can take as its complement a finite clause, in which the verb contains the information of tense and/or _____(A)_____, or a non-finite clause, in which the verb does not. Consider further the following sentences:

③ Max told Mary that there was a rose in the garden.

④ Max told Mary to have chocolate.

The verb *tell* can take two complements, as in ③, where the NP *Mary* functions as the object of the main clause. Given ② and ④, it appears that the verbs *believe* and *tell* behave alike. But, a sharp contrast arises between ⑤ and ⑥ when the NP is replaced by the expletive *there*.

⑤ Max believed there to be a rose in the garden.

⑥ *Max told there to be a rose in the garden.

Traditionally, the ungrammaticality of ⑥ is due to (B) <u>the constraint on the type of object</u> that the verb *tell* takes, as shown in ④ and ⑦.

④ Max told Mary to have chocolate.

⑦ *Max told the tree to have chocolate.

Another way of accounting for the difference in ⑤ and ⑥ is to rely on the distribution of the expletives. The sentences in ⑧ and ⑨ indicate that expletives always occupy the subject position.

⑧ a. There is a rose in the garden, isn't there?

   b. It is raining, isn't it?

⑨ a. *I talked about there. (expletive *there*)

   b. *I saw it. (expletive *it*)

Given both the difference of the number of complements that the verb can take and the constraint on the distribution of expletives, it can be concluded that the difference in grammaticality between ⑤ and ⑥ is based on the fact that _____(C)_____.

(1) 빈칸 (A)에 들어갈 말을 한 단어로 쓰시오.

_____

(2) 밑줄 친 (B)에서 말하는 제약(constraint)의 내용을 10자 내외의 우리말로 쓰시오.

_____

(3) 빈칸 (C)에 들어갈 내용을 50자 이내의 우리말로 쓰시오.

_____

_____

_____

_____

_____

02 Read the following and answer the questions. 2009년 29번

Compare the two sets of sentences in (1) and (2).

(1) a. John was said to have solved all of the questions.

    b. John was told to solve all of the questions.

(2) a. The earthquake was said to have hit the city.

    b. *The earthquake was told to hit the city.

(The sentence with an asterisk '*' is unacceptable.)

The two sentences in (1) contain an NP-movement; an NP moves from the position after the main verb to the subject position. The subject can be interpreted as identical with that of *to*-infinitive. We may assume that the verbs *say* and *tell* take the same type of complement. This assumption, however, cannot be tenable because of the contrast shown in (2). The contrast indicates that the subject in (2a) is not selected by the verb *say*, while that in (2b) must be selected by the verb *tell*.

Here are some more examples whose structure is identical either with (1a)-type construction or with (1b)-type construction as discussed above.

a. The gladiators were supposed to survive brutal fights.

b. The passengers were reminded to fasten their seat belts.

c. The Amish people are reported to live and dress very simply.

d. The company's workers were found to have organized a union.

e. The flood victims were advised to prepare food in hygienic conditions.

f. The listeners were invited to see the world in a different perspective.

Which of the following correctly classifies the above examples a~f?

	(1a)-type	(1b)-type
①	a, b, c	d, e, f
②	a, c, d	b, e, f
③	b, d, e	a, c, f
④	b, d, f	a, c, e
⑤	c, e, f	a, b, d

03 Read <A> and <B> and answer the question.

2013년 34번

┤ A ├

A group of verbs occurring in main verb position followed by infinitive complements may be described as involving some kind of commitment to future action. From a structural perspective, a commitment can be either SELF-DIRECTED (e.g., *decide*) or OTHER-DIRECTED (e.g., *order*). That is, you yourself (self-directed) can *decide to go* (*Structure I* : *V to-V*), or someone else (other-directed) can *order you to go* (*Structure II* : *V NP to-V*). When the commitment is self-directed, there is usually no need for an object NP, as in (1). When the commitment is other-directed, the structure will include an object NP, as in (2).

(1) I decided (*me) to go.
(2) He ordered *us* to get out.

Other-directed verbs also occur with 'for NP' followed by infinitive complements (*Structure III* : *V for NP to-V*), as in (3).

(3) She prayed for him to return.

┤ B ├

Cases	Types of structures
a. Can you <u>allow (we come in)</u>?	II
b. She <u>longed (he would visit her)</u>.	I
c. I <u>threatened (I would leave)</u>.	I
d. We <u>arranged (he would leave at once)</u>.	II
e. They <u>expect (we will come early)</u>.	III

Which of the following lists all and only the cases in <B> that correctly illustrate the types of structures described in <A> when the underlined part is changed into a verb plus infinitive clause sequence?

① a, b
② a, c
③ b, c
④ c, d
⑤ d, e

Mentor Linguistics
멘토영어학
기출분석

Chapter 05

Binding Theory /
Relative Clauses /
Complementizers

Unit
01

Preview & Review

01 Binding Theory

1.1. The Basic Concepts of Binding Theory

1.1.1. Dominance (Domination)

Node A dominates node B if and only if A is higher up in the tree than B and if you can trace a line from A to B going only downwards.

1.1.2. C-command

A node c-commands its sisters and all the daughters (and granddaughters and great-granddaughters, etc.) of its sisters.

1.1.3. Binding Principle

Binding Principle A	An anaphor must be bound in its binding domain.
Anaphor	An **NP** that obligatorily gets its meaning from another NP in the sentence. ⇨ reflexives, reciprocals, etc.
Binding Principle B	A pronoun must be free in its binding domain.
Pronoun (pronominal)	An **NP** that may (but need not) get its meaning from another NP in the sentence. ⇨ he, she, him, her, etc.
Binding Principle C	An R-expression must be free in all domains.
R-expression (Referential-expression)	An **NP** that gets its meaning by referring to an entity in the world. ⇨ Mary, Steve, Bill, etc

1.2. Binding Theory

1.2.1. The Notions Coindex and Antecedent

We're going to start with the distribution of anaphors. First, we need some terminology to set out the facts. An NP that gives its meaning to another noun in the sentence is called the *antecedent*:

(1) *Antecedent* : An NP that gives its meaning to another NP.

For example, in sentence (2), the NP *Heidi* is the source of the meaning for the anaphor *herself,* so *Heidi* is called the antecedent:

(2) <u>Heidi</u> bopped <u>herself</u> on the head with a zucchini.

    ↑   ↑

  antecedent   anaphor

We use a special mechanism to indicate that two NPs refer to the same entity. After each NP we write a subscript letter. If the NPs refer to the same entity, then they get the same letter. If they refer to different entities they get different letters. Usually we start (as a matter of tradition) with the letter i and work our way down the alphabet. These subscript letters are called *indices* or *indexes* (singular: *index*).

(3) (a) [Colin]$_i$ gave [Andrea]$_j$ [a basketball]$_k$.
   (b) [Art]$_i$ said that [he]$_j$ played [basketball]$_k$ in [the dark]$_l$.
   (c) [Art]$_i$ said that [he]$_i$ played [basketball]$_k$ in [the dark]$_l$.
   (d) [Heidi]$_i$ bopped [herself]$_i$ on [the head]$_j$ with [a zucchini]$_k$.

In (3a), all the NPs refer to different entities in the world, so they all get different indexes. The same is true for (3b). Without the indices, this sentence is ambiguous; *he* can refer to Art or to someone else. But with indexing, we disambiguate this form. (3b) only has the meaning where is not Art, but someone else—the pronoun *he* and *Art* have different indexed. The indexing in sentence (3c), by contrast, has *he* and *Art* referring to the same person. In this sentence, *Art* is the antecedent of the pronoun *he,* so they have the same index. Finally in (3d), the anaphor *herself* refers back to *Heidi* so they get the same index. Two NPs that get the same index are said to be ***coindexed***. NPs that are coindexed with each other are said to *corefer* (i.e., refer to the same entity in the world).

(4) *Coindexed*: Two NPs are said to be coindexed if they have the same index.

In (3c) *Art* and *he* are coindexed; in (3b) *Art* and *he* are not coindexed.

1.2.2. Binding

The notions of coindexation, coreference, and antecedence are actually quite general ones. They hold no matter what structural position an NP is the sentence. It turns out, however, that the relations between an antecedent and a pronoun or anaphor must bear particular structural relations. Contrast the three sentences in (5).

(5) (a) Heidi$_i$ bopped herself$_i$ on the head with a zucchini.

    (b) [Heidi$_i$'s mother]$_j$ bopped herself$_j$ on the head with a zucchini.

    (c) *[Heidi$_i$'s mother]$_j$ bopped herself$_i$ on the head with a zucchini.

In particular notice the pattern of indexes on (5b) and (5c). These sentences show that, while the word *herself* can refer to the whole subject NP *Heidi's mother,* it can't refer to an NP embedded inside the subject NP, such as *Heidi.* Similar facts are seen in (6).

(6) (a) [The mother of Heidi$_i$]$_j$ bopped herself$_j$ on the head with a zucchini.

    (b) *[The mother of Heidi$_i$]$_j$ bopped herself$_i$ on the head with a zucchini.

Look at the trees for (5a and b), shown in (7a and b) below, and you will notice a significant difference in terms of the position where the NP immediately dominating *Heidi* is placed.

(7) a)

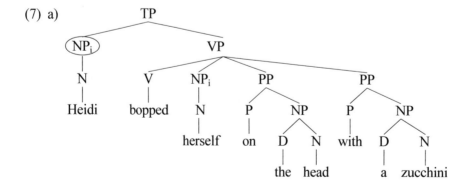

b)

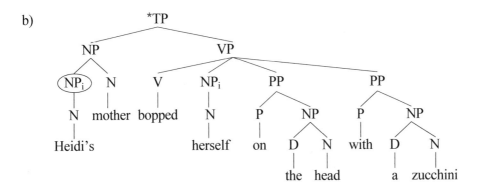

In (7a), the circled NP c-commands the NP dominating *herself,* but in (7b) it does not. It appears that the crucial relationship between an anaphor and its antecedent involves c-command. So in describing the relationship between an anaphor and an antecedent we need a more specific notion than simple coindexation. This is ***binding***:

(8) *Binds* : A binds B if and only if A c-commands B and A and B are coindexed.

Binding is a special kind of coindexation. It is coindexation that happens when one of the two NPs c-commands the other. Notice that coindexation alone does not constitute binding. Binding requires both coindexation and c-command.

Now we can make the following generalization, which explains the ungrammaticality of sentences (9a) and (9b):

(9) (a) *Herself$_i$ bopped Heidi$_i$ on the head with a zucchini.
    (b) *[Heidi$_i$'s mother]$_j$ bopped herself$_i$ on the head with a zucchini.

In neither of these sentences is the anaphor bound. In other words, it is not c-commanded by the NP it is coindexed with. This generalization is called ***Binding Principle A***. Principle A determines the distribution of anaphors:

(10) *Binding Principle A (preliminary)* : An anaphor must be bound.

1.2.3. Locality Conditions on the Binding of Anaphors

Consider now the following fact about anaphors:

(11) *Heidi$_i$ said that herself$_i$ discoed with Art.

    (cf. Heidi$_i$ said that she$_i$ discoed with Art.)

A tree for sentence (11) is given below. As you can see from this tree, the anaphor is bound by its antecedent: [$_{NP}$ *Heidi*] c-commands [$_{NP}$ *Herself*] and is coindexed with it. This sentence is predicted to be grammatical by the version of Principle A presented in (10), since it meets the requirement that anaphors be bound. Surprisingly, however, the sentence is ungrammatical.

(12)   *

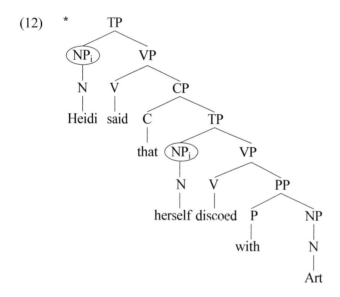

Notice that the difference between a sentence like (11) and a sentence like (5a) is that in the ungrammatical (11) the anaphor is in an embedded clause. The anaphor seems to need to find its antecedent in the same clause. This is called a ***locality constraint***. The anaphor's antecedent must be near it or "local" in some way. The syntactic space in which an anaphor must find its antecedent is called a ***binding domain***. For the moment let's just assume that the binding domain is the clause (TP).

(13) *Binding domain* : The clause containing the NP (anaphor, pronoun, or R-expression).

With this in mind, let's revise Principle A:

(14) *Binding Principle A (revised)* : An anaphor must be bound in its binding domain.

1.2.4. The Distribution of Pronouns

Anaphors are not the only NP type with restrictions on their syntactic position. Pronouns can also be restricted in where they may appear:

(15) (a) Heidi$_i$ bopped her$_j$ on the head with the zucchini.

    (b) *Heidi$_i$ bopped her$_i$ on the head with the zucchini.

Pronouns like her in the sentences in (15) may not be bound. (They may not be coindexed by a c-commanding NP.) The sentence in (15) may only have the meaning where the *her* refers to someone other than *Heidi*. Contrast this situation with the one in which the pronoun is in an embedded clause:

(16) (a) Heidi$_i$ said [$_{CP}$ that she$_i$ discoed with Art].

    (b) Heidi$_i$ said [$_{CP}$ that she$_k$ discoed with Art].

In this situation, a pronoun may be bound by an antecedent, but it doesn't have to be. It can be bound, as in (16a), or not bound, as in (16b). Unlike the case of anaphors, which *must* be bound in a particular configuration, pronouns seem only to have a limitation on where they *cannot* be bound. That is, a pronoun cannot be bound by an antecedent that is a clause-mate (in the same immediate clause). You'll notice that this is exactly the opposite of where anaphors are allowed. This restriction is called ***Principle B*** of the binding theory. It makes use of the term free. ***Free*** is the opposite of bound.

(17) *Free* : Not bound.

(18) *Principle B* : A pronoun must be free in its binding domain.

Given that the binding domain is a clause, the ungrammaticality of (15b) is explained. Both *Heidi* and *her* are in the same clause, so they may not be bound to each other. The pronoun must be free. In (16) both indexings are allowed by Principle B. In (16b) the pronoun isn't bound at all (so is free within its binding domain). In (16a), the situation is little trickier: The pronoun is bound, but it isn't bound within its binding domain (the embedded clause). Its binder lies outside the binding domain, so the sentence is grammatical.

1.2.5. The Distribution of R-Expressions

R-expressions have yet another distribution. R-expressions don't seem to allow any instances of binding at all, not within the binding domain and not outside it either.

(19) (a) *$Heidi_i$ kissed $Miriam_i$.
    (b) *Art_i kissed $Geoff_i$.
    (c) *She_i kissed $Heidi_i$.
    (d) *She_i said that $Heidi_i$ was a disco queen.

In none of these sentences can the second NP (all R-expressions) be bound by a c-commanding word. This in and of itself isn't terribly surprising, given the fact that R-expressions receive their meaning from outside the sentence (i.e., from the context). That they don't get their meaning from another word in the sentence (via binding) is entirely expected. We do have to rule out situations like (19), however. The constraint that describes the distribution of R-expressions is called **Principle C**.

(20) *Principle C*: An R-expression must be free.

Notice that Principle C says nothing about a binding domain. Essentially R-expressions must be free everywhere. They cannot be bound at all.

A Relative Pronoun vs. A Pure Complementizers

The use of *that* as both a relative pronoun and a pure complementizer can lead to confusion between appositive *that*-clauses and relative clauses:

a. The suggestion <u>that he might fail</u> is disturbing.
b. The suggestion <u>that he made</u> is disturbing.

In (a) is a clause functioning as a complement of N (equivalent to a direct object of the verb *suggest*: Someone suggested that he might fail). The complementizer *that* has no function in its own clause, and the embedded clause is complete without *that* and can stand alone as a complete sentence *He might fail*. The *that*-clause can also function as an NP: *That he might fail is disturbing*. In (b) is a clause functioning as a modifier of N′. The relative *that* has the function of direct object in its own clause, and hence the embedded clause is not complete without the relative: **He made*. The embedded clause cannot function as an NP: **That he made is disturbing*. Note that *which* can substitute for *that* in this case but not in the other: *The suggestion which he made is disturbing*, **The suggestion which he might fail is disturbing*.

03 Restrictives vs. Non-restrictives

All the relative clauses considered so far are restrictive relative clauses. The other kind of relative clause is described as non-restrictive. The internal structure of these two kinds of clause is identical. **The difference between restrictives and non-restrictives lies in the way they relate to the head noun within the overall NP.** In the following sentences, all the subject NPs contain relative clauses. Those in the [a]s are restrictive, those in the [b]s are non-restrictive.

[55a] The books which John has consulted are out of date.
[55b] The books, which John has consulted, are out of date.
[56a] The dogs which have rabies are dangerous.
[56b] The dogs, which have rabies, are dangerous.

As you can see, the non-restrictives are distinguished in writing from restrictives by being marked off by commas. The difference between them, though, does not consist in the presence vs. absence of commas, so we need to ask what the commas in the [b] examples are telling us about the relation between the main clause and the relative clause. This can be brought out by showing that <u>certain relative clauses can only be used non-restrictively in certain contexts</u>:

[57a] *The dogs which are mammals need treatment.
[57b] The dogs, which are mammals, need treatment.
[58a] *Triangles which have three sides are fascinating.
[58b] Triangles, which have three sides, are fascinating.

The oddity of the (restrictive) [a] examples is due to the fact that **restrictive relative clauses specify more exactly which of the things picked out by the head noun are being mentioned.** In [55a], for example, the relative clause tells us *which* books are out of date. It is described as 'restrictive' because it serves to restrict the set of books to a sub-set of books, namely those consulted by John. It is that more restricted set of books that are said, in [55a], to be out of date. But the relative clauses in [57] and [58] cannot be used to pick out a more highly specified set of dogs or triangles, because all dogs are mammals—and all triangles three-sided—anyway. So, you cannot (as in [58a]) use *which have three sides* to pick out a sub-set of triangles.

Nevertheless, there is nothing to stop us, parenthetically, adding the extra information that triangles have three sides or that dogs are mammals. This is precisely what the non-restrictive clause allows us to do. **Non-restrictive relative clauses serve to add extra—parenthetical— information, without restricting the set of things (triangles, dogs, books, etc,) being mentioned.**

In the light of this, compare [56a] and [56b]. [56a], with the restrictive clause, does not imply that all the relevant dogs are dangerous; it is only the rabid ones that are said to be dangerous. But [56b], with the non-restrictive clause, does imply that all the relevant dogs are dangerous—and it adds the further information that they also have rabies.

The big difference, then, is that [56a] makes just ONE statement—a statement about the rabid dogs to the effect that they dangerous—but [56b] makes TWO separate statements: (1) that the dogs are dangerous, (2) that the dogs have rabies.

04 Infinitival Relative Clauses

The types of restrictive relative clauses considered earlier in the chapter all have verbs with tense. The sentences in (57) have what appear to be infinitive clauses (with verbs in infinitive forms) following and modifying a head noun. These are examples of *infinitival (INFIN) relative clauses*. Notice that the particular examples in (57) are similar to OP (Object of the preposition) relatives; the head noun modified corresponds to a prepositional object in the infinitival relative clause.

(57) a. Here is a chair *to sit on.*

    b. We need a sack *to carry the money in.*

    c. John is not the right person *to confide in.*

Although the clauses in (57) do not have relative pronouns, they have versions that do have relative pronouns, shown in (58). In each case, the preposition and its object have been moved to the front of the infinitive clause by *wh*-movement, as illustrated in (58a). Thus, the versions in (57) can be considered INFIN relative clauses that have undergone relative pronoun deletion.

(58) a. Here is a chair [*on which* to sit _____].

    b. We need a sack *in which to carry the money.*

    c. John is not the right person *in whom to confide.*

Notice that a relative pronoun is possible only if the preposition moves to the front; we cannot add relative pronouns to the stranded versions in (57) (e.g., **Here is a chair which to sit on*).

The infinitival relative clauses in (59) are similar to O relatives; in each sentence in (59) the head noun corresponds to the object of the relative clause verb. The sentences in (59) also show that infinitival relative clauses can optionally have subjects, shown in parentheses, that follow *for*.

(59) a. I found something interesting *(for us/you) to read*.

    b. That is not a very good way *(for you/him) to begin*.

There are also infinitive relative clauses similar to S relatives, as illustrated by (60), in which the clause subject corresponds to the noun the clause modifies, *the first person.* The sentence therefore has no alternative version with *for,* but the infinitive clause has an S relative clause paraphrase: *John is not the first person who (has) noticed that.*

(60) He is not the first person *to notice that.*

05 Complementisers

Complementisers can be classified into types on the basis of two different criteria: (i) syntactic (whether they are used in interrogative or noninterrogative Clauses), and (ii) morphological (whether they serve to introduce finite or nonfinite Clauses). So, for example, we might classify *that* as a noninterrogative finite Complementiser, since it only introduces finite Clauses, not Infinitives: cf.

(48) (a) I am anxious [*that* you should arrive on time]
  (b) *I am anxious [*that* you to arrive on time]

Conversely, we might classify *for* as a noninterrogative infinitive Complementiser, since it can introduce infinitive Clauses, but not finite Clauses—cf. e.g

(49) (a) I am anxious [*for* you to arrive on time]
  (b) *I am anxious [*for* you should arrive on time]

By contrast, *whether* is an interrogative Complementiser which can introduce finite and nonfinite Clauses alike; whereas *if* by is an interrogative Complementiser which can only introduce finite Complement Clauses: cf.

(50) (a) I don't know [*whether/if* I should agree]
  (b) I don't know [*whether/*if* to agree]

If we were to use the feature [±WH] to indicate whether a Complementiser is interrogative or not, and the feature [±FINITE] to indicate whether a Complementiser can introduce a finite or nonfinite Clause (or both), then we could analyse each of the four Complementisers discussed above as having the feature structure (51) below:

(51) *that* = [−WH, +FINITE]
 for = [−WH, −FINITE]
 whether = [+WH, ±FINITE]
 if = [+WH, +FINITE]

We might further assume that the constituent C can be expanded into a feature complex by a feature rule such as (52) below:

(52) C → [±WH, ±FINITE]

and this rule would then generate the feature complexes specified in (53) below:

(53) [+WH, +FINITE] (can be filled by *whether/if*)
    [+WH, −FINITE] (can be filled by *whether*)
    [−WH, +FINITE] (can be filled by *that*)
    [−WH, −FINITE] (can be filled by *for*)

Answer Key p.490

01 Read <A> and <B> and answer the question.

2013년 35번

┤ A ├

A reflexive (e.g., *himself*) or a reciprocal (e.g., *each other*) in general meets both of the two constraints below.

The Binding Constraint (BC)

A reflexive or a reciprocal (Y) must be bound by its antecedent (X).

[X binds Y if and only if X c-commands Y and X and Y are co-indexed (thereby co-referring); a constituent X c-commands its sister constituent Y and any constituent Z that is contained within Y.]

The c-command relation is represented in the tree diagram below.

The Locality Constraint (LC)

A reflexive or a reciprocal must find its antecedent within the local binding domain. [The local binding domain is the smallest clause containing a reflexive or a reciprocal.]

For example, in (1), the reflexive violates the BC, and in (2), it violates the LC.

(1) *Mary hopes Michael$_i$'s father represents himself$_i$.
(2) *John$_i$ thinks Mary should marry himself$_i$.

| | B | |
Cases	Types of constraints violated
a. *Mary expects each other$_i$'s mothers will dance with the two boys$_i$.	LC only
b. *Their$_i$ teacher thinks Bill hit each other$_i$'s friends.	both BC and LC
c. *Each other$_i$ persuaded their$_i$ sons to leave.	BC only
d. *John wanted the girls$_i$ to know that he would help with each other$_i$'s homework.	both BC and LC

Which of the following lists all and only the cases in <B> that correctly illustrate the violation(s) of the constraint(s) described in <A>?

① a, b   ② a, c   ③ b, c

④ b, d   ⑤ c, d

02 **Read the passage and fill in the blank with ONE word.** [2 points] 2015년 A형 10번

The sentences in (1) show three types of NPs: the reflexive pronoun, the ordinary pronoun, and the proper noun.

(1) a. John likes himself.

    b. Mary met him.

    c. John came.

The reflexive pronoun should have the antecedent in the sentence from which it picks up its reference as shown in (2), with the coindexed NPs indicating the same referent. This sharply contrasts with the ordinary pronoun and the proper noun in (3).

(2) a. John$_i$ introduced himself$_i$ to Mary.

    b. *Himself came.

(3) a. John$_i$ introduced him$_j$ to Mary.

    b. John introduced Bill to Mary.

The existence of the antecedent in the sentence, however, is not a sufficient condition to license the reflexive pronoun, as shown in (4).

(4) a. *John$_i$ thinks that himself$_i$ is intelligent.

    b. John told Mary$_i$ about herself$_i$.

The examples in (2) and (4) show that the reflexive pronoun finds its antecedent in the smallest _____ that contains it. The sentences in (2b) and (4a) are thus ungrammatical in contrast to those in (2a) and (4b).

Note : * indicates that the sentence is ungrammatical.

03 Read the passage in <A> and the sentences in <B>, and follow the directions. [5 points]

2017년 B형 6번

───┤ A ├───

Anaphors such as *each other* have to be bound by their antecedent. An anaphor must satisfy two conditions to be bound. An anaphor can be bound if it is coindexed (i.e., coreferential) with its antecedent and is also c-commanded by that antecedent within the smallest clause or noun phrase containing the anaphor. A node c-commands its sister and all the descendents of its sister. For example, in (1), B c-commands C, D, E, F, G, H, I, J, and K; however, I c-commands only H, which is its sister. It does not c-command any other nodes.

(1)

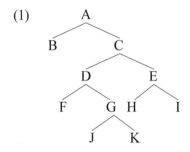

Consider the two structures for the verb phrase in the double object construction (2). (3) is a ternary (three) branching structure, which is a kind of multiple branching structure, and (4) a binary branching structure.

(2) Tom will give Mary a book.

(3)   (4)

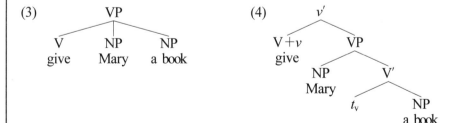

In (3) and (4), the direct and indirect objects have different structural relations.

┤ B ├

(i) Mary showed the boys$_i$ each other$_i$.

(ii) *Mary showed each other$_i$ the boys$_i$.

(In the examples *the boys* and *each other* refer to the same people.)

Note : * indicates that the sentence is ungrammatical.

Identify which VP structure, (3) or (4), can account for the ungrammaticality of sentence (ii) in <B>. Then, explain why one, but not the other structure, can account for the ungrammaticality by using the c-command relation described in <A>.

_____

_____

_____

_____

_____

04 다음 (1)과 (2)의 구조적 차이점을 2가지만 우리말로 쓰시오. [5점]   2003년 전국 16번

---

(1) a. the claim that the proof was false

　　b. the claim that John is a genius

(2) a. the claim that John has made

　　b. the claim that John found upsetting

---

① _____

_____

_____

② _____

_____

_____

05 Read <A> and <B> and follow the directions. [2.5 points]   2013년 2차 논술 3번

┤ A ├

A noun phrase can have one or multiple modifiers. The modifiers can precede or follow the noun, and the modification can be restrictive or nonrestrictive. Restrictive modifiers serve to identify the entity that the noun phrase refers to by providing information to narrow down the reference. On the other hand, nonrestrictive modifiers do not serve for identification, since their head noun is viewed as unique or as a member of a class that has been independently identified. The modifiers simply provide additional information about the head. The relative clauses in (1a) and (1b) are restrictive and nonrestrictive, respectively. In formal writing, (1b) is slightly unacceptable, and it is indicated with "#".

(1) a. John introduced me to the writer who sat behind me.

b. #John introduced me to his mother who sat behind me.

(2)   Picture-A   Picture-B

┤ B ├

Ted Baker ① <u>who explored many remote places</u> wrote a lot of travel books. In his ② <u>brilliant</u> last book, he described the lifestyle of the people on an islet ③ <u>he visited with his beautiful wife</u>. The islet has an active volcano, and the people deify it. Every year they sacrifice a ④ <u>young</u> girl to this volcano ⑤ <u>of great value to them</u>. In addition to the cherished volcano, since chimpanzees

⑥ <u>who share 99 percent of our DNA</u> exhibit behaviors similar to humans, the islanders consider them special creatures. Holding the belief ⑦ <u>that the creatures are their guardians sent from God</u>, the people revere the chief of the island ⑧ <u>who can communicate with chimpanzees.</u>

Note : Some punctuation marks have intentionally been left out of this passage.

Write one paragraph for each of the following three questions.

First, explain how restrictive and nonrestrictive relative clauses are distinguished in terms of punctuation and prosodic features. Second, write a sentence to describe each picture with five girls in (2). Each sentence should be about who is dancing and begin with *The girls* followed by a relative clause about what they are wearing. Then, explain why each sentence corresponds to its picture. Third, identify all and only the nonrestrictive modifications from the underlined modifiers in <B>, and specify why each of those modifiers is nonrestrictive.

06 Read the passage and follow the directions. [2 points]

In post-modification, *to*-infinitives can be interpreted as relative clauses or appositive clauses. When a *to*-infinitive is interpreted as a relative clause, the modified head noun corresponds to the relative pronoun, which is implicit in most cases, in the internal structure of the *to*-infinitive.

(1) a. I will buy <u>books</u> to read.

　　b. I will buy <u>books</u> which I will read.

The meaning of (1a) is equivalent to that of (1b). Since *books* is the antecedent of the object relative pronoun in (1b), it can be interpreted as the object of the verb in the internal structure of the *to*-infinitive in (1a). The modified head noun can also correspond to an implicit relative pronoun with other functions: the subject as in (2a), the object of the preposition as in (2b), and the object of the omitted preposition as in (2c).

When a *to*-infinitive is interpreted as an appositive clause as in (2d), there is no implicit relative pronoun in the *to*-infinitive that corresponds to the head noun.

(2) a. I need <u>someone</u> to help me with my homework.

　　b. Let's think about <u>issues</u> to deal with tomorrow.

　　c. We did not have <u>money</u> to buy food.

　　d. Do you have <u>plans</u> to travel abroad?

Analyze the sentences below and fill in the blanks with words from the passage. Write your answers in the correct order.

(i) The couples found <u>places</u> to stay before having dinner.

(ii) I am looking for <u>doctors</u> to consult regarding my mother's health.

The underlined head nouns in (i) and (ii) correspond to ① _____ and ② _____ in the internal structures of the *to*-infinitives, respectively.

---

07 다음 A를 읽고 지시에 따라 답하시오.

2005년 전국 24번

┤ A ├

Traditional grammarians have classified *whether* and *if* as the same grammatical category, i.e., subordinate conjunction. If we look at the two grammatical sentences below, it might seem as if there is a potential parallelism between *whether* and *if*, since they appear to occupy the same position.

I don't know *whether* he will come here.
I don't know *if* he will come here.

Do *whether* and *if* actually belong to the same grammatical category? There are arguments that *whether* and *if* belong to different grammatical categories.

다음 <B>의 문장들을 읽고, (1) 비문법적인 문장을 모두 찾아 그 기호를 쓰시오. (2) *whether, if*가 의문부사(wh-adverb)와 같은 문법 범주에 속하는지, 아니면 보문소(complementizer) *that*과 같은 문법 범주에 속하는지, 주어진 자료에 기초하여 쓰고, (3) 그 판단의 통사적 근거를 우리말로 쓰시오. [6점]

┤ B ├

(a) I wonder *whether* to go.
(b) I wonder *if* to go.
(c) I wonder *when* to go.
(d) I wonder *that* to go.
(e) I'm not certain about *whether* he'll come here.
(f) I'm not certain about *if* he'll come here.
(g) I'm not certain about *when* he'll come here.
(h) I'm puzzled at *that* he should have resigned.
(i) I don't know *whether* or not he will turn up.
(j) I don't know *if* or not he will turn up.

(1) 비문법적인 문장의 기호 : _____

	whether	if
(2) 문법 범주		
(3) 통사적 근거		

08 **Read the passage and follow the directions.** [4 points]   2018년 A형 12번

It is well known that coordinate conjunctions can conjoin constituents of the same grammatical category but cannot conjoin constituents of different grammatical categories, as exemplified in (1) and (2).

(1) a. fond of a dog and afraid of a tiger

   b. very slowly and very steadily

   c. a princess of Denmark and a prince of the United Kingdom

   d. I think that Mary likes poems and Susan novels.

   e. I think that Mary likes poems and that Susan likes novels.

(2) a. *like a dog and afraid of a tiger

   b. *slowly and the car

   c. *a princess of Denmark and with long hair

   d. *I believe Mary to be honest and that Susan is kind.

   e. *I believe that Mary is honest and Susan to be kind.

AP can conjoin with another AP, AdvP with another AdvP, NP or DP with another NP or DP, TP with another TP, and CP with another CP.

TP, meaning Tense Phrase, is a clause that does not include a complementizer like *Mary likes poems* in (3a). CP, meaning Complementizer Phrase, is a clause that includes a complementizer. The embedded clause of sentence (3a) has the structure in (3b).

(3) a. I think that Mary likes poems.

   b.

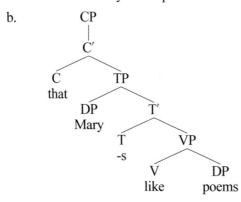

   Note : * indicates the ungrammaticality of the sentence.

State whether sentence (4) and sentence (5) can be conjoined with the coordinate conjunction *but* as in sentence (6). Then, explain why, identifying the grammatical category of sentence (4) and that of sentence (5).

---

(4) I am feeling thirsty.

(5) Should I save my last cola till later?

(6) I am feeling thirsty but should I save my last cola till later?

MEN
TOR

Mentor Linguistics

멘토영어학
기출분석

Chapter 06

Case Theory /
Theta Roles /
Ambiguity

Unit
01

Preview & Review

 Theta Roles

1.1. Thematic Roles

Arguments are participants in what one linguist has called 'the little drama' that a proposition expresses. To be a participant in a drama you must be playing a role. What sort of roles are we talking about here? We have already alluded to the notion of participant roles in an earlier chapter. We talked there about Agents and Patients, and we saw that these roles are typically fulfilled by Subjects and Objects, respectively. We now elaborate on this, and say that each argument carries at most one *thematic role* (as we will call participant roles from now on). Apart from Agents and Patients, there are a number of other roles. Linguists don't agree exactly how many there are, nor do they agree exactly which roles we should recognise. However, the following thematic roles are widely accepted:

Thematic roles (also known as theta roles, Θ-roles and semantic roles)

Agent	The 'doer' or instigator of the action denoted by the predicate.
Patient	The 'undergoer' of the action or event denoted by the predicate.
Theme	The entity that is moved by the action or event denoted by the predicate.
Experiencer	The living entity that experiences the action or event denoted by the predicate.
Goal	The location or entity in the direction of which something moves.
Benefactive	The entity that benefits from the action or event denoted by the predicate.
Source	The location or entity from which something moves.
Instrument	The medium by which the action or event denoted by the predicate is carried out.
Locative	The specification of the place where the action or event denoted by the predicate is situated.
Proposition	The specification of a state of affairs.

1.2. Exercise

Consider the sentences below and determine which thematic roles the bracketed phrases can be said to carry.

(i) [His mother] sent [David] [a letter].
(ii) [David] smelled [the freshly baked bread].
(iii) [We] put [the cheese] [in the fridge].
(iv) [Frank] threw [himself] [onto the sofa].
(v) [Greg] comes [from Wales].

In (i) the Subject noun phrase carries the role of Agent, as do the Subjects in (iii) and (iv). The role of *David* in (ii) is that of Experiencer. Sentence (v) illustrates that it is by no means always easy to determine the thematic role of a particular phrase: which theta role do we assign to the NP *Greg?* None of the roles on our list is quite appropriate. We can adopt two possible solutions to this problem. Either we say that *Greg* carries one of the theta roles on our list, though marginally so, say Theme, or we invent a new role altogether, say Topic. The first solution has the advantage that we keep our list of thematic roles short; the second solution allows us to make finer distinctions. In this book we won't worry too much about such problems, and we will use the list as given above. What's important is to know which elements bear a thematic role in a particular sentence.

We have yet to discuss the roles of the non-Subject phrases in the exercise. In (i) *David* is the Goal of the act of sending. The NPs *a letter* in (i), *the cheese* in (iii) and *himself* in (iv) are Themes. They could also be said to be Patients, and it is for exactly this reason that you will often find the Theme and Patient theta roles lumped together in textbooks. *In the fridge* and *onto the sofa* are Goals (or perhaps locative in the case of *in the fridge),* while *from Wales* in (v) clearly carries the role of Source. There only remains one case, and that is the NP *the freshly baked bread* in (ii). Again, it is not entirely clear which thematic role we are dealing with here. Is it a Patient, or some other role? We won't rack our brains too much, and settle for Patient. Once again, the important thing is to be aware that this NP carries a thematic role.

02 Case Theory

2.1. Key Points

We came up with the Case Filter:

(1) Every NP with a phonetic matrix gets Case.

We also came up with some principles for Structural Case Assignment: The rule of Structural Case Assignment is from a Case-assigner onto an NP that it governs.

(2) The Case-Assigners for English are [+Tense], V, and P.
(3) The Case-Assigner must govern the phrase it gives Case to.
(4) The Case-Assigners V and P must be adjacent (linearly) to the phrase they give Case to.

In addition to Structural Case Assignment, there are three other rules of Case assignment in English:

(5) Genitive rule : An NP in the specifier position of NP gets genitive Case *(Bill's house)*.
(6) Double-Object Rule : The second NP in the Double-Object construction gets Objective Case *(gave Mary a ring)*.
(7) Exceptional Case-Marking : Certain verbs can assign Case to the Subject of an infinitival clause that is adjacent to them if that infinitival clause is the complement of the V.

2.2. Morphological Case and Abstract Case

Consider the examples in (1):

(1a) The butler attacked the robber.
(1b) [That the butler attacked the robber] is surprising.
(1c) [For the butler to attack the robber] would be surprising.

(1a) is a simple sentence, containing two NPs, *the butler* and *the robber*. In (1b), the simple sentence (1a) is used as the subject clause of an adjectival predicate (surprising). In (1c) we find the non-finite parallel of (1a) used as the subject of the adjectival predicate.

Let us replace the argument NPs in (1) by the corresponding pronouns:

(3a) *He* attacked *him.*

(3b) That *he* attacked *him* is surprising.

(3c) For *him* to attack *him* would be surprising.

Depending on their positions in the sentences, the third person pronouns appear in different forms. When the pronoun is the internal argument of *attack,* it takes the form *him.* Adopting the terminology of traditional grammar, we call this form the ACCUSATIVE case. When the third person pronoun is the external argument of *attack,* it takes either the form *he* or the form *him.* The latter form is again the ACCUSATIVE case of the pronoun; the form *he* will be called the NOMINATIVE case. Pronouns thus can be seen to have different case forms: *he* is NOMINATIVE, *him* is ACCUSATIVE. A third case form found in English NPs is the GENITIVE, illustrated in (4a) and (4b).

(4a) *The butler's* coat was too big.

(4b) *His* coat was too big.

As can be seen in (3), the NOMINATIVE case (he) is reserved for the NP in the subject position of finite clauses. The ACCUSATIVE case (him) is used both for the object NP of a transitive verb [(3a), (3b) and (3c)] and for the subject NP of an infinitival subordinate clause (3C). We also find ACCUSATIVE case realized on the NP complement of a preposition.

(8) Jeeves moved towards him / *he.

Adopting the concepts of traditional grammar, we can say that subjects of finite clauses have NOMINATIVE case and that NPs that are complements of prepositions or verbs as well as NPs that are subjects of infinitival clauses appear in the ACCUSATIVE. But this informal system needs some discussion.

2.3. Adjectives and Nouns: *Of*-insertion

So far we have looked at case assignment by finite I—NOMINATIVE—and by verbs and prepositions (including *for*)—ACCUSATIVE. Nouns and adjectives are not case assigners in English:

(35a) Poirot envies Miss Marple.

(35b) *Poirot is envious Miss Marple.

(35c) Poirot is envious of Miss Marple.

(35d) *Poirot's envy Miss Marple.

(35e) Poirot's envy of Miss Marple.

All the examples in (35) contain a main predicate morphologically and semantically related to the verb *envy*. In (35a) *envy,* the verb, is used; in (35b) and (35c) we find the related adjective *envious;* in (35d) and (35e) the noun *envy*.

Let us consider how the case filter (25) [Every overt NP must be assigned abstract case] applies to these examples. In (35a) case assignment is straightforward: *Poirot* is assigned NOMINATIVE by the finite inflection and *Miss Marple* is assigned ACCUSATIVE by the transitive verb *envy*.

(35b) is ungrammatical. If we compare it with the grammatical (35a) the only difference is that we have replaced the verb *envy* by the adjective *envious*. Apparently (35b) can be rescued by the insertion of the preposition *of* as seen in (35c). How can we account for these data?

We shall try to explain the ungrammaticality of (35b), without *of,* and the grammatically of (35c), with *of,* also in terms of the case filter. **If adjectives like *envious* cannot case-mark their complement then (35b) is ruled out by the case filter since the NP *Miss Marple* will not be assigned case.**

Let us turn to (35d) and (35e). First of all, we see that these NPs contain a GENITIVE NP, Poirot's, in front of their head N. We shall not discuss GENITIVE assignment in the pre-nominal position. Let us assume that there is an element POSS in the specifier position of NPs which is able to assign GENITIVE to the NP in that position.

We turn to the post-nominal complement of *envy,* the NP *Miss Marple.* Analogously to (35b) and (35c), we shall try to account for the ungrammaticality of (35d) and the grammaticality of (35e) in terms of case theory. If nouns fail to assign case to their complements (35d) violates the case filter. *Of*-Insertion in (35e) enables the complement NP to receive case.

2.4. Adjacency and Case Assignment

Consider the following examples:

(42a) Poirot speaks [NP English] fluently.

(42b) *Poirot speaks fluently [NP English].

(42c) Poirot sincerely believes [IP English to be important].

(42d) *Poirot believes sincerely [IP English to be important].

(42e) Poirot believes sincerely [CP that English is important].

In (42a) the verb *speak* takes an NP complement *English* and VP further includes an adjunct *fluently.* The NP *Poirot* is case-marked by the finite INFL; the NP *English* is case-marked by the transitive verb. In (42b) the constituents of the sentence are not altered and yet the sentence is ungrammatical. The only contrast with (42a) is that the V *speak* and the complement NP *English* are **no longer next to each other or adjacent.**

A similar pattern is found in (42c) and (42d). In both sentences *believe* takes an IP complement. In (42c) the verb *believe* case-marks the subject NP of the lower clause (English) and the sentence is grammatical, while in (42d) the non-adjacency of the verb and the NP to which it should assign structural case leads to ungrammaticality.

The data in (42) have led linguists to propose that government is not a sufficient condition for case assignment in English and that a further structural requirement is that **the case assigner and the element to which case is assigned should be adjacent.** By the **adjacency requirement** case assigners must not be separated from the NPs which they case-mark by intervening material and hence (42b) and (42d) are ungrammmatical. In (42b) the verb *speak* would not be able to case-mark the NP *English* because there is intervening material; the NP *English* will violate the case filter (25). In (42d) the verb *believe* must case-mark the subject of the non-finite clause, hence ought not be separated from it; again the NP *English* violates the case filter.

The adjacency requirement has nothing to say about (42e). On the one hand, a finite clause does not need to be case-marked. **The case filter applies to NPs, not to clauses.** On the other hand, the subject of the finite clause, the NP *English,* will satisfy the case filter because it receives NOMINATIVE from the finite I.

2.5. Case and Passivization

Let us return to some of the earlier examples of case assignment.

(46a) Italy beat Belgium in the semi-finals.

According to the case filter (25) all overt NPs in the sentence above must be assigned case. The reader can verify that the case filter is satisfied in (46a). Now consider (46b), the passive pendant of (46a).

(46b) Belgium were beaten in the semi-finals.

The effects of passivization will be familiar from the traditional literature. First, passivization affects the morphology of the verb: in (46b) the verb *beat* turns up in its participial form and is accompanied by the auxiliary *be.* Furthermore, in the passive sentence the AGENT of the activity is not expressed by an NP. If we wish to refer to the AGENT of the action we need to use an adjunct PP headed by the preposition by, which itself carries the notion of AGENTIVITY.

(47) Belgium were beaten by Italy in the semi-finals.

(50a) *It was beaten Belgium.
(50b) *There was beaten Belgium.

Let us turn to (50b). In our account NPs have one crucial property that distinguishes them from clauses: NPs need case. We capitalize on this difference and try to explain the ungrammaticality of (50b) in terms of case theory. We shall assume that **a passivized verb loses the ability to assign structural ACCUSATIVE case to its complement**. Given the assumption that passive verbs absorb structural case. The object NP *Belgium* will not be able to receive ACCUSATIVE case from the verb *beaten.* Hence (50b) violates the case filter: the object NP fails to be case-marked. Given this assumption, (50a) will also be ruled out for case reasons: here too the NP *Belgium* cannot be assigned ACCUSATIVE case. Consider the examples in (52):

(52) a. I believe [Emsworth to have attacked Poirot].
         └── ACC ↑   └── ACC ↑

   b. I believe [Poirot to have been attacked].
         └── ACC ↑

   c. *It was believed [Emsworth to have attacked Poirot].
                                   └── ACC ↑

   d. It was believed [that Emsworth had attacked Poirot].
                          ↑ NOM │

2.6. The Double Object Construction

If it is a property of **inherent case** that it survives passivization then it could be argued that GENITIVE is not the only inherent case in English. Consider (56).

(56a) I gave John a book.
(56b) John was given a book.

We have not said anything about verbs like give in (56a) which appear to take two internal arguments. The question we address here is how both VP-internal NPs in (56a) are assigned case.

One approach would be to say that in (56a) the direct object is inherently case-marked. Inherent case is not lost under passivization.

03 Ambiguity

Our syntactic knowledge crucially includes rules that tell us how words form groups in a sentence, or how they are *hierarchically* arranged with respect to one another. Consider the following sentence:

The captain ordered all old men and women off the sinking ship.

This phrase "old men and women" is ambiguous, referring either to old men and to women of any age or to old men and old women. The ambiguity arises because the words *old men and women* can be grouped in two ways. If the words are grouped as follows, *old* modifies only *men* and so the women can be any age.

[old men] and [women]

When we group them like this, the adjective *old* modifies both *men* and *women.*

[old [men and women]]

The rules of syntax allow both of these groupings, which is why the expression is ambiguous. The following hierarchical diagrams illustrate the same point:

In the first structure *old* and *men* are under the same node and hence *old* modifies *men.* In the second structure *old* shares a node with the entire conjunction *men and women,* and so modifies both.

This is similar to what we find in morphology for ambiguous words such as *unlockable,* which have two structures, corresponding to two meanings.

Many sentences exhibit such ambiguities, often leading to humorous results. Consider the following two sentences, which appeared in classified ads:

For sale: an antique desk suitable for lady with thick legs and large drawers.
We will oil your sewing machine and adjust tension in your home for $10.00.

In the first ad, the humorous reading comes from the grouping [a desk] [for lady with thick legs and large drawers] as opposed to the intended [a desk for lady] [with thick legs and large drawers], where the legs and drawers belong to the desk. The second case is similar.

Because these ambiguities are a result of different structures, they are instances of **structural ambiguity**.

Contrast these sentences with:

This will make you smart.

The two interpretations of this sentence are due to the two meanings of smart—"clever" or "burning sensation."

Often a combination of differing structure and double word-meaning creates ambiguity (and humor) as in the cartoon:

Rhymes With Orange (105945) © Hilary B. Price. King Features Syndicate

Syntactic rules reveal the grammatical relations among the words of a sentence as well as their order and hierarchical organization. They also explain how the grouping of words relates to its meaning, such as when a sentence or phrase is ambiguous. In addition, the rules of the syntax permit speakers to produce and understand a limitless number of sentences never produced or heard before—*the creative aspect of linguistic knowledge.* A major goal of linguistics is to show clearly and explicitly how syntactic rules account for this knowledge. A theory of grammar must provide a complete characterization of what speakers implicitly know about their language.

Questions

Answer Key p.493

01 글 <A>를 읽고 <B>에서 비문법적인 문장을 모두 찾아 기호를 쓰고 비문법적인 이유를 <A>의 설명을 바탕으로 15단어 이내로 쓰시오. (단, 영어와 우리말 혼용 가능) [4점]

2008년 전국 19번

┤ A ├

Adopting the concepts of traditional grammar, we can say that subjects of finite clauses have Nominative Case and that NPs that are complements of prepositions or verbs appear in the Accusative. Let us postulate that there is a universal requirement that all overt NPs must be assigned abstract Case to satisfy the Case filter.

(1) Case Filter
Every overt NP must be assigned abstract Case.

To pass the Case filter NPs must be assigned Case by Case assigners such as a finite Tense, a transitive verb, a preposition, or a prepositional complementizer *for*. (The prepositional complementizer can appear in the infinitival clause to assign Accusative Case, since infinitival *to* can't assign Case to the overt subject of an infinitival clause.)

(2) a. He likes *her*.
b. She moved toward *him*.
c. For *her* to like *him* is surprising.

B

(a) It is likely Mary to be innocent.

(b) I persuaded him to go to college.

(c) She believes sincerely that he is smart.

(d) I don't know whether John to go to the party.

(e) She seems to me to be intelligent.

• 비문법적인 문장의 기호 : (   )

• 비문법적인 이유 : _____

02 Read <A> and <B> and follow the directions. [2.5점]

2010년 31번

---| A |---

Consider the sentences in (1).

(1) a. John is sure <u>that he will succeed</u>.
    b. John is sure <u>to succeed</u>.
    c. *John is sure <u>his success</u>.

The example (1c) is ungrammatical, though its underlined complement is legitimate. The ungrammaticality of (1c) is attributable to the following constraint on NPs: NPs in sentences should have a case either inherently or through being assigned by finite inflection, a transitive verb, or a preposition. Sentences with a caseless NP are ruled out. In (1c) the underlined complement lacks its case assigner.

---| B |---

a. *The child is difficult to travel alone.
b. *The city's recent dumping the garbage made people upset.
c. *I was pleased my sister to be pregnant.
d. *Not surprisingly did they miss the train.
e. *It turned out the suspect to be innocent.
(‘*’ indicates that the sentence is ungrammatical.)

Choose all the sentences in <B> which have a caseless overt NP.

① a, c, d   ② a, c, e   ③ b, c, e
④ b, e   ⑤ d, e

03 Read the passage and fill in each blank with ONE word from the passage. Write your answers in the correct order. [2 points]   2014년 A형 13번

Every predicate is associated with an argument structure, which specifies the number of arguments it requires. The predicate assigns its arguments thematic roles including the following:

- Agent : the instigator of the action
- Theme : the entity affected by the action or state
- Experiencer : the entity experiencing the psychological state
- Instrument : the means by which the action or event is carried out

Thematic roles do not have a one-to-one relationship with grammatical functions such as the subject, the object, and so on. For example, the argument *the ball* is the object in (1a) and the subject in (1b), but it retains the same thematic role, Theme, in both sentences. Other examples can be seen in (2).

(1) a. David kicked the ball.
   b. The ball was kicked by David.

(2) a. A brick smashed the window.
   b. They expected the ship to sink.
   c. David opened the door slowly.
   d. Bob cut the tree with a saw.

The subject in (2a) and the object of the preposition in (2d) carry the role of _____①_____, whereas the subject of the subordinate clause in (2b) and the object in (2c) have the role of _____②_____.

04 Read the passages and follow the directions. [5 points] 2018년 B형 6번

┤ A ├

Sentences must satisfy various principles to be grammatically correct. Consider the following sentences.

(1) a. It seems that Tom admires Mary.

b. *Tom seems that he admires Mary.

Sentence (1a) is grammatical but sentence (1b) is ungrammatical since the matrix subject *Tom* has no theta role.

Next, consider sentences containing an anaphor.

(2) a. Tom thinks that Mary$_i$ admires herself$_i$.

b. *Tom$_i$ thinks that Mary admires himself$_i$.

(3) a. Tom expects Mary$_i$ to admire herself$_i$.

b. *Tom$_i$ expects Mary to admire himself$_i$.

Sentences (2a) and (3a) are grammatical since the reflexive pronoun *herself* is in the same clause as, and bound by, the antecedent *Mary*. However, sentences (2b) and (3b) are ungrammatical since the reflexive pronoun *himself* does not occur in the same clause as the antecedent *Tom*, violating the binding condition, which requires a reflexive pronoun to be bound by its antecedent in its binding domain, which is the smallest clause containing the anaphor.

Finally, consider the following sentences.

(4) a. It seems that Tom is believed to admire Mary.

b. *Tom seems that it is believed to admire Mary.

Sentence (4a) is grammatically correct since no violation of grammatical principles has occurred. However, sentence (4b) is ungrammatical since the movement of the matrix subject has violated a constraint which bans a subject from crossing another subject.

Note : * indicates the ungrammaticality of the sentence.

| B |

Consider the following sentence.

(5) Tom$_i$ appears to Mary to be believed by his friends to brag about himself$_i$.

In the above sentence, the reflexive pronoun *himself* is in the lowest embedded clause, whereas its antecedent *Tom* is in the subject position of the matrix clause.

State whether sentence (5) in <B> is syntactically well-formed or ill-formed. Then, explain why, discussing whether the matrix subject can be assigned a theta role, whether it violates any movement constraint, and whether the anaphor can be bound.

_____

_____

_____

_____

_____

05 <A>의 밑줄 친 문장은 (a)~(d)의 구조로 해석될 수 있다. <B>의 (1)과 (2)가 보여주는 상황이 (a)~(d) 중에서 어떤 구조로 해석된 것인지 각각 그 기호를 쓰시오. [4점] 2007년 전국 24번

⊣ A ⊦

The cowboy rode the horse from the town with spirit.

a. *with spirit* modifies the NP headed by *town* and *from the town* modifies the NP headed by *horse*.

b. *with spirit* modifies the NP headed by *town* and *from the town* modifies the VP headed by *rode*.

c. *with spirit* modifies the NP headed by *horse* and *from the town* modifies the NP headed by *horse*.

d. *with spirit* modifies the VP headed by *rode* and *from the town* modifies the NP headed by *horse*.

⊣ B ⊦
---

(1) With spirit, the cowboy rode the horse that was from the town.
(2) The cowboy rode the horse away from the town that had spirit.

(1) _____

(2) _____

06 Read <A> and <B> and follow the directions. [2 points]

┤ A ├

Structural ambiguity results when more than one phrase-structure tree can be assigned to a sentence. In other words, if the sentence is associated with more than one surface structure representation, it is structurally ambiguous (e.g., *The father of the boy and the girl will travel to India.*). Here the sentence can be associated with two different surface structure representations. In one representation, only one person, the father, will travel. In the other representation, two people will travel: the girl and the father of the boy.

┤ B ├

a. Mrs. Coleman gave her dog biscuits this morning.

b. My brother told the teacher that he ran into something.

c. Who do you think Jim believes Judy wants to meet the mayor?

d. The boys have been waiting for more than an hour by the bank.

e. Under no circumstances are passengers permitted to open the doors.

f. The pilot said that flying airplanes is really dangerous.

Based on <A>, choose all and only the sentences in <B> that are structurally ambiguous.

① a, b   ② a, b, f   ③ a, c

④ c, d, e   ⑤ c, d, f

07 Read the passage in <A> and the sentence in <B>, and follow the directions. [5 points]

2015년 A형 4번

| A |

Linguistic expressions are often ambiguous, and homonymy is one source of ambiguity. Homonyms are words that have different meanings but are pronounced the same, and may or may not be spelled the same. Another source of ambiguity is structure. Sometimes, homonymy creates even more ambiguity in combination with different structures.

(1) John admires intelligent professors and students.
(2) They are pitchers from America.
(3) Mary observed the man at the bank.

The ambiguity in (1) is created by different structures. The source of the ambiguity in (2) is homonymy, whereas (3) is ambiguous due to different structures and homonymy.

| B |

Mary saw John's nose ring.

Identify the source(s) of the ambiguity of the sentence in <B>. Then explain why the sentence is ambiguous and write the two readings of sentence.

_____

_____

_____

_____

_____

08 Read the passage and follow the directions. [4 points]

2020년 A형 6번

┤ A ├

There is a class of words, such as *yet* and *any*, called 'Negative Polarity Items (NPIs).' They are allowed in sentences containing a negative word such as *not*, as illustrated below.

(1) a. The defense strategy had not been determined yet.
   b. *The defense strategy had been determined yet.

However, there is an additional structural condition for an NPI to be licensed by the negation *not*. As shown in (2), the negation has to c-command the NPI.

(2) *Any defense strategy had not been determined.

(3) A node c-commands its sister nodes and all the daughter nodes of its sister nodes.

In (2), given the definition of c-command in (3), *not* does not c-command *any*. Hence, the sentence is ungrammatical.

Temporal and locational adverbials can be structurally ambiguous in that they can modify either a matrix element or an embedded element. In (4a) below, *yesterday* can modify the embedded *knew the answer*, as illustrated in (4b). Let us refer to this reading as 'embedded reading.' In the embedded reading, it is asked whether Mark knew the answer yesterday. By contrast, *yesterday* can also modify the matrix predicate *wondered*, as shown in (4c). Let us refer to this reading as 'matrix reading.' In the matrix reading, yesterday is when Celin wondered about Mark.

(4) a. Celin wondered if Mark knew the answer yesterday.
   b. [Celin wondered [if Mark knew the answer yesterday]] : embedded reading
   c. [Celin wondered [if Mark knew the answer] yesterday] : matrix reading

Note : '*' indicates the ungrammaticality of the sentence.

B

(i) Mary said that Justin did not sing in any room.

(ii) Mary did not say that Justin sang in any room.

For the sentences in <B>, identify whether each sentence has a matrix reading, embedded reading, or both. Then, explain your answer on the basis of the description in <A>.

_____

_____

_____

_____

_____

MEN
TOR

Mentor Linguistics

멘토영어학
기출분석

Part 02

Grammar

Chapter 01
School Grammar

MEN
TOR

Mentor Linguistics
**멘토영어학
기출분석**

Chapter 01

School Grammar

Preview & Review

01 Four Basic Aspectual Classes

1.1. STATES

The first aspectual class is the class of states. Examples of sentences that report states are given in (147).

(147) a. Roger had a rash.

b. Karen felt happy.

c. Jonah owned a horse.

d. Fred's grandfather weighed two hundred pounds.

e. This tree is dead.

f. Thor has a tumor on his toe.

g. Nora liked the book.

As noted above, states characteristically are interpreted as being more or less uniform throughout an interval; consequently, **they do not have natural endpoints**. In addition, they generally do not involve any action on the part of their subject.

1.2. ACTIVITIES

The aspectual class consisting of activity sentences is one whose members, at first glance, look very much like states. Here are some examples:

(148) a. Karen talked to Martha.

b. Jonah pestered the cat.

c. Mavis snored.

d. Martin wandered around.

As their name implies, activities are in general more "active" than states. However, they are similar to states in **not having any natural endpoints**. For instance, there is no point at which an episode of "talking to Martha" would necessarily come to a conclusion, as "eating a peach" would have to.

1.3. ACCOMPLISHMENTS

The next aspectual class of verb phrases is generally referred to by the term *accomplishment*. In contrast with states and activities, **accomplishments have natural endpoints**. We have already seen two examples of accomplishment verb phrases: *write a sonnet* and *eat a peach*. Other accomplishment verb phrases occur in the following sentences:

(149) a. Ron peeled the carrot.

     b. Jody repaired the toaster.

     c. Dorothy built a house.

     d. Heifetz performed the Third Partita.

     e. Georgia wrote a sonnet.

     f. A man traveled from Jerusalem to Jericho.

The definable endpoints here are the point at which the carrot is completely peeled, the point at which the toaster works again, the point at which the house is finished, and so on.

1.4. ACHIEVEMENTS

The final aspectual class of verb phrases consists of *achievements*. Verb phrases of this class are like accomplishment verb phrases in **having a clear natural endpoint**. Yet, as we will see more clearly below, they **differ from accomplishments in attaching much greater importance to the endpoint** than to any earlier point. Several examples are given in (150).

(150) a. Linda finished her dissertation.

     b. Joel arrived at the meeting.

     c. Fred's goldfish died.

     d. Carol got to Boston.

02 Rules Concerning Aspectual Adverbial Phrases

Two kinds of adverbial phrases are commonly used to indicate the duration of a state or event. One kind is headed by *in*, the other by *for*.

As a preliminary matter, we need to observe that phrases such as *in four minutes* can be used in two distinct ways, only one of which is relevant in what follows. These phrases can indicate how long a certain event goes on, or they can indicate how long it is before a certain state or event begins. Both readings are possible in the following ambiguous sentence:

(151) Roger Bannister will run a mile in four minutes.

On one reading, the sentence means that the task of running a mile will require four minutes from start to finish. On the other reading, the sentence means that the running of the mile is scheduled to begin four minutes after utterance time. The former interpretation is aspectual in nature, having to do with the time internal to the event itself, whereas the latter interpretation is relational, having to do with the time of the event relative to another time. In what follows, we will be interested exclusively in the aspectual interpretation.

We turn now to the matter of primary concern. *In* phrases are most acceptable in situations in which natural endpoints exist (accomplishments and achievements).

(152) a. Ron peeled the carrot *in three minutes (?for three minutes)*. [accomplishment]
     b. Linda finished her thesis *in three months (?for three months)*. [achievement]

By contrast, *for* phrases are most natural in situations in which such endpoints do not exist (states and activities).

(153) a. Roger had a rash *for three days (?in three days)*. [state]
     b. Karen talked to Martha *for thirty minutes (?in thirty minutes)*. [activity]

The above discussion affords a practical dividend that merits special attention: the differing hospitality to *for* phrases and *in* phrases provides an effective means for distinguishing between states and activities on one hand, and accomplishments and achievements on the other. For instance, suppose that we want to determine the class membership of the two sentences in (154).

(154) a. Simon treated Roger's rash.

     b. Simon healed Roger's rash.

When we add aspectual adverbials of these two kinds to the two sentences, we get a clear result.

(155) a. Simon *treated Roger's rash* for three weeks (*in three weeks).

     b. Simon *healed Roger's rash* in three weeks (*for three weeks).

We conclude from this experiment that treating Roger's rash is a state or an activity, whereas healing Roger's rash is an accomplishment or an achievement. (Tests described later will show that the former is an activity rather than a state, and that the latter is an accomplishment rather than an achievement.)

Applied to a variety of verb phrases, this test yields some surprises. In particular, we find many examples in which two nonstate verb phrases are headed by the same verb but nevertheless have to be placed in different classes. One group of examples is given in (156) and (157).

(156) a. Brenda *drove to San Francisco* in an hour (*for an hour).

     b. Brenda *drove toward San Francisco* for an hour (*in an hour).

(157) a. Gordon *rowed two miles* in an hour (*for an hour).

     b. Gordon *rowed* for an hour (*in an hour).

The contrast between (156a) and (156b) derives from the fact that in the former but not in the latter, a specific goal is attained. Similarly, (157a) asserts that a definite distance was covered, whereas (157b) does not. These examples, then, can be accounted for by the following rule:

(158) Motion verb phrases in which a definite goal is reached or a definite distance is covered count as accomplishments or achievements, whereas motion verb phrases in which neither of these conditions hold count as activities.

The examples in (159)-(162) illustrate another contrast between accomplishments and activities.

(159) a. Freddy *ate a pancake* in two minutes (*for two minutes).
 b. Freddy *ate pancakes* for two hours (*in two hours).

(160) a. Linda *drank a glass of beer* in thirty seconds (*for thirty seconds).
 b. Linda *drank beer* for thirty minutes (*in thirty minutes).

(161) a. Frances *read a story* in thirty minutes (*for thirty minutes).
 b. Frances *read stories* for three hours (*in three hours).

(162) a. Grant *wrote a poem* in three weeks (*for three weeks).
 b. Grant *wrote poetry* for three months (*in three months).

In each of these pairs of examples, the first sentence involves some definite unit or amount of something, whereas the second does not. These examples can be accounted for by the following rule:

(163) If a certain verb phrase has a direct object that denotes a definite number or amount, and the verb phrase is an accomplishment, then a corresponding verb phrase in which the object denotes an indefinite number or amount will count as an activity.

03 In Adverbials

The most frequently used test for telicity is modification of the event duration by an adverbial of the form *in ten minutes* or *for ten minutes*, in a sentence in the simple past tense. Telic predicates take *in* adverbials; atelic predicates take *for* adverbials.

With an accomplishment an *in* adverbial expresses the duration of the event, as shown in (8):

(8) **accomplishment**

    a. He can **eat** a meat pie **in** 60 seconds.

    b. They **built** the barn **in** two days.

    c. Jones **walked** to town **in** 45 minutes.

Recall that the main difference between accomplishments and achievements is that achievements have no duration. It follows that an adverbial of duration cannot generally express the duration of the event itself with an achievement predicate. Instead, the *in* adverbial is interpreted as stating the time which elapses before the event, and the event occurs at the end of the stated interval. This is illustrated in (9). Sentences like (9b, c) may sound more natural with *within five minutes* or *within three days*.

(9) a. He **recognized** her <u>in a minute or so</u>.

    b. Jones **noticed** the marks on the wallpaper **in** five minutes at most.

    c. Jones **lost** his keys **in** three days.

An atelic predicate is usually anomalous with an *in* adverbial, as illustrated in (10) and (11). For some examples, a possible 'repair' reading is that the stated time elapsed before the event began. For example, (10a) might be interpreted as 'After two years the couple began to be happy'. Even with this interpretation the sentence is usually awkward.

(10) **state**

    a. #The couple **were happy** in two years.

    b. #The room **was sunny** in an hour.

    c. #Jones **knew** him well in five years.

(11) **process**

    a. #They **walked** in the park in half an hour.

    b. #People waiting to buy tickets **chatted** in half an hour.

    c. #Jones **pushed** a supermarket trolley in 90 seconds.

It is essential with the *in* adverbial test to use simple past tense sentences, as *in* adverbials with future tense can modify any class of predicate, with the 'delay before event begins' reading. This is illustrated in (12)-(15). **With the accomplishment in (14) the adverbial is ambiguous between expressing the actual duration of the event and the time to pass before the event begins.**

(12) **state**

    a. They will **be happy** in a year.

    b. The room will **be sunny** in an hour.

    c. Jones will **know** him in five years.

(13) **process**

    a. We will **walk** in the park in an hour.

    b. They'll **chat** in a few minutes.

    c. Jones will **push** the supermarket trolley in 90 seconds.

(14) **accomplishment**

    a. He'll **eat** a meat pie in an hour.

    b. They'll **build** the barn in two weeks.

    c. Jones will **walk** to town in 45 minutes.

(15) **achievement**

    a. He will **recognize** her in a minute.

    b. Jones will **notice** the marks on the wallpaper in a few minutes.

    c. Jones will **lose** his keys in three days.

04 The Distinction Between Prepositional Verbs and Phrasal Verbs

Type I prepositional verbs resemble transitive phrasal verbs superficially, but the differences are both syntactic and phonological. The contrast is exemplified for the prepositional verb *call on* ('visit') and the phrasal verb *call up* ('summon').

(a) The particle of a prepositional verb must precede the prepositional object, but the particle of a phrasal verb can generally precede or follow the direct object:

She *called on* her friends.   She *called up* her friends.
~ *She *called* her friends *on*.   ~ She *called* her friends *up*.

(b) When the object is a personal pronoun, the pronoun follows the particle of a prepositional verb but precedes the particle of a phrasal verb:

She *called on* them.   She *called* them *up*.
~ *She *called* them *on*.   ~ *She *called up* them.

(c) An adverb (functioning as adjunct) can often be inserted between verb and particle in prepositional verbs, but not in phrasal verbs:

She *called* angrily *on* her friends.
~ *She *called* angrily *up* her friends.

(d) The particle of a phrasal verb cannot precede a relative pronoun or wh-interrogative:

the friends *on* whom she *called*.   *the friends *up* whom she *called*.
~ *On* which friends did she *call*?   ~ **Up* which friends did she *call*?

(e) The particle of a phrasal verb is normally stressed, and in final position normally bears the nuclear tone, whereas the particle of a prepositional verb is normally unstressed and has the 'tail' of the nuclear tone that falls on the lexical verb:

Which friends did she CALL on?
~ Which friends did she call UP?

05 Type II Prepositional Verbs (Ditransitive): Passivization

Type II prepositional verbs are ditransitive verbs. They are followed by two noun phrases, normally separated by the preposition: the second noun phrase is the prepositional object:

He *deprived* the peasants *of* their land.

They *plied* the young man *with* food.

Please *confine* your remarks *to* the matter under discussion.

This clothing will *protect* you *from* the worst weather.

Jenny *thanked* us *for* the present.

May I *remind* you *of* our agreement?

They have *provided* the child *with* a good education.

The direct object becomes the subject in the corresponding passive clause:

The gang *robbed* her *of* her necklace.

~ She was *robbed of* her necklace (by the gang).

[NOTE]

There are two minor subtypes in which the direct object is part of the idiomatic combination:

(1) The first is exemplified by *make a mess of, make allowance for, take care of, pay attention to, take advantage of.* It allows a second less acceptable passive in which the prepositional object becomes subject:

They have *made a (terrible) mess of* the house.

→ A (terrible) *mess* has been *made of* the house.

~(?) The house has been *made a (terrible) mess of.*

(2) The second is exemplified by *catch sight of, keep pace with, give way to, lose touch with, cross swords with, keep tabs on, give rise to.* Only the prepositional object can become the passive subject, though it is considered somewhat clumsy:

Suddenly they *caught sight of* the life boat.

→ The lifeboat was suddenly *caught sight of.*

06 English Participles

English verbs may appear in two different participial forms: present participles (sinking, taking, painting) and past participles (sunk, taken, painted). In this chapter we have discussed the apparent ambiguity of gerunds, which seem to have grammatical properties of both nouns and verbs. In the same way, participles in English appear to be **ambiguous between the categories Adjective and Verb.** In this exercise we will examine various uses of participial forms to see whether they can be unambiguously classified as either adjectives or verbs, or whether there are some instances where a single form seems to have characteristic features of both categories. For your convenience, some of the characteristic grammatical properties of adjectives and verbs are summarized below:

Summary of criteria for class membership

Verbs :

a. inflectional forms, marking tense, aspect, and agreement

b. may take NP, PP, AdjP, or clausal complements (depending on subcategorization)

Adjectives :

a. can be marked for comparative and superlative forms (bigger, biggest; more beautiful, most beautiful)

b. can function as modifier of nouns, and as the predicate complement of verbs like *be, seem, become, consider, find,* etc., e.g.

John seems nice/hungry/Italian/*sing/*eat/*fell.
I find her stories funny/dull/sad.

c. can be modified by adverbs of degree (*too, very, quite, rather, less,* etc.); note the following contrast:

(i) *That is a <u>very nice</u> picture.*
(ii) *John <u>really/*very works</u> when he is facing a deadline.*

Task 1 : For each of the following examples, state whether the underlined participial form should be assigned to category V or Adj. Briefly indicate the reason for each decision.

(A1) a. John fixed the <u>squeaking</u> hinge.

b. The captain's <u>laughing</u> daughter was a favorite with all the soldiers.

c. Mary found a <u>broken</u> guitar in the attic.

d. The king's <u>pampered</u> daughter kept her toys in a brightly <u>painted</u> box.

e. Peter is the most <u>respected</u> economist in his department.

(A2) a. Those noisy motorcycles are extremely <u>annoying</u>.

b. John considers cold showers <u>invigorating</u>.

c. I found the proposal very <u>appealing</u>.

(A3) a. The winner looked <u>elated</u>.

b. John seems quite <u>annoyed</u> at his mother.

c. The president did not sound <u>convinced</u>.

(A4) a. That child has the most <u>charming</u> smile I have ever seen.

b. Max is (*very) <u>charming</u> a snake.

(A5) a. He made me a very <u>tempting</u> offer.

b. Mary is (*very) <u>tempting</u> the child with a piece of chocolate.

(A6) a. The queen was <u>riding</u> a bicycle.

b. Christopher Robin is <u>feeding</u> buns to the elephant.

c. Yeltsin's statements are <u>alarming</u> American officials.

Task 2 : Each of the following examples involves a participle used as the complement of a verb of perception. Based on this data, state whether the participial form in this construction belongs to category V or Adj. Briefly state the reasons for your decision.

(A7) a. I saw the Prime Minister <u>riding</u> a bicycle.

    b. I saw a young child (*very) <u>appealing</u> for help.

    c. No one heard the serpent (*very) <u>tempting</u> Eve to eat the apple.

    d. I heard the ambassador (*very) <u>insulting</u> his interpreter.

    (cf. *He made a very <u>insulting</u> gesture.*)

(A8) a. I have seen suspects much/*very <u>abused</u> by the police.

    b. John heard his wife (*very) <u>insulted</u> by a policeman.

    c. King Louis saw his palace (*very) <u>destroyed</u> by the mob.

Task 3 : The following examples contain participial relative clauses, which immediately follow the modified noun. Based on this data, state whether the participial forms in this construction belong to category V or Adj. Briefly state the reasons for your decision.

(A9) a. The child <u>riding</u> a bicycle is my nephew.

    b. The woman (*very) <u>tempting</u> the governor is a former Miss America.

    c. The statements currently (*very) <u>alarming</u> American officials are not coming from the Kremlin.

    (cf. *Yeltsin holds some very <u>alarming</u> views.*)

Adjectives and Participles

Often the difference between the adjective and the participle is not clear cut. The verbal force of the participle is explicit for the *-ing* form when a direct object is present. Hence, the following *-ing* forms are participles that constitute a verb phrase with the preceding auxiliary:

> Her views were *alarming* her audience.
> You are *frightening* the children.
> They are *insulting* us.

Similarly, the verbal force is explicit for the *-ed* form when a *by*-agent phrase with a personal agent is present, indicating the correspondence to the active form of the sentence:

> The man was *offended* by the policeman.
> He is *appreciated* by his students.
> She was *misunderstood* by her parents.

For both participle forms, premodification by the intensifier *very* is an explicit indication that the forms have achieved adjective status:

> Her views were very *alarming*.
> You are very *frightening*.
> The man was very *offended*.

We might therefore expect that the presence of *very* together with an explicit indicator of verbal force would produce an unacceptable sentence. This is certainly so for the *-ing* participle form:

> *His views were very *alarming* his audience.

However, with the -*ed* participle, there appears to be divided usage, with increasing acceptance of the cooccurence of *very* with a *by*-agent phrase containing a personal agent:

?The man was very *offended* by the policeman.

Generally, -*ed* participle forms accepting *very* can retain *very* when they cooccur with a *by*-phrase containing a nonpersonal noun phrase that expresses the notion of cause or reason.

I'm *very disturbed* by your attitude.

We were *very pleased* by his behavior.

08 Ambiguity: Adjectives and Participles

Sometimes there is a corresponding verb, but it has a different meaning. We can therefore have ambiguous sentences where the ambiguity depends on whether the word is a participle or a participial adjective:

ADJECTIVE : She is (very) *calculating* (but her husband is frank).
PARTICIPLE : She is *calculating* (our salaries). ['···so don't disturb her while she is doing the arithmetic'.]

ADJECTIVE : They were (very) *relieved* (to find her at home).
PARTICIPLE : They were *relieved* (by the next group of sentries).

09 Syntactic Differences of Adjectives

Type I   true

    (1) (He is a genius) is true.

    (2) It is true that he is a genius.

    (3) *It is true for him to be a genius.

    (4) *He is true to be a genius.

       apparent, (un)clear, evident, obvious, plain, (im)probable, well-known, etc.

Type II   certain

    (1) (He will pass the test) is certain.

    (2) It is certain that he will pass the test.

    (3) He is certain to pass the test.

    (4) *It is certain for him to pass the test.

       sure, likely, etc.

Type III essential

(1) (We take three meals a day) is essential.

(2) It is essential that we take three meals a day.

(3) It is essential for us to take three meals a day.

(4) *We are essential to take three meals a day.

advisable, compulsory, crucial, desirable, expedient, imperative, important, (un)necessary, obligatory, preferable, proper, vital, etc.

Type IV easy

(1) (we please him) is easy.

(2) It is easy for us to please him.

(3) He is easy for us to please.

(4) *It is easy that we please him.

(5) *We are easy to please him.

difficult, hard, impossible, (un)pleasant, tough, etc.

Type V foolish

(1) (You make such a mistake) is foolish.

(2) It is foolish of you to make such a mistake.

(3) You are foolish to make such a mistake.

(4) *It is foolish for you to make such a mistake.

(5) *It is foolish that you make such a mistake.

brave, careful, careless, clever, crazy, cruel, generous, good, greedy, kind, nice, polite, reasonable, rude, selfish, sensible, silly, stupid, wicked, wise, etc.

10 The Grammatical Functions of Adverbials

10.1. Subjuncts

Subjuncts have a subordinate and parenthetic role in comparison with adjuncts. There are two main types. Those with *narrow orientation* are chiefly related to the predication or to a particular part of the predication. Those with *wide orientation* relate more to the sentence as a whole, but show their subjunct character in tending to achieve this through a particular relationship with one of the clause elements, especially the subject.

10.1.1. Wide orientation
10.1.1.1. Viewpoint subjuncts

The subjuncts which express a viewpoint are largely concerned with the semantic concept of respect, are predominantly expressed by nongradable adverb phrases, and are characteristically placed at *I (Initial)*. For example:

Architecturally, the plans represent a magnificent conception.

But there can be other forms of realization:

From a personal viewpoint, he is likely to do well in this post.
Looked at politically, the proposal seems dangerous.

Especially in AmE, we find adverbs in *-wise:*

Weatherwise, the outlook is dismal.

NOTE

Scientifically, the expeditions was planned. (I-position)   [subjunct]
The expeditions was planned *scientifically*. (E-position)   [adjunct]
The lawyer advised *legally*. (E-position)   [adjunct]

10.1.1.2. Courtesy subjuncts

A small number of adverbs in *-ly*, along with *please*, serve to convey a formulaic tone of politeness to a sentence. They normally occur at *M* (medial):

> You are *cordially* invited to take your places.
> He asked if I would *please* read his manuscript.

Courtesy subjuncts obviously involve the semantic category manner but are quite distinct from manner adjuncts. Contrast:

> She *kindly* [subjunct] offered me her seat.
> ('She was kind enough to offer ...')
> She offered me her seat *kindly* [adjunct].
> ('She offered me her seat in *a kind manner.*')

10.1.2. Narrow orientation

10.1.2.1. Item subjuncts

The commonest item to be associated with subjuncts is the *subject* of a clause, with the subjunct operating in the semantic area of *manner* but distinguished from the corresponding manner adjunct by being placed at *I* or *M*:

> She has *consistently* opposed the lawyers's arguments.

This does not mean that her own arguments have been conducted consistently but that she has been consistent in always opposing the lawyer's.

Many such subjuncts express volition, as in:

> *Intentionally,* they said nothing to him about the fire.
> *With great reluctance,* he rose to speak.

Paraphrase:

(a) *Bitterly,* he buried his child.

    → He was bitter when he buried his child.

(b) *With great pride,* he accepted the award.

    → He was very proud to accept the award.

(c) He *deliberately* misled us.

    → He was being deliberate when he misled us.

(d) *With great unease,* they elected him as their leader.

    → They were very uneasy when they elected him as their leader.

10.2. Disjuncts

Where adjuncts are seen as on a par with such sentence elements as S and O, while subjuncts are seen as having a lesser role, disjuncts have by contrast a superior role to sentence elements, being somewhat detached from and superordinate to the rest of the sentence. There are two broad types. First we have the relatively small class of (1) **STYLE disjuncts**, conveying the speaker's comment on the style and form of what is being said and defining in some way the conditions under which 'authority' is being assumed for the statement. Thus where [1] is stated as an unsupported fact, [2] is conditioned by a style disjunct:

    Mr Forster neglects his children.   [1]

    From my personal observation, Mr Forster neglects his children.   [2]

The second type is the much larger class of (2) **CONTENT disjuncts**, making an observation on the actual content of an utterance and on its truth conditions:

    To the disgust of his neighbours, Mr Forster neglects his children. [3]

Although not restricted as to position (and while some, as we shall see are often at *M*), most disjuncts appear at *I.*

10.2.1. Style disjuncts

Many style disjuncts can be seen as abbreviated clauses in which the adverbial would have the role of manner adjunct:

> Frankly, I am tired.
> (cf: 'I tell you *frankly* that I am tired'.)

Sometimes the disjunct has full clausal form:

> If I *may say so without giving you offence,* I think your writing is rather immature.

More often, a clausal disjunct is nonfinite, as in *to be frank, putting it bluntly, considered candidly.*

The semantic roles of disjuncts fall under two main heads:

(a) Manner and modality, thus involving items such as *crudely, frankly, honestly, truthfully; eg* :

> *(To put it) briefly,* there is nothing I can do to help.
> You can, *in all honesty,* expect no further payments.

(b) Respect, thus involving items such as *generally, literally, personally, strictly; eg* :

> *Strictly (in terms of the rules),* she should have conceded the point to her opponent.
> I would not, *(speaking) personally,* have taken offence at the remark.
> *From what he said,* the other driver was in the wrong.

10.2.2. Content disjuncts

Comment on the content of an utterance may be of two kinds:

(a) relating to certainty;

(b) relating to evaluation.

Both can be expressed by a wide range of adverb phrases, by prepositional phrases and—especially those in (a)—by clauses.

(a) *Certainty*. These disjuncts comment on the truth value of what is said, firmly endorsing it, expressing doubt, or posing contingencies such as conditions or reasons. For example, beside the statement 'The play was written by Francis Beaumont', we may have:

The play was *undoubtedly (apparently/perhaps)* written by Francis Beaumont.

Compare also:

In essence, the judge called her evidence in question.
Since she had no time to have the car fixed, Rachel telephoned for a taxi.
The proposal would have been accepted *if the chairman had put it more forcibly.*

(b) *Evaluation*. These disjuncts express an attitude to an utterance by way of evaluation. Some express a judgment on the utterance as a whole, including its subject:

Wisely, Mrs Jensen consulted her lawyer.
('Mrs Jensen was wise in consulting her lawyer.')

So also *correctly, cunningly, foolishly, justly, rightly, stupidly,* etc. Other evaluation disjuncts carry no implication of comment on the subject:

Naturally, my husband expected me home by then.
('It was natural for my husband to expect me back by then'—not 'My husband was natural...')

So also *curiously, funnily (enough), strangely, unexpectedly, predictably, understandably, disturbingly, pleasingly, regrettably, fortunately, happily, luckily, sadly, amusingly, hopefully* <esp AmE>, *significantly.* Prepositional phrases and relative clauses (sentential and nominal) involving such lexical bases are also used:

To my regret, she did not seek nomination.
What is especially fortunate, the child was unhurt.
We were not, *which is surprising,* invited to meet the new members of staff.

NOTE

(a) The prisoner answered the questions *foolishly.*   [Adjunct]
(b) *Foolishly,* the prisoner answered the questions.   [Disjunct]
(c) *Wisely,* he answered the question *foolishly.*   [Disjunct / Adjunct]

Unit 02 Questions

Answer Key p.495

01 다음 예문 중 비문법적인 문장을 찾아 그 번호를 쓰고, 그 문장들이 왜 비문법적인지 설명하시오. [4점]

2002년 전국 17번

(1) Sharon had been to Boston, hadn't she?

(2) Sharon had been to Boston, didn't she?

(3) Sharon had the dentist examine her son, hadn't she?

(4) Sharon had the dentist examine her son, didn't she?

_____

_____

_____

_____

_____

02 다음 'prefer'의 용례를 분석하고, 3가지 유형으로 구분하여 <보기>처럼 쓰시오. [3점]

① Many *prefer* a familiar authority figure to a young achiever.

② Whenever she visits her parents, Jane *prefers* traveling by train to driving alone.

③ Airlines would *prefer* to update rather than retrain crews.

④ For obvious reasons, I *preferred* my house to his.

⑤ I would far *prefer* to drive rather than go by train.

⑥ I much *prefer* playing in the open air to reading indoors.

⑦ Many parents *prefer* tissues to handkerchiefs, but they are not without problems.

⑧ I *prefer* placing orders over the phone to using websites to buy new items.

⑨ He *prefers* to study in the library rather than stay at home playing computer games.

─┤ 보기 ├─

⑩, ⑪, ⑫ → give NP NP 또는 give 명사구 명사구

해당 문장 번호 　　　　　　　　　　　　　　유형

(1) _____ → _____

(2) _____ → _____

(3) _____ → _____

03 Read a piece of written work by a student. Identify TWO UNGRAMMATICAL parts, according to the context in the passage. Write down the original and corrected versions for each part. [4점]   2004년 서울/인천 11번

Yesterday Minju called me to go to the movie theater. I told her that it would be a good idea to go to see a movie early in the morning. When I was going out without a coat this morning, Mom said, "It's cold today. The temperature will fall below zero. With no warm coat on will you catch a cold." But I ignored her advice, as I often did.

Minju was supposed to be at the box office by 7:30, but she did not show up on time. It was very windy this morning and I felt as if it were 10 degrees below zero. I kept waiting with a runny nose, but she did not come till 8:30. When Minju finally came, I was coughing as well.

In the evening, my coughing got worse and I had a high fever. I had a bad cold. I should listen to Mom, but my regret was too late.

Ungrammatical Parts	Your Corrections

04 각 문장의 밑줄 친 부분들이 동일 대상을 나타낸다고 가정할 때, 비문법적인 문장이 하나 있다. 그 기호를 적고 문법적인 문장으로 고쳐 쓰시오. [2점] 2005년 전국 11번

(a) When *the doctor* had examined the patient, *she* picked up the telephone.

(b) When *she* had examined the patient, *the doctor* picked up the telephone.

(c) *She* examined the patient, and then *the doctor* picked up the telephone.

(d) There is *a good doctor* here, and you should go to see *her*.

---

(1) 비문법적인 문장 : (   )번

(2) 문법적인 문장 : _____

_____

05 다음 글을 읽고, 밑줄 친 단어 중 어법상 잘못 사용된 3개를 찾아 바르게 고쳐 쓰시오. [3점]

2006년 전국 2번

There are still some Bostonians who <u>consider</u> their city the center of the world. One of my father-in-law's favorite stories concerns a European traveler <u>arrived</u> at Boston's Logan Airport in mid-December sometime back in the '70s. <u>Coming</u> out of the airport, he found an empty cab waiting to take him to his hotel in the city. As they drove along, the passenger <u>asking</u> the driver whether he could recommend some sights that a first-time visitor to Boston should see.

"All right," said the driver. "Let's see. You certainly ought to visit our great universities—Harvard and MIT—and at this time of year you ought to go to the planetarium. There is an exhibit showing how the stars were <u>arranging</u> in the sky on the night when Jesus was born."

"Over Bethlehem?" asked the visitor.

"No," said the driver with some exasperation. "Over Boston, of course."

잠못 사용된 단어   바르게 고친 단어

(1) (   ) → (   )

(2) (   ) → (   )

(3) (   ) → (   )

06 다음 (1), (2), (3)의 밑줄 친 것 중에서 어법상 잘못 쓰인 단어를 각각 하나씩 찾아 바르게 고쳐 쓰시오. [3점]

2007년 전국 22번

---

(1)

Jane was about to knock on the door but stopped <u>short</u>. Her eyes opened <u>widely</u> in shock when a voice screamed <u>loudly</u> from somewhere in the house. She decided to leave <u>immediately</u>.

(2)

Old Mr. Elkins is over ninety but is still going <u>strong</u>. Although he <u>convincingly</u> says that he can reach a hundred, he admits that he may be aiming a bit <u>highly</u>. However, there is a <u>widely</u> held belief in the village that he will get there.

(3)

When I took my driving test, the examiner said that I had done everything <u>right</u> except reversing when I had turned too <u>sharply</u> and mounted the pavement. He <u>strongly</u> recommended that I practice in a car smaller than the one I'd been using <u>late</u>.

　　　　잘못 사용된 단어　　　　바르게 고친 단어

(1) (　　　　　　　) → (　　　　　　　)

(2) (　　　　　　　) → (　　　　　　　)

(3) (　　　　　　　) → (　　　　　　　)

07 Read the passage and complete the examples in (2)-(4) in the answer space provided below.

2007년 서울/인천 16번

The difference between <formal> and <informal> uses is best seen as a scale, rather than as a simple 'yes or no' distinction. Consider the following example.

(1) There are many selfish people with whom one would hesitate to converse.

Sentence (1) is towards the formal end of the scale for a number of reasons:

- Use of *there are*, which (unlike the less formal *there's*) maintains the plural concord with *many selfish people* as subject.
- Use of *many selfish people* itself, rather than the more informal *a lot of selfish people* or *lots of selfish people*.
- Use of the initial preposition to introduce a relative clause (*with whom*), rather than a construction with a final preposition *whom ... with*.
- Use of *whom*, which is itself a rather formal pronoun compared with *who*.
- Use of the generic personal pronoun *one*, rather than the more informal use of generic *you*.

If we replaced all these features of (1) by informal equivalents, the sentence would run as in (2).

(2) ① _____ you would hesitate to ② _____.

However, it is significant that this sentence seems very unidiomatic. The reason is that a translation from one variety to another cannot be treated as a mechanical exercise. In practice, informal English prefers its own typical features, which include, for example, contracted forms of verbs (*there's* rather than *there is*, etc.), omission of the relative pronoun *who/whom/that*, and informal vocabulary rather than more formal vocabulary such as *converse*. As an example of informal English, (3) is a more natural-sounding sentence than (2).

(3) There's ③ _____.

   However, we could make more lexical changes to increase or decrease the formality of this sentence. For example, replacing *people* by *guys* would make the sentence even more informal:

(4) There's ④ _____.

① _____

② _____

③ _____

④ _____

08 **Read the passage and follow the directions.** [3점]   2008년 서울/인천 19번

Nominalization has the effect of changing the categorial status of the verb *destroyed* into the noun *destruction*, of the noun phrase *the enemy* into the prepositional phrase *by the enemy*, and of the noun phrase *the city* into the prepositional phrase *of the city* in (1) below.

(1) a. They reported that the enemy had destroyed the city.

b. They reported the destruction of the city by the enemy.

Not all grammatical functions of the sentence need be realized in derived nominals, as in (2a), and the grammatical function expressed by an *of*-phrase can be marked by a genitive noun, as in (2b). Occasionally, a specific preposition selected by a derived noun must be used, as in (3).

(2) a. the destruction of the city

b. the city's destruction

(3) a. The war was widely opposed.

b. wide opposition (①) the war

The nominalization process allows several simple sentences to be combined into one, and increases the density of information transmitted.

(4) a. Dr. Manning discovered something.

b. Bacteria exist in the mouth.

c. This is what Dr. Manning discovered.

d. Someone reported this event last month.

(5) (②) discovery of (③) in the mouth was reported last month.

The four sentences in (4) are condensed into one, reducing the number of words from twenty one to fifteen, but at the expense of introducing the abstract noun discovery and increasing the syntactic complexity of the resulting sentence in (5).

Fill in blank ① with one word, and blanks ② and ③ with one phrase each, that best completes the passage.

① _____

② _____

③ _____

09 Read the following and choose the UNACCEPTABLE expression.

2009년 33번

Once upon a time there lived a man who wished to have a parrot but couldn't afford to buy one because he was too poor. One day he prayed to God, ⓐ "If you will help me get a parrot, I'll really appreciate it and I'll tell other people what you did for me." The next day there suddenly appeared three lovely parrots in his house. He couldn't see ⓑ where they came from. His wife said to him, "God seems to have answered your prayer even though you have done nothing good for Him. Why don't we keep them?" He was so thankful and happy that he took good care of them. ⓒ The parrots, he thought, were like his children and they were priceless assets to him. When his neighbors asked him how he came to get them, he said, "You know, I did so much good work for God that He gave me a prize." ⓓ The minute he said that, he felt a pang in his heart. ⓔ The next day he found there suddenly disappeared a parrot. He said to himself, "Oh, I shouldn't have told a lie." Then he made a resolution not to tell a lie again.

① ⓐ   ② ⓑ   ③ ⓒ

④ ⓓ   ⑤ ⓔ

10 Read this excerpt from an autobiographical novel and follow the directions.
[3 points]

2009년 2차 논술 3번

"Why won't you talk?" I started to cry. What if I couldn't stop, and everyone would want to know what happened? "Now look what you've done," I scolded. "You're going to pay for this. I want to know why. And you're going to tell me why. You don't see I'm trying to help you out, do you? Do you want to be like this, dumb (do you know what dumb means?), your whole life? Don't you ever want to be a cheerleader? Or a pompom girl? What are you going to do for a living? Yeah, you're going to have to work because you can't be a housewife. Somebody has to marry you before you can be a housewife. And you, you are a plant. Do you know that? That's all you are if you don't talk. If you don't talk, you can't have a personality. You'll have no personality and no hair. You've got to let people know you have a personality and a brain. You think somebody is going to take care of you all your stupid life? You think you'll always have your big sister? You think somebody's going to marry you, is that it? Well, you're not the type that gets dates, let alone gets married. Nobody's going to notice you. And you have to talk for interviews, speak right up in front of the boss. Don't you know that? You're so dumb. Why do I waste my time on you?" Sniffling and snorting, I couldn't stop crying and talking at the same time. I kept wiping my nose on my arm, my sweater lost somewhere (probably not worn because my mother said to wear a sweater). It seemed as if I had spent my life in that basement, doing the worst thing I had yet done to another person. "I'm doing this for your own good," I said. "Don't you dare tell anyone I've been bad to you. Talk. Please talk."

When speaking or writing in English, Korean high school students frequently make mistakes with stative verbs like *know* and dynamic verbs like *wipe*. Your task is to explain how the two types of verbs differ in usage. First, explain the semantic difference between stative and dynamic verbs. Second, using your own examples, explain how and why the two types of verbs behave differently with respect to manner adverbs, progressives, and imperatives. Use approximately 200 words (20 lines). [1.5 points]

11 Read <A> and <B> and follow the directions. [1.5점]   2010년 28번

---| A |---

Sentences in (1) and (2) exemplify prepositional verbs of the structure 'V NP$_1$ P NP$_2$.' (1) and (2), however, are different in that NP$_2$ in (1) can be the subject of a passivized sentence, but NP$_2$ in (2) cannot.

(1) a. They took good care of <u>Mary</u>.

    b. <u>Mary</u> was taken good care of.

(2) a. They deprived Jenny of <u>the land.</u>

    b. *<u>The land</u> was deprived Jenny of.

('*' indicates that the sentence is ungrammatical.)

---| B |---

a. I have made a mess of our friendship.

b. We thanked Mr. Brown for the presentation.

c. Two men robbed Jack of all his possessions.

d. They took advantage of his passion.

e. He blamed me for the failure of the project.

f. The children paid attention to the teacher.

Choose all the sentences in <B> where NP$_2$ CANNOT be the subject of a passivized sentence.

① a, c, d   ② b, c, e   ③ b, d, f

④ c, d, e   ⑤ c, e, f

12 The following is a conversation extract from a communication-oriented middle school English classroom. They are discussing the demographic statistics of Asian countries. Examine the extract and follow the directions below. [35 points]

2010년 2차 논술 3번

Teacher	: What happened to the birth rate in Korea over the last few years?
Student A	: It was | fallen by 2.4%.
Student B	: 　　　| It was dropped.
Teacher	: Okay. Then, what about the birth rate in Singapore?
Student A	: The rate was also dropped.
Teacher	: _____

It has been said that intransitive verbs are grouped into two classes. Verbs like *fall* and *drop* in the above extract differ from verbs like *work* and *swim*. Providing appropriate examples, explain how these two types of verbs differ in terms of the possibility of a resultative reading exemplified by a sentence like *John painted the wall black*, where the resultative phrase *black* denotes the state achieved by the referent of *the wall* as a result of the action denoted by the verb *painted.* Then, explain why Student B's utterance *It was dropped* in the extract is not acceptable even if we assume that it is a passive sentence derived from the transitive verb *drop*. Answer in well-formed paragraphs. [15 points]

_____

_____

_____

_____

_____

_____

_____

_____

_____

_____

13 Read the description below and follow the directions. [1.5점]

Each of the sentences below contains a past participle preceded by a form of *be*, but some of them are not really passive sentences in that they don't have their active counterparts. In other words, they are not "derived from" active sentences.

a. I am done with the chemistry assignment.

b. Dr. Jackson was given a birthday present yesterday.

c. That situation was taken advantage of by a shrewd guy.

d. The problem is going to be dealt with after all.

e. The safe in the president's room is gone.

f. Some issues were talked about at the last meeting.

Choose all and only the sentences that do NOT have their active counterparts.

① a, e   ② a, e, f   ③ b, c, d

④ b, f   ⑤ c, d, e

14 Read <A> and <B> and answer the question. [2.5점] 2011년 34번

---| A |---

Consider the following sentences:

(1) Jimmy was looking <u>at</u> it.

(2) Jimmy was looking <u>into</u> it.

   (= Jimmy was investigating it.)

  Superficially, both *at* in (1) and *into* in (2) appear to be prepositions following an intransitive verb. However, they are clearly distinguishable in terms of certain syntactic patterns. In a wh-question, for instance, we can front *at* in (1), but not *into* in (2), as seen below.

(1a) What was Jimmy looking <u>at</u>?

(1b) <u>At</u> what was Jimmy looking?

(2a) What was Jimmy looking <u>into</u>?

(2b) *<u>Into</u> what was Jimmy looking?

  This contrast suggests that *into* in (2) makes up a syntactic unit with the verb *look* rather than with the object *it*. Notice that (2) is also different from (3) below in terms of the possibility of separating verb phrases: *Up* in (3) must be separated from the verb, whereas *into* in (2) must not.

(2) Jimmy was looking <u>into</u> it.

(2′) *Jimmy was looking it <u>into</u>.

(3) *Jimmy was looking <u>up</u> it.

(3′) Jimmy was looking it <u>up</u>.

---| B |---

a. The captain doesn't seem to <u>agree with</u> the sergeant major.

b. We couldn't but <u>put off</u> the softball game due to the terrible weather.

c. Susan <u>came across</u> an old picture of her mother in the desk drawer.

d. The customs officer <u>checked out</u> everything I brought from China.

e. I think I will <u>go over</u> this article and write a summary.

Based on <A>, which of the underlined phrases in <B> show the same pattern as *look into* in (2)?

① a, b, d   ② a, c   ③ a, c, e   ④ b, d, e   ⑤ c, e

15 Clauses can express different types of situations such as activities and accomplishments as exemplified below. 2011년 2차 논술 4번

---

(1) a. John walked in the park.　　[activities]

　　b. Mary danced in the party.

(2) a. John ate an apple.　　[accomplishments]

　　b. Mary built the house last year.

　The situations described by the sentences in (2) have an inherent terminal point beyond which they cannot continue, but those expressed by the sentences in (1) have no such terminal point.

Explain why (3a) is grammatical but (3b) is not and how the meaning of the verb *painted* in (3c) is different from the one in (3d). [15 points]

---

(3) a. John painted for two weeks.

　　b. *John painted in two weeks.

　　c. John painted the wall for two weeks.

　　d. John painted the wall in two weeks.

---

16 Read <A> and <B> and answer the question. [1.5점]   2012년 30번

| A |

The adverbials *briefly* and *wisely* in sentences (1a) and (1b) are not integrated into the sentences in which they occur and they are understood as being superordinate to the sentences. Thus, sentences (1a) and (1b) can be paraphrased as (2a) and (2b), respectively.

(1) a. Briefly, there is nothing I can do to help.
　　b. Wisely, Mrs. Jensen consulted her lawyer.
(2) a. If I put it briefly, there is nothing I can do to help.
　　b. It was wise for Mrs. Jensen to consult her lawyer.

Adverbials of this kind are called DISJUNCTS. Notice, however, that the way the sentences are paraphrased is not the same. As we can see in (2), the adverbial *briefly* conveys the speaker's comment on the style and form of what is being said, while the adverbial *wisely* conveys the speaker's comment on the actual content of the utterance and on its truth condition. Adverbials of the former type are called STYLE disjuncts and adverbials of the latter are called CONTENT disjuncts.

| B |

a. With respect, he doesn't deserve the award.
b. To my regret, he was hesitant to help her.
c. Honestly, the movie was a little boring.
d. Fortunately, his application has arrived in time.
e. Stupidly, Bill dropped out of college.

Which of the following lists all and only sentences with a style disjuncts adverbial in <B>?

① a, c　　　　　　② a, d　　　　　　③ b, c, e
④ b, d, e　　　　　⑤ d, e

17 Read <A> and <B>, and answer the question. 2012년 32번

---| A |---

Noun phrases are maximally comprised of four parts: determiner, pre-modifier, head, and post-modifier. The head noun is obligatory, but the other parts can be optional or multiple. In example (1), the head *student* combines with the determiner *a* and the pre-modifier *serious* on its left side. On its right side, it combines with the post-modifiers *of music* and *from Monaco*.

(1) a serious student of music from Monaco

There are many rules and constraints English learners should know to produce well-formed noun phrases. Some of them are concerned with the category of the modifier, the relative order of modifiers, the type of determiner, and the contribution of the modifier to narrowing down the set of what the head refers to.

---| B |---

a. We found the boy's notebooks under the table.

b. The ladies didn't like the detergent glass container.

c. John gave me a book you might be interested in.

d. He wouldn't admit his wife's high standing in the office.

e. Josh Groban who had achieved fame and fortune didn't need anything.

Which of the following lists all and only sentences with a well-formed underlined NP in <B>?

① a, b, d   ② a, c   ③ a, c, d

④ b, c, e   ⑤ d, e

18 Read the dialogue and follow the directions. [30 points]

Tom : There will be a big tennis match taking place, won't there?

Mary : Yes, there is going to be a semi-final for the Continental Grand Prize.

Tom : Who do you think is going to win?

Mary : <u>Susan is likely to win, I guess.</u>

John : What makes you think so?

Mary : The fact is, Susan has practiced very hard and with great passion. She is really strong, so she will be tough to defeat.

John : I know it is tough that other players defeat her. But they have to beat her to make it into the final.

Tom : Do you really believe Susan to be so strong?

Mary : Yes, I am her fan. I want her to win and somehow I feel like it's going to happen.

Tom : Do you know where the final will be?

Mary : Yes. <u>In the Central Stadium is a tennis court.</u> That's where the match will be taking place next Friday afternoon. Let me show you on this map. You see, the stadium is behind City Hall. Here is the tennis court.

Tom : Oh, I see.

First, locate one ungrammatical expression in the above dialogue and discuss why it is ungrammatical, suggesting how it has to be corrected. Second, explain why (1a) and (2a) would not sound natural in place of the underlined sentences above, whereas (1b) and (2b) do sound natural. Third, note that (4a) is grammatical but (4b) is ungrammatical while (3a) and (3b) are both grammatical. Focusing on *here* and *there*, discuss why (4b) is ungrammatical, comparing it with (4a) in terms of their syntactic, semantic, and phonological features.

(1) a. It is likely that Susan will win, I guess.

    b. Susan is likely to win, I guess.

(2) a. A tennis court is in the Central Stadium.

    b. In the Central Stadium is a tennis court.

(3) a. There will be a big tennis match on Friday afternoon.

    b. Here will be a big tennis match on Friday afternoon.

(4) a. There will be a big tennis match on Friday afternoon, won't there?

    b. *Here will be a big tennis match on Friday afternoon, won't here?

(* indicates the ungrammaticality of the sentence.)

19 Read <A> and <B>, and answer the question. 2013년 32번

┤ A ├

Type I *so* occurs in clause-initial position, as in (1). In this type of construction, *so* introduces an emphasis that might otherwise be conveyed by *indeed* or *in fact*.

(1) You asked me to leave, and *so* I did.

Type II *so* also occurs in clause-initial position, as in (2). In this type of construction, however, *so* is an additive adverb equivalent in meaning to *too* or *also*.

(2) You asked him to leave, and *so* did I.

┤ B ├

Cases	Types of so
a. A : It's starting to snow. 　 B : So it is.	II
b. A : I saw the movie last week. 　 B : So did I.	II
c. A : You've spilled coffee on your dress. 　 B : Oh dear, so I have.	I
d. A : The corn is ripening. 　 B : So are the apples.	I

Which of the following lists all and only the cases in <B> that correctly illustrate the types of *so* described in <A>?

① a, b   ② a, d   ③ b, c

④ b, d   ⑤ c, d

20 Read the passage in <A> and the sentences in <B>, and follow the directions. [5 points]

2015년 B형 4번

┤ A ├

Preverbal adverbs sometimes behave differently in terms of scope. The sentence in (1a) with the adverb *usually* can be paraphrased into (1b) and (1c). One can represent the two paraphrases using the schemata in (2a) and (2b), respectively.

(1) a. John usually comes late for class.

    b. It is usual that John comes late for class.

    c. It is usually the case that John comes late for class.

(2) a. It be _____X_____ that _____Y_____.

    b. It be ____X____ the case that ____Y____.

In (2a), X stands for the adjective form of the adverb, and Y for the rest of the original sentence. In (2b), X stands for the adverb, and Y for the rest of the original sentence. In the meantime, sentences with a preverbal adverb such as *carefully* cannot be so paraphrased as illustrated in (3).

(3) a. John carefully drives his car in winter.

    b. *It is careful that John drives his car in winter.

    c. *It is carefully the case that John drives his car in winter.

Note : * indicates that the sentence is ungrammatical.

┤ B ├

(i) John <u>rarely</u> talks with philosophers.

(ii) The fish <u>slowly</u> swims.

Based on the discussion of the two types of adverbs in <A>, a *usually* type and a *carefully* type, identify the type of the underlined adverbs in <B>. Then verify their type by writing the paraphrases of (i) and (ii), using the schemata in (2).

_____

_____

_____

_____

_____

21 Read the passage in <A> and the sentences in <B>, and follow the directions. [4 points]

2016년 A형 10번

┤ A ├

There are two kinds of events or situations that predicates describe in sentences: One is telic and the other atelic. A telic event is the kind of event that has a natural finishing point and once it is completed, it cannot go on any further as shown in (1). In contrast, an atelic event does not have a natural finishing point and it can go on and on as shown in (2).

(1) a. They built the barn.
   b. They reached the summit.
(2) a. The room was sunny.
   b. The choir sang.

One of the tests for telicity is modification of the event duration by an adverbial led by *in* or *for*. Telic predicates take *in* adverbials; atelic predicates take *for* adverbials, as shown in (3-5) below. In the sentences describing a telic event in (3-4), *in* adverbials have either the event duration interpretation as in (3a) or the event delay interpretation as in (4a). In the latter interpretation, the time which elapses prior to the event is specified by *in* adverbials, and the event occurs at the end of the stated interval. Meanwhile, in the sentences describing an atelic event as in (5), *for* adverbials have the event duration interpretation only.

(3) a. They built the barn in two days.
   b. #They built the barn for two days.
(4) a. They reached the summit in half an hour.
   b. #They reached the summit for half an hour.
(5) a. #The room was sunny in an hour.
   b. The room was sunny for an hour.

It is essential to use simple past tense sentences when we do the above adverbial test; if *in* adverbials occur in future tense sentences, they can modify any type of predicate, including atelic predicates, and produce the event delay interpretation, as shown in (6a). This in turn leads to the following; certain unambiguous sentences with *in* adverbials may become ambiguous in the future tense as in (6b).

(6) a. The room will be sunny in an hour.
    b. They will build the barn in two days.

Note : # indicates that the sentence is anomalous.

┤ B ├

(i) a. John walked to the park.
    b. John walked in the park.
(ii) a. John will arrive at the station in five minutes.
    b. John will eat the pizza in five minutes.
    c. John will play football in five minutes.

Based on the description in <A>, identify the type of event, telic or atelic, that each sentence of (i) in <B> describes. Then choose ONE ambiguous sentence in (ii) in <B> and explain why it is ambiguous.

_____

_____

_____

_____

_____

22 Read the passages and follow the directions. [4 points] 2017년 B형 5번

┤ A ├

The English article system seems deceptively simple because there are only two articles: the indefinite article *a(n)* and the definite article *the*. There are, however, many situations in which a noun phrase is considered definite and thus requires the definite article. Described below are five common uses for the definite article:

(1) second mention—when the speaker wants to refer to something that has already been mentioned, e.g., *She has a brother and a sister: The brother is a university student. The sister is still in high school.*

(2) situational use—when the speaker wants to refer to something specific that is present in the environment and visible to the listener, e.g., *Can you pass me the salt?*

(3) associative use—when the speaker can assume that the listener knows about the relationships that exist between certain objects and things usually associated with them, e.g., *I bought a book yesterday, and I spoke to the author today.*

(4) post-modification—when relative clauses are used to define or specify something, making it specifically identifiable and hence definite, e.g., *She's never met the girl I dated in college.*

(5) generic reference—when a noun refers generally to members of a species or class, e.g., *The penguin is a flightless bird.*

┤ B ├

A taxi was involved in a terrible accident last night. Luckily, neither the driver nor the passengers were injured.

Identify which of the five uses of the definite article described in <A> best accounts for the use of the two definite articles in <B>. Then explain the reason.

_____

_____

_____

_____

_____

23 Read the passage in <A> and the dialogue in <B>, and follow the directions. [4 points]

2018년 B형 4번

| A |

The modal auxiliary *will* can be used to express a neutral prediction of what will happen in the future or have a volitional meaning for describing what one will do, as exemplified in (1).

(1) a. It will snow tomorrow.

　　b. I will go to the U.S. next year for further studies.

However, the simple present tense is used instead of the auxiliary *will* to express future time in adverbial time clauses, as in (2a).

(2) a. He will help the scientists when he gets to the research center.

　　b. *He will help the scientists when he will get to the research center.

Note : * indicates the ungrammaticality of the sentence.

| B |

W : You're going to attend the international conference, aren't you?

M : Yes, I am.

W : How do you feel about the conference?

M : I am glad I can go to the conference with you. I'll be excited when the conference will begin.

W : Do you think Helen will come, too?

M : I don't know if she will come. Have you finished your preparation for the presentation?

W : Not yet. I need to work on it several more hours. It will be nice if it's finished by tomorrow, but I am not sure if it will be possible.

M : I hope you'll have it finished by tomorrow.

W : But it seems very difficult. Could you help me?

M : Sure. I'll be happy to.

W : Thank you very much. With your help I'll be able to complete it by tomorrow.

M : Don't worry. I'll help you until you will finish it.

Note : M = man, W = woman

Identify TWO ungrammatical sentences that contain incorrect usages of the auxiliary *will* in <B>. Then, explain why they are incorrect, based on the description given in <A>.

_____

_____

_____

_____

_____

24 Read the passages and follow the directions. [4 points]

---| A |---

The vast majority of adjectives in English can appear in both attributive and predicative positions. Attributive adjectives modify the head noun in an NP and occur before that head noun (e.g., That elephant has a really *big* trunk). In contrast, predicative adjectives appear after a verb, not in an NP, and function as a predicate (e.g., That elephant's trunk is really *big*). However, a number of adjectives function only as attributive. Listed below are four types of attributive-only adjectives.

(1) Adjectives of Degree—describe the degree of the property expressed by the head noun, e.g., a *complete* ballplayer

(2) Quantifying Adjectives—indicate the amount, quantity, or frequency of the head noun, e.g., an *occasional* cloud

(3) Adjectives of Time and Location—place a head noun within a particular time frame or location, e.g., a *previous* version

(4) Associative Adjectives—do not express literal properties of a head noun but instead describe it in terms of some entity that is associated with it, e.g., a *nuclear* physicist

---| B |---

It was a hot and humid day when a cool, crisp breeze came over the mountain. The wind brought sweet relief; it was an absolute welcome, piercing the scorching humidity and cooling the sweat dripping down my brow. Nature—in its stunning beauty, with the ebb and flow of its continuous cycles—once again provided in a time of need. I'm so thankful to our urban planners for keeping this park.

Based on the description in <A>, identify TWO attributive-only adjectives in <B>. Then, state what type of adjectives each belongs to.

25 Read the passage and follow the directions. [4 points]   2020년 B형 8번

┤ A ├

Sentences containing [*be* + past participle] can fall into two subtypes, based on whether the past participle form is a verb or an adjective, as shown in (1).

(1) a. The cat was bitten by the mouse.

    b. He had always been interested in Korean history.

In (1a), *bitten* is a verb, and in (1b), *interested* is an adjective.

There are two syntactic properties that distinguish adjectives from verbs. First, adjectives can be modified by degree modifiers, whereas verbs cannot, as shown in (2).

(2) a. I couldn't stand his overly offensive behavior.

    b. She was so embarrassed by his demeaning attitude toward her.

    c. *He very solved the difficult problem.

    d. *The ball was very bounced against the wall several times.

The fact that *offensive* and *embarrassed* in (2a) and (2b) can be modified by degree modifiers whereas *solved* and *bounced* in (2c) and (2d) cannot suggests that the former are adjectives and the latter are verbs. For an adjective to be modified by a degree modifier, it should be gradable. Such modification is not possible with non-gradable adjectives. This is illustrated in (3).

(3) a. The meeting was rather serious.

    b. *The situations were too impossible.

Second, other than *be*, verbs such as *remain* can be followed by adjectives, but not by verbs, as given in (4).

(4) a. The visitors remained assembled outside the museum for over an hour.

    b. *The safe remained broken by the burglars.

Note : '*' indicates the ungrammaticality of the sentence.

┤ B ├

(i) They were married at the church.

(ii) They were married until last Christmas.

Identify whether *married* in (i) and (ii) is an adjective or a verb, respectively. Then, for the sentence containing the adjective *married*, provide TWO sentences, each of which has a property described in <A>. Each sentence should have a different property. Put an '*' before the ungrammatical sentence.

---

26 Read the passage and follow the directions. [4 points]   2021년 A형 7번

| A |

'Locative inversion' involves the preposing of a locative phrase before the verb and the postposing of the subject after the verb, as illustrated below.

(1) a. John ran into the house.

    b. Into the house ran John.

(2) a. A woman stood on the corner.

    b. On the corner stood a woman.

Note that (1b) can be derived from (1a) by moving the locative phrase *into the house*' to the front of the sentence and by inverting the verb *ran* and the subject *John*. Likewise, we can derive (2b) from (2a). Meanwhile, there is some restriction with 'locative inversion.' Consider the following examples.

(3) a. My friend Mary seated my mother among the guests of honor.

    b. *Among the guests of honor seated my mother my friend Mary.

    c. *Among the guests of honor seated my friend Mary my mother.

(4) a. The women danced beautiful dances around the fire.

    b. *Around the fire danced beautiful dances the women.

    c. *Around the fire danced the women beautiful dances.

All the examples above clearly show that the basic verb types affect the grammaticality of 'locative inversion.'

Note : '*' indicates the ungrammaticality of the sentence.

| B |

(i) Out of the house came an old lady.

(ii) Under the bridge lived a troll a good life.

Based on <A>, state whether or not each sentence in <B> is grammatical. Then, explain why each sentence is grammatical or ungrammatical on the basis of the description in <A>.

_____

_____

_____

_____

_____

27 Read the passage in <A> and the examples in <B>, and follow the directions. [4 points]

2023년 B형 5번

A

Coordination by *and, but,* and *or* can be divided into clausal and phrasal coordination types, as demonstrated in (1a) and (1b), respectively.

(1) a. [Jim speaks Spanish poorly] but [he got good scores on the Spanish exam].

b. Jim speaks [French or German] poorly.

In many cases, a phrasal coordination can be expanded into a logically equivalent clausal one. Compare sentence (2a) with (2b). If (2a) is true, then (2b) is true, and vice versa. The two sentences are logically equivalent and they can also be said to share the same truth conditions.

(2) a. Alice$_i$ introduced me to her$_i$ [mother and father].

b. [Alice$_i$ introduced me to her$_i$ mother] and [she$_i$ introduced me to her$_i$ father].

There are, however, some pairs of coordination sentences that do not share the same truth conditions. Consider the examples in (3), for instance. Under the condition where Sue had coffee but not tea, (3b) is true but (3a) is false. Sentence (3a) is true when it denotes that Sue had neither coffee nor tea.

(3) a. Sue didn't have any [coffee or tea].

b. [Sue$_i$ didn't have any coffee] or [she$_i$ didn't have any tea].

Note : The subscript 'i' indicates coreferentiality.

B

(4) a. Your car keys are [in your purse or on the dresser].

b. The [last and most telling] objection concerned the cost.

c. Fred [noticed but didn't mention] Bill's inconsistencies.

d. [Two perfect and four slightly damaged] copies were found.

Based on the description in <A>, first, identify the ONE phrasal coordination in the sentences in <B> that shows different truth conditions from the clausal coordination, and then change it into an appropriate clausal coordination. Second, explain how the phrasal coordination you chose and the clausal coordination you created differ in their truth conditions.

_____

_____

_____

_____

_____

MEN
TOR

Mentor Linguistics

멘토영어학
기출분석

Part 03

Phonetics and Phonology

MEN
TOR

Mentor Linguistics

멘토영어학
기출분석

Chapter 01

Phonemes and
Their Allophones

Unit 01 Preview & Review

01 Phonemes: The Phonological Units of Language

Phonemes are the basic form of a sound as sensed mentally rather than spoken or heard. Each phoneme—a mental abstraction in itself—is manifested aurally by one or more sounds, called **allophones**, which are the perceivable sounds corresponding to the phoneme in various environments.

For example, the phoneme /p/ is pronounced with the aspiration allophone [pʰ] in *pit* but without aspiration [p] in *spit*.

Phonological rules operate on **phonemes** to make explicit which **allophones** are pronounced in which environments.

Consider the voiceless alveolar stop /t/ along with the following examples:

(1)

Spelling	Phonemic representation	Phonetic representation
tick	/tɪk/	[tʰɪk]
stick	/stɪk/	[stɪk]
blitz	/blɪts/	[blɪts]
bitter	/bɪtər/	[bɪɾər]

In *tick* we normally find an **aspirated** [tʰ], whereas in *stick* and *blitz* we find an **unaspirated** [t], and in *bitter* we find the **flap** [ɾ].

(2)

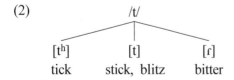

We account for this knowledge of how *t* is pronounced by positing a **phoneme** /t/ with three **allophones** [tʰ], [t], and [ɾ].

We also note **phonological rules** to the effect that the **aspirated voiceless stop** [tʰ] occurs initially in a stressed syllable, the **unaspirated** [t] occurs directly before or after /s/, and the **flap** [ɾ] occurs between a stressed vowel and an unstressed vowel.

02 Phonemes and How to Find Them

Phonemes are not physical sounds and directly observable. They are abstract mental representations of the phonological units of a language, the units used to represent words in our mental lexicon.

2.1. Minimal Pairs

The process of substituting one sound for another in a word to see if it makes a difference is a good way to identify the phonemes of a language. Here are twelve words differing only in their vowels:

(3)

beat	[bit]	[i]	boot	[but]	[u]
bit	[bɪt]	[ɪ]	but	[bʌt]	[ʌ]
bait	[bet]	[e]	boat	[bot]	[o]
bet	[bɛt]	[ɛ]	bought	[bɔt]	[ɔ]
bat	[bæt]	[æ]	bot	[bat]	[a]
bite	[baɪt]	[aɪ]	bout	[baʊt]	[aʊ]

Any two of these words form a **minimal pair**: two different words that differ in one sound in the same position. The two sounds that cause the word difference belong to different phonemes.

When two sounds are capable of occurring in the same environment, we say that these sounds are in **overlapping distribution**.

When two sounds are found in an overlapping distribution and the substitution of one sound for the other changes the meaning of the word ([lek] vs. [ɹek], [kɪn] vs. [kɪŋ]), we say that they are in **contrast**, and they are the manifestations of different phonemes.

We can add a phoneme corresponding to [ʊ] resulting from **minimal pairs** such as *book* [bʊk] and *beak* [bik]; and we can add one for [ɔɪ] resulting from **minimal pairs** such as *boy* [bɔɪ] and *buy* [baɪ].

(4) book   [bʊk]   [ʊ]   boy   [bɔɪ]   [ɔɪ]
     beak   [bik]   [i]   buy   [baɪ]   [aɪ]

Our minimal pair analysis has revealed eleven monophthongal and three diphthongal vowel phonemes, namely, /i/, /ɪ/, /e/, /ɛ/, /æ/, /u/, /ʊ/, /o/, /ɔ/, /a/, /ʌ/, and /aɪ/, /aʊ/, and /ɔɪ/.

A particular realization (pronunciation) of a phoneme is called a **phone**. The aggregate of phones that are the realizations of the same phoneme are called the **allophones** of that phoneme.

To distinguish graphically between a phoneme and its allophones, we use slashes / / to enclose **phonemes** and continue to use square brackets [ ] for **allophones** or **phones**. For example, [i] and [ĩ] are allophones of the phoneme /i/.

2.2. Complementary Distribution

Some sounds are **non-contrastive** and cannot be used to make different words. The sounds [tʰ] and [ɾ] were cited as examples that do not contrast in English, so [ɹaɪtʰəɹ] and [ɹaɪɾəɹ] are not a minimal pair, but rather alternate ways in which *writer* may be pronounced.

Oral and nasal vowels in English are also non-contrastive sounds. What's more, the oral and nasal allophones of each vowel phoneme never occur in the same phonological context.

Where oral vowels occur, nasal vowels do not occur, and vice versa. In this sense the phones are said to complement each other or to be in **complementary distribution**.

Aspirated and unaspirated voiceless stop consonants are in **complementary distribution**. In general, then, the allophones of a phoneme are in complementary distribution—never occurring in identical environments.

Two sounds are in complementary distribution if /X/ never appears in any of the phonetic environments in which /Y/ occurs.

If two sounds are in complementary distribution, then they are the **allophones of the same phoneme**.

2.3. Phonetic Similarity

Complementary distribution alone is insufficient for determining the allophones when there is more than one allophone in the set. The phones must also be **phonetically similar**, that is, share most phonetic features.

In English, the velar nasal [ŋ] and the glottal fricative [h] are in complementary distribution; [ŋ] does not occur word-initially and [h] does not occur word-finally.

But they share very few phonetic features; [ŋ] is a voiced velar nasal stop; [h] is a voiceless glottal fricative.

Therefore, they are not allophones of the same phoneme; [ŋ] and [h] are allophones of different phonemes.

Two or more sounds are **allophones of the same phoneme**, if (a) they are in complementary distribution, and (b) they are phonetically similar.

2.4. Free Variation

Free variation is, most commonly, the phenomenon in which any of two or more **phones** can appear in the same position without any effect upon meaning. For example, a single speaker of English may at various times pronounce the word *eat* with two or more of aspirated [tʰ], unaspirated [t], glottalized [ʔt], or unreleased [t˺].

Less commonly, the phenomenon in which either of two or more **phonemes** may be used in the same position in the same word without affecting meaning, as when *economics* or *evolution* may be pronounced either with initial /i/ or initial /e/.

The first type of free variation is related to the allophones of the same phoneme (*allophonic free variation*, as in [k] and [k˺] of *back*). The second type of free variation is related to the realizations of separate phonemes (*phonemic free variation*, as in [i] and [aɪ] of *either*).

Questions

Answer Key p.501

01 Read the passage and fill in each blank with TWO words. (Use the SAME answer for both blanks.) [2 points]   2017년 A형 7번

S : Could you give me some advice on how I can improve my pronunciation?

T : Yes, of course. Are you having trouble pronouncing a particular word?

S : I can't think of any right now, but there are a lot of sounds in English that I can't pronounce.

T : Can you give me an example?

S : The word *right*. *R* is very difficult for me.

T : Oh, that's because the consonant *r* doesn't exist in the Korean sound system. Then, you should practice pronunciation with a lot of _____. For example, the words *river* and *liver* have only one sound difference in the same position, but it makes a big difference in meaning.

S : Oh, I see. So, I guess *fine* and *pine* would be another example of _____, right?

T : Yes, you're right. If you want to be able to pronounce *right*, you first need to be able to hear the difference between *right* and *light*. There are so many other examples, like *rice* and *lice*, *rode* and *load*, etc.

S : I can't hear the difference between those words, either.

T : I know they are difficult, but with enough practice, you will be able to hear the difference and pronounce them correctly.

Note : T = teacher, S = student

---

02 Read the passage and fill in each blank with ONE word. Write your answers in the correct order. [2 points]   2015년 A형 7번

A glottal stop is the sound that occurs when the vocal cords are held tightly together. In many accents of English, a glottal stop is often realized as a(n) _____①_____ of /t/ in the words given in (1).

(1) Ba<u>t</u>man   ca<u>t</u>nap   bu<u>t</u>ler   a<u>t</u>las
   /t/   /t/   /t/   /t/

While the /t/ in the words in (1) can be produced as a glottal stop, the /t/ in the words in (2) cannot be realized as a glottal stop.

(2) a<u>t</u>rocious   a<u>tt</u>raction   a<u>t</u>rophic   pa<u>t</u>rol
   /t/   /t/   /t/   /t/

The data given in (1) and (2) show that, unlike the /t/ in the words in (1), the /t/ in the words in (2) is in a(n) _____②_____ position of a syllable, and thus it cannot be produced as a glottal stop.

Note : In the words in (1) and (2), the underlined spelling of t or tt represents /t/.

---

03 Read <A> and <B> and answer the question. 2012년 31번

┤ A ├

When a sound [X] and a sound [Y] occur in the same environment, we say these sounds are in *overlapping distribution*. On the other hand, if a sound [X] never appears in any of the phonetic environments in which a sound [Y] occurs, the two sounds are in *complementary distribution*. When the two sounds in overlapping distribution are not involved in the meaning difference of the word pair, it is termed a *free variation*. If the two sounds in overlapping distribution contribute to the meaning difference of the word pair, the two sounds are in *contrastive distribution*. When phonetic realizations of two sounds are in contrast with each other, the two sounds are *allophones of different phonemes*.

┤ B ├

(a) style [sta̠ɫ] — latter [lǽɾɚ]

(b) seat [si̠t˺] — sit [sɪ̠t˺]

(c) economy [ɪkʰánõmi] — economy [ɛkʰánõmi]

(d) feel [fiəɫ] — lake [le̠ɪk]

(e) hit [hɪ̠t˺] — hint [hɪ̃nt˺]

(f) ram [rǽm̠] — rang [rǽŋ̠]

(g) neither [níðɚ] — neither [náɪðɚ]

("~" over the vowel indicates vowel nasalization and "˺" marks unreleasing of a stop.)

Which of the following is a correct statement about <A> and <B>?

① The underlined pairs of sounds in each word pair (b) and (e) are in overlapping distribution.

② The underlined pairs of sounds in each word pair (c), (f), and (g) are in complementary distribution.

③ The underlined pairs of sounds in each word pair (a), (d), and (g) are in free variation.

④ The underlined pairs of sounds in each word pair (c), (e), and (f) are in contrastive distribution.

⑤ The underlined pairs of sounds in each word pair (b) and (f) are allophones of different phonemes.

04 Read <A> and <B> and follow the directions. [1.5점]

┤ A ├

Student A's Worksheet

Directions : Read sentences 1-4 to your partner, and then circle the words you hear in sentences 5-8 as they are read by your partner.

1. He gave me a hug.
2. Hand me the pin.
3. This room is full of cats.
4. The men will come soon.
5. I'd like to see the chimp/champ.
6. That's my luck/lock.
7. They spun/spin around.
8. I fell over a rock/rack.

Student B's Worksheet

Directions : Circle the words in sentences 1-4 as they are read by your partner, and then read sentences 5-8 to your partner.

1. He gave me a hug/hog.
2. Hand me the pen/pin.
3. This room is full of cots/cats.
4. The man/men will come soon.
5. I'd like to see the champ.
6. That's my lock.
7. They spun around.
8. I fell over a rock.

┤ B ├

a. The activity focuses on phonemic differences of vowel sounds.

b. The activity requires students to distinguish suprasegmental features.

c. The activity places greater importance on accuracy than on fluency.

d. The activity forces students to practice different registers.

Choose all and only the correct statements about the activity in <A> from the list in <B>.

① a, b ② a, c ③ a, c, d

④ b, c ⑤ b, d

05 다음 글을 읽고, 빈칸에 알맞은 것을 쓰시오. [3점]

2005년 전국 21번

> In English, aspirated voiceless stops occur at the beginning of a stressed syllable, as in *pie* and *appear*, but unaspirated voiceless stops are produced when preceded by [s] as in *spy* and *spat*. If [p] is pronounced instead of [pʰ] in *pie*, it does not make a difference in meaning since these two phonetically different sounds count as the same thing in English. That is, though they are phonetically distinct, they belong to the same mental representation and correspond to a single mental category, which is phonologically referred to as a ____(1)____. The two stops, [pʰ] and [p], are allophones of / (2) / .

(1) _____

(2) /_____/

06 다음 글을 읽고 ( ) 안에 가장 알맞은 말을 쓰시오. 빈칸 하나에 영어 단어 하나씩 쓰시오.

1999년 추가 21번

> Some speakers of English substitute a glottal stop for the [t] at the end of words such as *don't* or *can't* or in the middle of words like *bottle* or *button*. The substitution of the glottal stop does not change the meaning; [dŏnt] and [dŏnʔ] do not contrast in meaning, nor do [batl] and [baʔl]. A glottal stop is therefore not a phoneme in English since it is not a distinctive sound. These sounds [t] and [ʔ] are in ( ) ( ) in these words.

Mentor Linguistics

멘토영어학
기출분석

Chapter 02

Segmental Classification and Phonological Features

Unit
01

Preview & Review

01 Consonants

The sounds of all languages fall into two classes: **consonants** and **vowels**.

Consonants are produced with **some restriction or closure** in the vocal tract that impedes the flow of air from the lungs.

1.1. Voiced and Voiceless Sounds

Sounds are **voiceless** when **the vocal cords are apart** so that air flows freely through the glottis into the oral cavity.

If **the vocal cords are together**, the airstream forces its way through and causes them to vibrate. Such sounds are **voiced**.

1.2. Place of Articulation

We classify consonants according to where in the vocal tract the airflow restriction occurs, called the **place of articulation**. Movement of the tongue and lips creates the constriction, reshaping the oral cavity in various ways to produce the various sounds.

Table 1. Places of Articulation of English Pronunciation

Bilabial	p	b	m	(w)				
Labiodental	f	v						
(Inter)dental	θ	ð						
Alveolar	t	d	n	s	z	l	ɹ	ɾ
Alveopalatal	ʃ	ʒ	ʧ	ʤ				
Palatal	j							
Velar	k	g	ŋ	(w)				
Glottal	h	(ʔ)						

Alveolars The **alveolar ridge** is the bony protrusion behind the top teeth before the arched roof of the mouth which forms the palate. This is the most commonly used passive articulator and the tip of the tongue is the most frequently used active one, as in such common sounds as /t, d, s, z, n, l/ and the /ɹ/ found in most varieties of English.

Alveopalatals The region immediately behind the alveolar ridge is used for the broad-grooved fricatives of English, /ʃ/ and /ʒ/, and found in the affricates /tʃ/ and /dʒ/ as well.

Palatals The palate is the arched roof of the mouth which consists of bone covered by a thin layer of skin. The typical sounds produced here are /j/, in *yes* /jɛs/, *year* /jɹ/.

Velars Another class of sounds is produced by raising **the back of the tongue** to **the soft palate** or **velum**. The initial and final sounds of the words *kick* [kɪk] and *gig* [gɪg] and the final sounds of the words *back* [bæk], *bag* [bæg], and *bang* [bæŋ] are all velar sounds.

If the air is stopped completely at the glottis by tightly closed vocal cords, the sound upon release of the cords is a **glottal stop** [ʔ].

1.3. Manner of Articulation

Speech sounds also vary in the way the airstream is affected as it flows from the lungs up and out of the mouth and nose. It may be **blocked** or **partially blocked**. We refer to this as the **manner of articulation**.

| 1. Stops | 2. Fricatives | 3. Approximants | 4. Vowels |

Figure 1. Apertures of Speech Sounds

Table 2. Manners of Articulation of English Pronunciation

Stops		p	b	t	d	k	g	ʔ		
Affricates		ʧ	ʤ							
Fricatives		f	v	θ	ð	s	z	ʃ	ʒ	h
Nasals (or Nasal Stops)		m	n	ŋ						
Approximants	Liquids	l	ɹ	ɻ						
	Glides	j	w							
Flaps		ɾ								

Glides [j] [w] The sounds [j] and [w], the initial sounds of you [ju] and we [wi], are produced with little obstruction of the airstream. After articulating [j] or [w], the tongue glides quickly into place for pronouncing the next vowel, hence the term **glide**.

The glide [j] is a **palatal** sound; the front tongue is raised toward the hard palate in a position almost identical to that in producing the vowel sound [i] in the word *beat* [bit].

The glide [w] is produced by both rounding the lips and simultaneously raising the back of the tongue toward the velum. It is thus a **labio-velar** glide. The position of the tongue and the lips for [w] is similar to that for producing the vowel sound [u] in *suit* [sut].

Flap [ɾ] Another r-sound is a flap and is produced by a flick of the tongue against the alveolar ridge. It sounds like a very fast *d*. Its IPA symbol is [ɾ]. Most American speakers produce a flap instead of a [t] or [d] in words like *writer* and *rider*, which then sound identical and are spelled phonetically as [ɹaɪɾəɹ].

Table 3. Consonants of English

	Bilabial	Labio-dental	Inter-dental	Alveolar	Alveo-palatal	Retroflex	Palatal	Velar	Glottal
Stops	p b			t d				k g	
Affricates				ʧ ʤ					
Fricatives		f v	θ ð	s z	ʃ ʒ				h
Nasals	m			n				ŋ	
Liquids				l		ɻ			
Glides	(w)						j	w	

NOTE Symbols between slashes / / are phonemic; those between square brackets [ ] are phonetic.

1.4. Phonetic Classes of Consonants

1.4.1. Noncontinuants and Continuants

Stops and affricates belong to the class of **noncontinuants**. There is a total obstruction of the airstream in the oral cavity. Nasal stops are included, although air does flow continuously out the nose.

All other consonants, and all vowels, are **continuants**, in which **the stream of air** flows continuously out of the mouth.

(1)

Noncontinuants	Stops, Affricates, Nasal stops
Continuants	Fricatives, Liquids, Glides, Vowels

1.4.2. Obstruents and Sonorants

The non-nasal stops, the fricatives, and the affricates form a major class of sounds called **obstruents**. The airstream may be **fully obstructed**, as in nonnasal stops and affricates, or **nearly fully obstructed**, as in the production of fricatives.

Sounds that are not obstruents are sonorants.

(2)

Obstruents	Stops, Affricates, Fricatives
Sonorants	Nasals, Liquids, Glides, Vowels

1.4.3. Consonantals and Nonconsonantals

Obstruents, **nasal stops**, **liquids**, and **glides** are all **consonants**. There is some degree of restriction to the airflow in articulating these sounds.

With **glides** (**[j]**, **[w]**), however, the restriction is minimal, and they are the most vowel-like, and the least consonant-like, of the consonants. Glides may even be referred to as **"semi-vowels"** or **"semi-consonants."**

In recognition of this fact, linguists place the obstruents, nasal stops, and liquids in a subclass of consonants called **consonantal**, from which the glides are excluded.

(3)

Consonantals	Stops, Affricates, Fricatives, Nasals, Liquids
Nonconsonantals	Glides, Vowels

Here are some other terms used to form subclasses of consonants.

Labials [p] [b] [m] [f] [v] [w]

Coronals [Ɵ] [ð] [t] [d] [n] [s] [z] [ʃ] [ʒ] [ʧ] [ʤ] [l] [ɹ] [ɻ]
Coronal sounds are articulated by raising the tongue tip or blade. Coronals include the interdentals [Ɵ] and [ð], the alveolars [t], [d], [n], [s], and [z], the alveopalatals [ʃ] and [ʒ], the affricates [ʧ] and [ʤ], and the liquids [l] and [ɹ].

Anteriors [p] [b] [m] [f] [v] [Ɵ] [ð] [t] [d] [n] [s] [z] [l] [ɹ]

Sibilants [s] [z] [ʃ] [ʒ] [ʧ] [ʤ]
This class of consonantal sounds is characterized by an **acoustic** rather than an **articulatory** property of its members. The friction created by **sibilants** produces a hissing sound, which is a mixture of high-frequency sounds.

(4)

Labials	[p] [b] [m] [f] [v] [w]
Coronals	[t] [d] [n] [Ɵ] [ð] [s] [z] [ʃ] [ʒ] [ʧ] [ʤ] [l] [ɹ] [ɻ]
Velars	[k] [g] [ŋ] [w]

(5)

Anteriors	[p] [b] [t] [d] [f] [v] [Ɵ] [ð] [s] [z] [m] [n] [l] [ɹ]
Posteriors	[k] [g] [ʃ] [ʒ] [h] [ʧ] [ʤ] [ŋ] [ɹ] [j]

02 Vowels

Vowels are sounds which are produced without any constriction of the vocal tract. They are nearly always voiced and are usually produced with airflow solely through the oral cavity.

2.1. Tongue Height, Tongue Position, and Lip Roundness

We classify vowels according to three questions:

(6) a. How high or low in the mouth is the tongue?

b. How forward or backward in the mouth is the tongue?

c. Are the lips rounded (pursed) or spread?

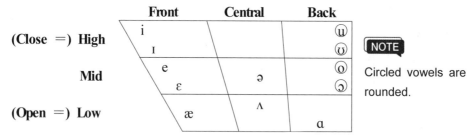

Figure 2. English Vowels (from AEP)

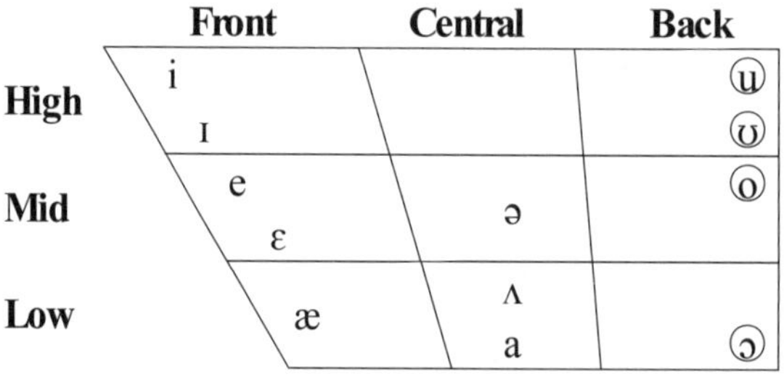

Figure 3. Classification of American English Vowels
(from *An Introduction to Language*)

2.2. Tense and Lax Vowels

The vowel [i] has a slightly higher tongue position than [ɪ]. This is also true for [e] and [ɛ]; and [u] and [ʊ]. The first vowel in each pair is generally produced with greater tension of the tongue muscles than its counterpart, and it is often a little longer in duration. These vowels can be distinguished by the features tense and lax, as shown in the first three rows of the following:

(7) Tense   Lax

i	beat		ɪ	bit
e	bait		ɛ	bet
u	boot		ʊ	put
o	boat		ʌ	hut
ɔ	saw		æ	hat
a	pa		ə	about
aɪ	high			
aʊ	how			
ɔɪ	boy			

Tense vowels may occur at the ends of words : [si], [se], [su], [so], [sɔ], [pa], [saɪ], [haʊ], and [sɔɪ] represent the English words *see, say, sue, sew, saw, pa, sigh, how,* and *soy.*

Lax vowels do not ordinarily occur at the ends of words : *[sɪ], *[sɛ], *[sʊ], *[sʌ], *[sæ], and *[sə] are not possible words in English.

2.3. Schwa

It is the first vowel sound which occurs in most speakers' pronunciation of the word *about.* This vowel is referred to as **schwa**; it is produced without lip rounding, and with the body of the tongue lying in the most central part of the vowel space, between high-mid and low-mid, and between back and front. Schwa is transcribed as [ə].

This vowel is typically even shorter than the short vowels, and it differs from those in that it may never occur in a stressed syllable.

2.4. Monophthongs and Diphthongs

A **diphthong** is a sequence of two vowel sounds "squashed" together. Diphthongs are present in the phonetic inventory of many languages, including English. The vowels we have studied so far are simple vowels, called **monophthongs**.

A diphthong is a sequence of two vowels run together as a single phonological unit: e.g., [aɪ], [aʊ], [ɔɪ] as in *bite, bout, boy.*

2.5. Oral Vowels and Nasalized Vowels

Vowels, like consonants, can be produced with a raised velum that prevents the air from escaping through the nose, or with a lowered velum that permits air to pass through the nasal passage. When the nasal passage is blocked, **oral vowels** result; when the nasal passage is open, **nasal** (or **nasalized**) **vowels** result. In English, **nasal vowels** occur for the most part before nasal consonants in the same syllable, and **oral vowels** occur in all other places.

The words *bean, bone, bingo, boom, bam,* and *bang* are examples of words that contain nasalized vowels. To show the nasalization of a vowel in a narrow phonetic transcription, an extra mark called a **diacritic**—the symbol ~ (tilde) in this case—is placed over the vowel, as in *bean* [bĩn] and *bone* [bõn].

03 Distinctive and Nondistinctive Features

When a feature distinguishes one phoneme from another, hence one word from another, it is a **distinctive feature** or, equivalently, a **phonemic feature**.

Phones and phonemes are not indissoluble units; they are composed of **phonetic features**, similar to the way that molecules are composed of atoms.

3.1. Phonemic Classes of English Phonemes

Table 4. Basic Classification of English Phonemes

True Consonants	Obstruents	Stops	Voiceless
			Voiced
		Affricates	Voiceless
			Voiced
		Fricatives	Voiceless
			Voiced
	Sonorants	Nasals	
		Liquids	Lateral
			Retroflex
Glides	Palatal/Velar		
Vowels	High/Mid/Low		
	Front/Central/Back		
	Rounded/Unrounded		
	Tense/Lax		

Table 5. More Specific Classification of English Phonemes

Consonantals	Obstruents	Noncontinuants	Stops	Voiceless
				Voiced
			Affricates	Voiceless
				Voiced
		Continuants	Fricatives	Voiceless
				Voiced
	Sonorants	Noncontinuants	Nasals	
		Continuants	Liquids	Lateral
				Retroflex
Nonconsonantals	Glides	Palatal/Velar		
	Vowels	High/Mid/Low		
		Front/Central/Back		
		Rounded/Unrounded		
		Tense/Lax		

3.2. Distinctive Features of English Consonants

A more explicit description of the phonemes /p/, /b/, and /m/ may thus be given in a **feature matrix** of the following sort.

(8)

	p	b	m
labial	+	+	+
voiced	−	+	+
nasal	−	−	+

Because the phonemes /b/, /d/, and /g/ contrast in English by virtue of **the place of articulation features**—*labial, alveolar,* and *velar*—these place features are also distinctive in English.

(9)

	b	m	d	n	g	ŋ
voiced	+	+	+	+	+	+
labial	+	+	−	−	−	−
alveolar	−	−	+	+	−	−
velar	−	−	−	−	+	+
nasal	−	+	−	+	−	+

Table 6. Feature Specification of Major Natural Classes of English Phonemes

Features	Obstruents	Nasals	Approximants		Vowels
			Liquids	Glides	
consonantal	+	+	+	−	−
syllabic	−	−	−	−	+
sonorant	−	+	+	+	+
nasal	−	+	−	−	−

Table 7. Classification of English Phonemes by Features

$\begin{bmatrix} + \text{ consonantal} \\ - \text{ syllabic} \end{bmatrix}$	$[-\text{ sonorant}]$	$\begin{bmatrix} - \text{ continuant} \\ - \text{ del. rel.} \end{bmatrix}$	$[-\text{ voiced}]$
			$[+\text{ voiced}]$
		$\begin{bmatrix} - \text{ continuant} \\ + \text{ del. rel.} \end{bmatrix}$	$[-\text{ voiced}]$
			$[+\text{ voiced}]$
		$\begin{bmatrix} + \text{ continuant} \\ - \text{ del. rel.} \end{bmatrix}$	$[-\text{ voiced}]$
			$[+\text{ voiced}]$
	$[+\text{ sonorant}]$	$[+\text{nasal}]$	
		$[-\text{ nasal}]$	$[+\text{lateral}]$
			$[-\text{ lateral}]$
$\begin{bmatrix} - \text{ consonantal} \\ - \text{ syllabic} \end{bmatrix}$	$[-\text{ back}]$ / $[+\text{ back}]$		
$\begin{bmatrix} - \text{ consonantal} \\ + \text{ syllabic} \end{bmatrix}$	$\begin{bmatrix} + \text{ high} \\ - \text{ low} \end{bmatrix}$ / $\begin{bmatrix} - \text{ high} \\ - \text{ low} \end{bmatrix}$ / $\begin{bmatrix} - \text{ high} \\ + \text{ low} \end{bmatrix}$		
	$\begin{bmatrix} - \text{ back} \\ - \text{ central} \end{bmatrix}$ / $\begin{bmatrix} - \text{ back} \\ + \text{ central} \end{bmatrix}$ / $\begin{bmatrix} + \text{ back} \\ - \text{ central} \end{bmatrix}$		
	$[+\text{ rounded}]$ / $[-\text{ rounded}]$		
	$[+\text{ tense}]$ / $[-\text{ tense}]$		

Part

03

Table 8. Feature Specifications for American English Consonants

Features	p	b	m	t	d	n	k	g	ŋ	f	v	θ	ð	s	z	ʃ	ʒ	ʧ	ʤ	l	ɹ	j	w	h
consonantal	+	+	+	+	+	+	+	+	+	+	+	+	+	+	+	+	+	+	+	+	+	−	−	+
syllabic	−	−	−	−	−	−	−	−	−	−	−	−	−	−	−	−	−	−	−	−	−	−	−	−
sonorant	−	−	+	−	−	+	−	−	+	−	−	−	−	−	−	−	−	−	−	+	+	+	+	−
continuant	−	−	−	−	−	−	−	−	−	+	+	+	+	+	+	+	+	−	−	+	+	+	+	+
delayed release	−	−	−	−	−	−	−	−	−	−	−	−	−	−	−	−	−	+	+	−	−	−	−	−
nasal	−	−	+	−	−	+	−	−	+	−	−	−	−	−	−	−	−	−	−	−	−	−	−	−
lateral	−	−	−	−	−	−	−	−	−	−	−	−	−	−	−	−	−	−	−	+	−	−	−	−
voiced	−	+	+	−	+	+	−	+	+	−	+	−	+	−	+	−	+	−	+	+	+	+	+	−
labial	+	+	+	−	−	−	−	−	−	+	+	−	−	−	−	−	−	−	−	−	−	−	+	−
alveolar	−	−	−	+	+	+	−	−	−	−	−	−	−	+	+	−	−	−	−	+	−	−	−	−
palatal	−	−	−	−	−	−	−	−	−	−	−	−	−	−	−	+	+	+	+	−	−	+	−	−
velar	−	−	−	−	−	−	+	+	+	−	−	−	−	−	−	−	−	−	−	−	−	−	+	−
anterior	+	+	+	+	+	+	−	−	−	+	+	+	+	+	+	−	−	−	−	+	−	−	−	−
coronal	−	−	−	+	+	+	−	−	−	−	−	+	+	+	+	+	+	+	+	+	+	−	−	−
sibilant	−	−	−	−	−	−	−	−	−	−	−	−	−	+	+	+	+	+	+	−	−	−	−	−

NOTE The phonemes /ɹ/ and /l/ are distinguished by the feature [lateral]. /l/ is the only phoneme that would be [+lateral].

3.3. Distinctive Features of English Vowels

Vowels, too, have distinctive features. For example, the feature [±back] distinguishes the vowel in *look* [lʊk] ([+back]) from the vowel in *lick* [lɪk] ([−back]) and is therefore distinctive in English. Similarly, [±tense] distinguishes [i] from [ɪ] (*beat* versus *bit*)—[u] from [ʊ] (*pool* versus *pull*)—and is also a distinctive feature of the English vowel system.

(10)

	u	ʊ	ɪ	i
high	+	+	+	+
back	+	+	−	−
tense	+	−	−	+

Table 9. Feature Specifications for American English Vowels

Features	i	ɪ	e	ɛ	æ	u	ʊ	o	ɔ	a	ʌ	ə
high	+	+	−	−	−	+	+	−	−	−	−	−
low	−	−	−	−	+	−	−	−	+	+	+	−
back	−	−	−	−	−	+	+	+	+	−	−	−
central	−	−	−	−	−	−	−	−	−	+	+	+
round	−	−	−	−	−	+	+	+	+	−	−	−
tense	+	−	+	−	−	+	−	+	+	+	−	−

3.4. Nondistinctive Features

As we saw, **aspiration** is not a distinctive feature of English consonants. It is a **nondistinctive** or **redundant** or **predictable** feature (all equivalent terms).

Some features may be distinctive for one class of sounds but nondistinctive for another. For example, **nasality** is a distinctive feature of English consonants but not a distinctive feature for English vowels. Thus the feature **nasal** is **nondistinctive** for *vowels*.

Another nondistinctive feature in English is aspiration for voiceless stops. The voiceless aspirated stops [pʰ], [tʰ], and [kʰ] and the voiceless unaspirated stops [p], [t], and [k] are in complementary distribution. The presence of this feature is predicted by rule and need not be learned by speakers when acquiring words.

04 Overview

4.1. Consonants of English

	Bilabial	Labio-dental	Inter-dental	Alveolar	Alveo-palatal	Retroflex	Palatal	Velar	Glottal
Stops	p b			t d				k g	
Affricates					ʧ ʤ				
Fricatives		f v	θ ð	s z	ʃ ʒ				h
Nasals	m			n				ŋ	
Liquids				l		ɹ			
Glides	(w)						j	w	

4.2. Classification of Consonants

(1)

Noncontinuants	Stops, Affricates, Nasal stops
Continuants	Fricatives, Liquids, Glides, Vowels

(2)

Obstruents	Stops, Affricates, Fricatives
Sonorants	Nasals, Liquids, Glides, Vowels

(3)

Consonantals	Stops, Affricates, Fricatives, Nasals, Liquids
Nonconsonantals	Glides, Vowels

(4)

Labials	[p] [b] [m] [f] [v] [w]
Coronals	[t] [d] [n] [Θ] [ð] [s] [z] [ʃ] [ʒ] [ʧ] [ʤ] [l] [ɹ] [ɹ]
Velars	[k] [g] [ŋ] [w]

(5)

Anteriors	[p] [b] [t] [d] [f] [v] [Θ] [ð] [s] [z] [m] [n] [l] [ɹ]
Posteriors	[k] [g] [ʃ] [ʒ] [h] [ʧ] [ʤ] [ŋ] [ɹ] [j]

4.3. English Vowels

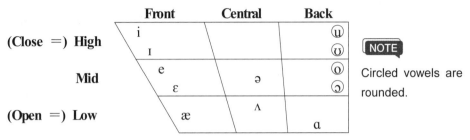

Figure 2. English Vowels (from AEP)

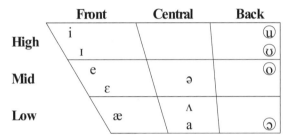

Figure 3. Classification of American English Vowels

4.4. Feature Specifications for American English Consonants

Features	p	b	m	t	d	n	k	g	ŋ	f	v	θ	ð	s	z	ʃ	ʒ	tʃ	dʒ	l	ɹ	j	w	h
consonantal	+	+	+	+	+	+	+	+	+	+	+	+	+	+	+	+	+	+	+	+	−	−	+
syllabic	−	−	−	−	−	−	−	−	−	−	−	−	−	−	−	−	−	−	−	−	−	−	−	−
sonorant	−	−	+	−	−	+	−	−	+	−	−	−	−	−	−	−	−	−	−	+	+	+	+	−
continuant	−	−	−	−	−	−	−	−	−	+	+	+	+	+	+	+	+	−	−	+	+	+	+	+
delayed release	−	−	−	−	−	−	−	−	−	−	−	−	−	−	−	−	−	+	+	−	−	−	−	−
nasal	−	−	+	−	−	+	−	−	+	−	−	−	−	−	−	−	−	−	−	−	−	−	−	−
lateral	−	−	−	−	−	−	−	−	−	−	−	−	−	−	−	−	−	−	−	+	−	−	−	−
voiced	−	+	+	−	+	+	−	+	+	−	+	−	+	−	+	−	+	−	+	+	+	+	+	−
labial	+	+	+	−	−	−	−	−	−	+	+	−	−	−	−	−	−	−	−	−	−	−	+	−
alveolar	−	−	−	+	+	+	−	−	−	−	−	−	−	+	+	−	−	−	−	+	−	−	−	−
palatal	−	−	−	−	−	−	−	−	−	−	−	−	−	−	−	+	+	+	+	−	−	+	−	−
velar	−	−	−	−	−	−	+	+	+	−	−	−	−	−	−	−	−	−	−	−	−	−	+	−
anterior	+	+	+	+	+	+	−	−	−	+	+	+	+	+	+	−	−	−	−	+	−	−	−	−
coronal	−	−	−	+	+	+	−	−	−	−	−	+	+	+	+	+	+	+	+	+	+	−	−	−
sibilant	−	−	−	−	−	−	−	−	−	−	−	−	−	+	+	+	+	+	+	−	−	−	−	−

4.5. Feature Specifications for American English Vowels

Features	i	ɪ	e	ɛ	æ	u	ʊ	o	ɔ	a	ʌ	ə
high	+	+	−	−	−	+	+	−	−	−	−	−
low	−	−	−	−	+	−	−	−	+	+	+	−
back	−	−	−	−	−	+	+	+	+	−	−	−
central	−	−	−	−	−	−	−	−	−	+	+	+
round	−	−	−	−	−	+	+	+	+	−	−	−
tense	+	−	+	−	−	+	−	+	+	+	−	−

Questions

Answer Key p.502

01 **Read the passages in <A> and <B>, and follow the directions.** [2 points]

2023년 A형 2번

┤ A ├

Distinctive features of speech sounds play a critical role in many morphological processes in English, including suffixation. One of the suffixation processes is verb formation with the suffix *-en*. Consider the following *-en* suffixed words.

(1) sadden whiten soften
  dampen sicken fasten
  quieten thicken toughen

One of the phonological characteristics shared in common among the adjective stems in (1) is that they are all monosyllabic, i.e., consisting of one syllable. The verb-forming suffix *-en* seems to attach to a wide range of monosyllabic adjectives, but it sometimes creates ill-formed suffixed words, as illustrated in (2). All adjective stems in (2) are monosyllabic, but they cannot combine with the verb-forming suffix ˗*en*.

(2) *grayen *meanen *pooren
  *freeen *tallen *slimen

To explain why the words in (2) are unattested, we need another phonological property that refers to one of the distinctive features that are used for vowels and consonants in English. The table in (3) provides some of the well-known distinctive features for vowels and consonants that the adjective stems in (1) and (2) end in.

(3)	vowel	glide	liquid	nasal	obstruent
[consonantal]	−	−	+	+	+
[continuant]	+	+	+	−	+/−
[syllabic]	+	−	+/−	+/−	−
[sonorant]	+	+	+	+	−

Note : '*' indicates an unattested word.

⊢ B ⊢

What differentiates the words in (1) from those in (2) is that the verb-forming suffix -*en* can attach to monosyllabic adjectives that end in a segment with the feature [＿＿＿＿＿＿].

Fill in the blank in <B> with the ONE distinctive feature from the passage in <A>. The feature value (i.e., '+' or '−') must be specified.

---

02 Read the passage and fill in the blank with the ONE most appropriate word. [2 points]

Diphthongs such as [aɪ] and [aʊ] are vowels that exhibit a change in quality within a single syllable. This is due to tongue movement from the initial vowel articulation toward another. In English, this combinatory sound is considered one vowel, as it behaves as a single unit. That is, the words *hide* [aɪ] and *loud* [aʊ] are monosyllabic, as are *heed* [i] and *hid* [ɪ]. Diphthong vowels are different from two consecutive monophthongs as in *seeing* [siɪŋ] and *ruin* [ɹuɪn], which are counted as two syllables.

A similar phenomenon is also observed among consonant sequences. Consider the following examples where two different consonants occur together at the end of a word:

(1) a. ni<u>nth</u> [nθ], war<u>mth</u> [mθ]   b. lau<u>ghs</u> [fs], twel<u>fth</u> [fθ]

    c. ma<u>ps</u> [ps], wi<u>dth</u> [dθ]   d. ma<u>tch</u> [tʃ], ba<u>dge</u> [dʒ]

When the words in (1) are followed by a word beginning with a vowel, such as *is/are* as in (2), the second member of the consonant sequences in (2a)-(2c) can move to the next syllable:

(2) a. Leaving on the ni<u>nth is</u> fine with me. ([nθ] or [n.θ])

    b. His lau<u>ghs are</u> heard from down the hall. ([fs] or [f.s])

    c. Ma<u>ps are</u> useful when you travel abroad. ([ps] or [p.s])

    d. A ma<u>tch is</u> found in the box. ([tʃ] but not [t.ʃ])

In (2a), for example, the second consonant of the underlined part [nθ] forms a new syllable in fast speech. That is, [θ] in *ninth* is a coda of the syllable, but it can move to the next syllable and in turn, it becomes the onset of [θɪz]. However, this resyllabification does not happen in (2d). That is, (2d) is pronounced [mæ.tʃɪz] and not [mæt.ʃɪz]. This is because English treats them differently: the consonant sequences in (2a)-(2c) are two consonant clusters while the one in (2d) is a single sound. This class of sounds is indeed inseparable just like diphthongs, and a member of this class is called a(n) _____.

Note : '.' represents a syllable boundary.

03 Read the passage and fill in the blank with the most appropriate IPA symbol. [2 points]

Two different definitions are employed for the tense-lax distinction. One is the phonetic definition given in (1).

(1) Phonetic definition
    a. A tense vowel has a higher tongue position than its lax counterpart.
    b. A tense vowel has greater duration than its lax counterpart.
    c. A tense vowel requires a greater muscular effort in production than a lax vowel.

The other is a phonologically defined tense-lax separation in terms of the different kinds of syllables in which the vowels can occur.

(2) Phonological definition
    Tense vowels can appear in open syllables with stress while lax vowels cannot.

The distributionally based phonological classification of tense-lax comes into conflict with the phonetically based classification in several respects. First of all, both /oʊ/ and /ɔ/ are tense in the phonological classification while they are separated as tense and lax, respectively, in the phonetic classification. Second, there is a problem with regard to duration, which the phonetically based criterion focuses on. While it is true that several of the lax vowels are short, _____ is not. Indeed, this vowel has equal duration with, or even greater duration than typically long and tense vowels.

04 Read the passage and fill in each blank with the ONE most appropriate word, respectively. [2 points]

2018년 A형 5번

> The examples in (1) show that word final consonant clusters formed by the addition of an inflectional suffix undergo voicing assimilation.
>
> (1) cats [kæts] dogs [dɔgz]
>   cans [kænz] bells [bɛlz]
>   baked [beɪkt] popped [pɑpt]
>   farmed [fɑɹmd] sealed [sild]
>
> The examples in (2) illustrate the voicing agreement patterns in word final consonant clusters of the underived lexical items.
>
> (2) a. apse [æps] *[æpz] adze [ædz] *[æds]
>   apt [æpt] *[æpd] lift [lɪft] *[lɪfd]
>   act [ækt] *[ækd] cast [kæst] *[kæsd]
>
>   b. mince [mɪns] *[mɪnz] belch [bɛltʃ] *[bɛldʒ]
>   purse [pəɹs] *[pəɹz] pump [pʌmp] *[pʌmb]
>   mint [mɪnt] *[mɪnd] elk [ɛlk] *[ɛlg]
>
> Unlike the lexical items with inflectional suffixes in (1), voicing agreement selectively occurs for the underived lexical items in (2). As can be seen in (2b), there are cases where clusters composed of _____ and _____ do not agree in voicing.
>
> *Note* : * indicates a non-permissible form.

05 Read the passage and fill in the blank with ONE word. [2 points] 2017년 A형 3번

While all vowels of English (except [ə]) can occur in stressed syllables, many of these vowels reveal alternations with an [ə] in reduced syllables in morphologically related words, as shown in (1).

(1) **Stressed Syllable**   **Reduced Syllable**

/i/	homogeneous	[hoʊmədʒiniəs]	homogenize	[həmɑdʒənaɪz]
/eɪ/	explain	[ɪkspleɪn]	explanation	[ɛkspləneɪʃən]
/ɛ/	perpetuate	[pəɹpɛtʃʊeɪt]	perpetuity	[pəɹpətʃuəti]
/ɑ/	demonstrable	[dɪmɑnstɹəbəl]	demonstration	[dɛmənstɹeɪʃən]
/ʌ/	confront	[kənfɹʌnt]	confrontation	[kɑnfɹənteɪʃən]
/ɑɪ/	recite	[ɹɪsɑɪt]	recitation	[ɹɛsəteɪʃən]

However, it is not uncommon to see an [ɪ] in reduced syllables of the words in (2).

(2) a. selfish   [sɛlfɪʃ]   b. metric   [mɛtɹɪk]

        sandwich [sændwɪʃ]   running [ɹʌnɪŋ]

        marriage [mæɹɪdʒ]   allegation [ælɪgeɪʃən]

In the examples in (2), [ɪ] occurs before palato-alveolars as in (2a) or before _____ as in (2b). (Your answer must account for all three examples in (2b).)

06 **Read the passage and fill in the blank with a distinctive feature.** [2 points]

2016년 A형 5번

In the syllable structure of English words, dependencies between peaks and codas provide evidence for the existence of rhyme as a constituent of syllable. For example, we can see the relationship between /aʊ/ peak and its coda as follows:

(1) town [taʊn]　　　　　　　　(2) *[taʊm]/*[taʊŋ]
　　house [haʊs]　　　　　　　　　　 *[haʊf]
　　rouse [raʊz]　　　　　　　　　　　*[raʊv]/*[raʊg]
　　sprout [spraʊt]　　　　　　　　　 *[spraʊp]/*[spraʊk]
　　loud [laʊd]　　　　　　　　　　　*[laʊb]/*[laʊg]
　　mouth [maʊθ]　　　　　　　　　 *[maʊf]
　　couch [kaʊʧ]　　　　　　　　　　*[kaʊg]

The examples in (1) show that the coda following /aʊ/ has to be _____, while those in (2) show that it cannot be [labial] or [dorsal] to form a rhyme.

Note : * indicates a non-permissible form.

07 Read the passage and follow the directions. [4 points]

There are two types of derivational suffix *-al* : the type that attaches to nouns and forms adjectives as in *central*, *coastal*, and *musical*, and the type that attaches to verbs and forms nouns as in *refusal, proposal*, and *recital*. The second type, called a deverbal suffix, can derive well-formed nouns only if three requirements are satisfied. One is that the final syllable of the verb it attaches to has stress, and based on this requirement, English lacks nouns like **fidgetal, *promisal,* and **abandonal.* The data in (1) and (2) exemplify the other two requirements.

Requirement 2 :

(1) betrothal, arrival, acquittal, *rebukal, *impeachal, *detachal

Requirement 3 :

(2) rental, dispersal, rehearsal, *acceptal, *resistal, *engraftal

Some Distinctive Features for Consonants

Distinctive Features	Labials	Dentals/ Alveolars	Palato- alveolars	Velars
[anterior]	+	+	−	−
[coronal]	−	+	+	−

Distinctive Features	Nasal stops	Oral stops	Fricatives	Liquids/ Glides
[sonorant]	+	−	−	+
[continuant]	−	−	+	+

Describe Requirements 2 and 3 based on the data in (1) and (2), respectively. For each requirement, use ONE or TWO distinctive features from the list above.

_____

_____

_____

_____

08 Read <A> and <B> and follow the directions. 2011년 35번

┤ A ├

We all make speech errors, and they tell us interesting things about language and its use. More than simply amusing, speech errors are linguistically interesting because they provide further evidence for phonological rules and for the decomposition of speech sounds into features. Consider the following speech errors:

Intended Utterance	Actual Utterance
1. cu<u>p</u> of coffee	cu<u>ff</u> of coffee
2. gave the <u>b</u>oy	gave the <u>g</u>oy
3. the <u>z</u>ipper is <u>n</u>arrow	the <u>n</u>ipper is <u>z</u>arrow
4. go<u>ne</u> to see<u>d</u>	go<u>d</u> to see<u>n</u>

┤ B ├

a. The first error is known as an anticipation error, where a segment that occurs later in a series is repeated in an earlier position. The bilabial stop of the first word *cup* was replaced by a labio-dental fricative of the third word *coffee*.

b. The second error is known as a preservation error, where a segment that occurs earlier in a series is repeated in a later position. The bilabial stop of the third word *boy* was switched with a velar fricative of the first word *gave*.

c. The third error is known as a metathesis error, where two segments switch places. The alveolar fricative of the second word *zipper* and the alveolar nasal of the fourth word *narrow* switched places.

d. In the fourth example, also a metathesis error, the coda consonants of the first and third words were reversed. Hence, the first vowel in the actual utterance lost nasalization because it no longer occurs before a nasal consonant. Instead, the third vowel in the actual utterance is nasalized because it is followed by a nasal consonant.

Choose all and only the statements in <B> that correctly explain the data in <A> in terms of phonological rules and features.

① a, b   ② a, c   ③ a, c, d

④ b, c, d   ⑤ b, d

09 Read the passage and follow the directions.

The plural suffix -s is pronounced as [əz] in words like *buses*, *bushes*, *benches*, *mazes*, *rouges*, and *garages*. These words end with the consonants [s, z, ʃ, ʒ, ʧ, ʤ]. These sounds differ with respect to voicing as well as place and manner of articulation. That is, they do not share any articulatory feature. They do, however, have an auditory property in common: they all have a high-pitched hissing sound quality. The high-pitched hissing sound quality is described by using the feature, *sibilant*. These sounds form the natural class of sibilant consonants in English. Using this feature makes it possible to state a generalization. If we state that [əz] occurs in six different situations, we treat the six consonants as if they were a random collection of sounds with no relation to each other. By referring to the natural class, however, we can state the generalization like this: _____.

Fill in the blank with about 12 words. [3점]

Chapter 03

Phonological Rules

Unit 01 Preview & Review

01 The Function of Phonological Rules

The relationship between the phonemic representation of a word and its phonetic representation, or how it is pronounced, is **rule-governed**. Phonological rules are part of a speaker's knowledge of the language.

Many rules change features from one value to its opposite or even add features not present in the phonemic representation.

The function of the phonological rules in a grammar is to provide the phonetic information necessary for the pronunciation of utterances. We may illustrate this point in the following way:

(1)　input　　　　　*Phonemic Representation of Words in a Sentence*
　　　　　　　　　　　　　↓
　　　　　　　　　　Phonological Rules (P-rules)
　　　　　　　　　　　　　↓
　　　output　　　*Phonetic Representation of Words in a Sentence*

The input to the P-rules is the phonemic representation. The P-rules apply to the phonemic strings and produce as output the phonetic representation.

The application of rules in this way is called a **derivation**. We have given examples of derivations that show how plurals are derived, how phonemically oral vowels become nasalized, and how /t/ and /d/ become flaps in certain environments. A derivation is thus an explicit way of showing both the effects and the function of phonological rules in a grammar.

For example, the word *tempest* is phonemically /tɛmpɛst/ (as shown by the pronunciation of *tempestuous* [tʰɛ̃mpʰɛsʧuəs]) but phonetically [tʰɛ̃mpəst]. Three rules apply to it: the aspiration rule, the vowel nasalization rule, and the schwa rule. We can **derive** the phonetic form **from** the phonemic representation as follows:

(2)

Underlying phonemic representation	/	t	ɛ	m	p	ɛ	s	t	/
Aspiration rule		tʰ							
Nasalization rule			ɛ̃						
Schwa rule						ə			
Surface phonetic representation	[	tʰ	ɛ̃	m	p	ə	s	t	]

02 Assimilation Rules

A particular kind of feature-changing rule is **assimilation**. Assimilation rules in languages reflect **coarticulation**—the spreading of phonetic features either in the anticipation or in the perseveration of articulatory processes.

2.1. Aspiration

The rule in English that aspirates voiceless stops at the beginning of a syllable simply **adds a nondistinctive feature**. Generally, **aspiration** occurs only if the following vowel is stressed. The /p/ in *pit* and *repeat* is an **aspirated** [pʰ], but the /p/ in *inspect* or *compass* is an **unaspirated** [p]. We also note that even with an intervening consonant, the aspiration takes place so that words such as *crib, clip,* and *quip* ([kʰhɹɪb], [kʰlɪp], and [kʰwɪp]) all begin with an aspirated [kʰ]. And finally, the affricate /ʧ/ is subject to the rule, so *chip* is phonetically [tʰʃɪp].

We can now state **the aspiration rule**:

(3) A voiceless noncontinuant has [+aspirated] added to its feature matrix at the beginning of a syllable when followed by a stressed vowel with an optional intervening consonant.

2.2. Vowel Nasalization

We have seen that nasalization of vowels in English is **nonphonemic** because it is predictable by rule. The vowel nasalization rule is an **assimilation rule** that makes neighboring segments more similar by **adding** the feature [+nasal] **to** the vowel.

We now wish to look more closely at **the vowel nasalization rule**:

(4) Vowels are nasalized before a nasal consonant within the same syllable.

This rule specifies the **class of sounds** affected by the rule:

(5) a.   *Vowels*

It states what **phonetic change** will occur by applying the rule:

(5) b.   *Change phonemic oral vowels to phonetic nasal vowels.*

And it specifies the **context** or **phonological environment**.

(5) c.   *Before a nasal consonant within the same syllable.*

A shorthand notation to write rules, similar to the way scientists and mathematicians use symbols, makes the rule statements more concise. We can use notations to state the nasalization rule as:

(6)   V → [+nasal] / _____ [+nasal] $

Let's look at the rule piece by piece.

(7)   **V**   →   **[+nasal]**   /   _____   **[+nasal]**   **$**

    Vowels become nasalized   in the environment   before   nasal segments   within a syllable

(8)

		"bob"			"boom"	
Phonemic representation	/b	ə	b/	/b	u	m/
Nasality: phonemic feature value	−	0*	−	−	0*	+
Apply nasal rule		NA			↓	
Nasality: phonetic feature value	−	−	−	−	+	+
Phonetic representation	[b	ə	b]	[b	ũ	m]

   * The 0 means not present on the phonemic level.

A word such as *den$tal* /dɛn$təl/ will be pronounced [dɛ̃n$təl]: we have showed the syllable boundary explicitly. However, the first vowel in *de$note*, /dɪ$not/, will not be nasalized, because the nasal segment does not precede the syllable boundary, so the "within a syllable" condition is not met.

2.3. Glottalization and Preglottalization

Mention should be made of **the glottal stop** or **the preglottalized /t/** and the contexts in which it manifests itself. A glottal stop is the sound that occurs when the vocal cords are held tightly together. In most speakers of American and British English, **glottal stops** or **the preglottalized /t/** are commonly found as allophones of /t/ in words such as:

(9) Batman [bæʔmæn]   Hitler [hɪʔlɚ]   atlas [æʔləs]

    Atlanta [əʔlæntə]   he hit me [hihɪʔmi]   eat well [iʔwɛl]

    hot water [hɑʔwɑɾɚ]

While the glottal stop can replace the /t/ in these words, it is not allowed in *atrocious* [ət̠ oʃəs] (not *[əʔɹoʃəs]), *attraction* [ət̠ɹækʃən] (not *[əʔɹækʃən]; the asterisk here means "wrong" or "unattested"). The reason for this is that the **glottal stop replacement** requires the target /t/ to be **in a syllable-final position** ([bæʔ.mæn], [əʔ.læn.tə]). The words that do not allow the replacement have their /t/ in the onset position ([ə.t̠o.ʃəs], [ə.t̠ɹæk.ʃən]), as /tɹ/ is a permissible onset in English.

The glottal stop replacement of syllable-final /t/ is also observable **before the syllabic nasal** (e.g. *beaten* [biʔn̩], *kitten* [kɪʔn̩]). The process under discussion is most easily perceived after short vowels (e.g. *put*, *hit*), and least obvious after consonants (e.g. *belt, sent*).

As pointed out above, in absolute final position, some speakers do not replace the /t/ with a glottal stop entirely, but insert a glottal stop before /t/, as in *hit* [hɪʔt] ("**preglottalization**" or "**glottal reinforcement**").

The only difference between **a glottal stop [ʔ]** and **a glottally reinforced [ʔt]** is that the tip of the tongue makes contact with the alveolar ridge in the latter case but not in the former. It is also worth pointing out that this **glottal reinforcement** may be applicable to **other voiceless stops** for many speakers, as shown in *tap* [tæʔp], *sack* [sæʔk].

2.4. /l/-Velarization

Let us turn to a phoneme /l/. /l/ has only two main allophones in English, depending on its position in the word. If you say *lull*, or *lilt*, you will notice that the first *l* in each case is pronounced with the tip of your tongue up behind your top front teeth, while the second additionally has the tongue raised further back.

In the case of /l/, what matters is whether the /l/ precedes or follows the vowel in the word. If /l/ comes first, it is pronounced as 'clear', fronter [l], as also in *clear*; and if the vowel comes first, /l/ is realized as 'dark', more back [ɫ], as in *dull*. The two are obviously **in complementary distribution**, and hence can both straightforwardly be assigned to the same phoneme, /l/, in Modern English.

The rule for velarization of /l/ was informally stated as:

(10) The liquid /l/ is velarized when it follows a vowel in a word.

This rule specification gives the correct results for *clear* versus *hill*, for instance. This works well enough when we are only dealing with word-initial versus word-final clusters, but it leaves a grey area in word-medial position, where we find dark [ɫ] in *falter, hilltop*, but clear [l] in *holy, hilly*.

This is resolvable if we state the rule in terms of the **syllable**:

(11) The liquid /l/ is velarized when it appears in coda position.

In fact, this process does not only provide evidence for the contrast between onset and coda position, but for the superordinate rhyme constituent, which consists of the nucleus plus the optional coda. In cases of **consonant syllabification**, where /l/ comes to play the role of a vowel and therefore occupies the nuclear position, as in *bottle, little*, we find the dark allophone. **/l/-velarization**, then, takes place in syllable rhymes.

2.5. Palatalization

Alveopalatal fricatives /ʃ, ʒ/ differ from the others by having an appreciable lip rounding (**labialization**). Another pair, alveolar fricatives /s, z/, echoing the alveolar stops, may undergo **palatalization** and turn into [ʃ, ʒ] respectively, when they occur before the palatal glide /j/. Commonly heard forms such as

(12) [aɪmɪʃju]   (I miss you)   [aɪpliʒju]   (I please you)

　　 [ðɪʃiɹ]   (this year)   [huʒjʊɹ bɑs]   (who's your boss?)

demonstrate this clearly. Thus, we can put together the behavior of /t, d, s, z/ and state that

(13) The **alveolar obstruents** of English become alveopalatal when followed by a word that starts with the palatal gide /j/

(since there are no alveopalatal stops in English, the replacements are affricates for /t, d/).

03 Dissimilation Rules

It is understandable that so many languages have **assimilation rules**; they permit greater **ease of articulation**. It might seem strange, then, to learn that languages also have feature-changing rules called **dissimilation rules**, in which certain segments becomes less similar to other segments. Ironically, such rules have the same explanation: it is sometimes **easier to articulate** dissimilar sounds.

3.1. Fricative Dissimilation

An example of easing pronunciation through dissimilation is found in some varieties of English, in which there is a fricative dissimilation rule. This rule applies to sequences /fΘ/ and /sΘ/, changing them to [ft] and [st]. Here the fricative /Θ/ becomes dissimilar to the preceding fricative by becoming a stop. For example, the words *fifth* and *sixth* come to be pronounced as if they were spelled *fift* and *sikst*.

3.2. Liquid Dissimilation

A classic example of the same kind of **dissimilation** occurred in Latin, and the results of this process show up in the derivational morpheme /-aɹ/ in English. In Latin a derivational suffix *-alis* was added to nouns to form adjectives. When the suffix was added to a noun that contained the liquid /l/, the suffix was changed to *-aris;* that is, the liquid /l/ was changed to the dissimilar liquid /ɹ/. These words came into English as adjectives ending in *-al* or in its dissimilated form *-ar,* as shown in the following examples:

(14) **-al**   **-ar**

    anecdot-al   angul-ar

    annu-al   annul-ar

    ment-al   column-ar

    pen-al   perpendicul-ar

    spiritu-al   simil-ar

    ven-al   vel-ar

All of the *-ar* adjectives contain /l/, and as *columnar* illustrates, the /l/ need not be the consonant directly preceding the dissimilated segment.

04 Segment Deletion Rules

Phonological rules may **add** or **delete** entire segments. These are **different from** the feature-changing rules, which affect only parts of segments.

4.1. Schwa Deletion

Segment deletion rules are commonly found in many languages and are far more prevalent than **segment insertion rules**. One such rule occurs in **casual** or **rapid speech**.

We often **delete** the unstressed vowels in words like the following:

(15) mystery   general   memory   funeral   vigorous   Barbara

These words in casual speech can sound as if they were written:

(16) mystry   genral   memry   funral   vigrous   Barbra

4.2. /g/-Deletion

The silent *g* that torments spellers in such words as *sign* and *design* is actually the result of a segment deletion rule. Consider the following examples:

(17)
A		B	
sign	[sãɪn]	signature	[sɪgnətʃər]
design	[dəzãɪn]	designation	[dɛzɪgneʃõn]
paradigm	[pʰærədãɪm]	paradigmatic	[pʰærədɪgmærək]

In none of the words in column A is there a phonetic [g], but in each corresponding word in column B a [g] occurs. Our knowledge of English phonology accounts for these phonetic differences.

The "[g] ~ no [g]" alternation is regular and is also seen in pairs like *gnostic* [nastɪk] and *agnostic* [ægnastɪk].

This rule may be stated as:

(18) Delete a /g/ word-initially before a nasal consonant or before a syllable-final nasal consonant.

Given this rule, the phonemic representations of the stems in *sign/signature, design/ designation, malign/malignant, phlegm/phlegmatic, paradigm/paradigmatic, gnostic/agnostic,* and so on will include a /g/ that will be deleted by the regular rule if a prefix or suffix is not added. By stating the class of sounds that follow the /g/ (nasal consonants) rather than any specific nasal consonant, the rule deletes the /g/ before both /m/ and /n/.

4.3. /t/-Deletion

Another characteristic of **American English** in **informal conversational speech** is the creation of homophonous productions for pairs such as *planner − planter* [plænɚ], *canner − canter* [kænɚ], *winner − winter* [wɪnɚ], *tenor − tenter* [tɛnɚ]. **The loss of /t/** in the second member of these pairs is also in many other words, as in *rental, dental, renter, dented, twenty, gigantic, Toronto*. In all these examples we see that the /t/ that is lost is following an /n/.

However, that such as *contain, interred, entwined*, in which /t/ following an /n/ can**not** be deleted. The difference between these words and the earlier ones is that **/t/ is deleted only in an unstressed syllable**.

4.4. Interdental Fricative Deletion

Interdental fricatives /θ, ð/ may undergo **the elision process** (i.e. they may be left out) when they occur before the alveolar fricatives /s, z/, as exemplified by *clothes* [kloz], *months* [mʌns].

(19) <u>clothes</u>   /kloð+z/   kloðz   —ð-Deletion→   [kloz]

    <u>months</u>   /mʌnθ+z/ —Devoicing→ mʌnθs   —θ-Deletion→   [mʌns]

4.5. /j/-Deletion

Words such as *music* [mjuzɪk] and *cube* [kjub] are pronounced in the same way in both American English and British English. However, words such as *tuition, endure,* and *annuity* vary, as shown in (20a) and (20b).

(20a) British English

    tuition [tjuɪʃən]   duration [dju̠ɹeɪʃən]

    endure [ɪnd̠jʊə]   annuity [ən̠juəti]

    perpetuity [pɜ:pət̠juəti]   voluminous [vəl̠jumənəs]

(20b) American English

    tuition [tuɪʃən]   duration [du̠ɹeɪʃən]

    endure [ɪnd̠ʊɹ]   annuity [ən̠uəti]

    perpetuity [pɜ:pət̠uəti]   voluminous [vəl̠umənəs]

While in British English we see a /j/ after the underlined consonants /t/, /d/, /n/, and /l/ in the words given in (20a), the expected American English pronunciations are without a /j/ after the same underlined consonants, as shown in (20b). The same difference is observed after the underlined consonants /s/ and /z/ for the words in (21a) and (21b).

(21a) British English

    assume [ə̠sjum]   superb [s̠jupɜ:b]

    exude [ɪgz̠jud]   résumé [ɹɛz̠jʊmeɪ]

(21b) American English

    assume [ə̠sum]   superb [s̠upɜ˞b]

    exude [ɪgz̠ud]   résumé [ɹɛz̠ʊmeɪ]

However, the words given in (22) show that the underlined alveolars /n/ and /l/ are followed by a /j/ in American English as well as in British English.

(22) British English and American English

| continue [kəntɪn̠ju] | biannual [baɪæn̠juəl] |
| voluble [vɑljʊbəl] | valuation [væljueɪʃən] |

These examples may suggest that /j/ may **not** follow an **alveolar** in the same morpheme in AmE (across morphemes this is possible, as in *would you, bet you*).

This generalization, however, has to be amended, because words such as *onion* [ɑnjən], *tenure* [tɛnjɚ], *annual* [ænjuəl], *value* [vælju], *failure* [feljɚ], *million* [mɪljən] have alveolars /n/ or /l/ followed by a /j/ in AmE as well as in BE. Thus, the correct characterization of the **AmE** restriction on alveolar should read as "**/j/ cannot follow an alveolar obstruent; it can follow an alveolar sonorant when in an unstressed syllable.**"

05 Segment Insertion Rules

The process of inserting a consonant or vowel is called **epenthesis**.

If you say *hamster* slowly and carefully, it will sound like [hæmstə] (or [hæmstəɹ]). If you say the word quickly several times, you will produce something closer to your normal, casual speech pronunciation, and it is highly likely that there will be an extra consonant in there, giving [hæmpstə] (or [hæmpstəɹ]) instead.

As the rate of speech increases, adjacent sounds influence one another even more than usual, because the same complex articulations are taking place in even less time. Here, the articulators are moving from a **voiced nasal stop** [m], to a **voiceless alveolar fricative** [s], so that almost every possible property has to change all at once.

In fast speech, not all these transitions may be perfectly coordinated: the **extraneous [p]** appears when the speaker has succeeded in switching off voicing, and raising the velum to cut off airflow through the nose, but has not yet shifted from stop to fricative, or from labial to alveolar.

A very similar process arises in words like *mince* and *prince*, which can become homophonous (that is, identical in sound) to *mints* and *prints* in fast speech. Here, the transition is from [n], a voiced alveolar nasal stop, to [s], a voiceless alveolar oral fricative, and the half-way house is [t], which this time shares its place of articulation with both neighbours, but differs from [n] in voicing and nasality, and from [s] in manner of articulation.

In both *hamster* and *mince/prince*, however, the casual speech process creating the **extra medial plosive** is an **optional** one.

06 Stem-Bounded Rule

Bounding effects can also be found in the interior of words. For studying such effects, it is useful to set up a linguistic unit which I will refer to as the stem. Although the word stem has multiple meanings in linguistics, for purposes of this discussion I will assume that it is the minimal constituent within a word that can stand as an independent word. Thus, in *jumping* [[dʒʌmp]ᵥ ɪŋ]ₙ, the stem is [dʒʌmp]ᵥ. In *identifier* [[[aɪdɛnt] ɪfaɪ]ᵥ ɚ]ₙ, the stem is [aɪdɛntɪfaɪ]ᵥ. Although we can recognize a smaller root morpheme [aɪdɛnt] within this word (compare *identity, identical*), we will not consider it to be the stem, since it cannot occur as an independent word. This definition of stem is only an approximation, but will serve for present purposes.

Consider now an example of a stem-bounded rule. The following rule occurs in some version in a number of English dialects:

Pre-/l/ Monophthongization

oʊ → o / ___ l

We can see the effects of the rule in the following data:

/oʊ/ before /l/: [o]				/oʊ/ in other environments: [oʊ]			
pole	[pol]	*Coltrane*	[koltʃɹeɪn]	*Poe*	[poʊ]	*propane*	[pɹoʊpeɪn]
hole	[hol]	*told*	[told]	*hope*	[hoʊp]	*toad*	[toʊd]
mole	[mol]	*fold*	[fold]	*moat*	[moʊt]	*phone*	[foʊn]
poultry	[poltʃɹi]	*mold*	[mold]	*Oakley*	[oʊkli]	*most*	[moʊst]

The above are all simple, monomorphemic forms. The more subtle effects occur when we add suffixes to stems that end in /oʊ/ or in /oʊ/ plus /l/.

First, if we add a suffix or compound member starting with /l/ to a stem that ends in /oʊ/, we get [oʊ], contrary to what we might have expected:

lowly	[loʊli]
slowly	[sloʊli]
lowlands	[loʊləndz]
toeless	[toʊləs]

There is nothing about suffixation per se that produces this result. Thus, if we add a vowel-initial suffix to a stem that ends in /oʊ/ plus /l/, then the monophthongal allophone appears:

goalie [goli]

hole-y [holi]

rolling [ɹolɪŋ]

Pol-ess [poləs] 'a female Pole'

These facts can be accounted for if we assume that Pre-/l/ Monophthongization is a stem-bounded rule. Below, I have labeled the stem morphemes within the full words.

lowly	*goalie*	
[[loʊ]stem li]word	[[goʊl]stem i]word	underlying forms
BLOCKED	o	Pre-/l/ Monophthongization
loʊli	goli	surface forms

It can be seen that underlying /oʊ/ gets monophthongized only if it is in the same stem as the immediately following /l/.

Another rule that seems to be stem-bounded in English is Vowel Nasalization, which converts underlying oral vowels to their nasal counterparts before a nasal consonant. I find that many English speakers have near-minimal pairs for nasality of the following type: ã õ ĩ ũ ɚ̃ ễ

Venus [vĩnəs]	*freeness* [fɹinəs]
bonus [bõũnəs]	*slowness* [sloʊnəs]
Uranus [jʊɹêĩnəs]	*greyness* [gɹeɪnəs]
Linus [lãĩnəs]	*dryness* [dɹaɪnəs]

These distinctions can be derived under the assumption that the rule that derives nasalization is stem-bounded:

Vowel Nasalization (refined)

[+syllabic] → [+nasal] / ___ [+nasal]   Domain: Stem

A stem-bounded rule will match up to an underlying representation like /[[vinəs]stem]word/ but not to /[[fɹi]stem nəs]word/.

Unit 02 Questions

Answer Key p.503

01 **Read the passage and follow the directions.** [4 points]   2022년 B형 4번

┤ A ├

Nucleus positions in syllables are usually taken by vowels. In the cases that syllables have no vowel, consonants stand as the nucleus. It is usual to indicate that a consonant is syllabic by means of a small vertical mark (ˌ) beneath or above the symbol. Even though syllabic consonants are observed word-medially (e.g., Hungary [hʌ́ŋgɹi]), most syllabic consonants are found word-finally as in (1). Note that some words can be realized in two phonetic forms.

(1) Syllabic consonants

<u>syllabic [n]</u>	<u>syllabic [m]</u>	<u>syllabic [ŋ]</u>	<u>syllabic [l]</u>
open [oʊpn̩]	~[oʊpm̩]		supple [sʌpl̩]
ribbon [ɹɪbn̩]	~[ɹɪbm̩]		rebel [ɹɛbl̩]
cotton [katn̩]			bottle [batl̩]
sudden [sʌdn̩]			muddle [mʌdl̩]
broken [bɹoʊkn̩]		~[bɹoʊkŋ̍]	uncle [ʌŋkl̩]
pagan [peɪgn̩]		~[peɪgŋ̍]	fungal [fʌŋgl̩]
question [kwɛstʃn̩]			satchel [sætʃl̩]
soften [sɔfn̩]			muffle [mʌfl̩]
lengthen [lɛŋΘn̩]	anthem [ænΘm̩]		lethal [liΘl̩]
lesson [lɛsn̩]	handsome [hænsm̩]		muscle [mʌsl̩]
ashen [æʃn̩]			bushel [bʊʃl̩]
column [kaləm],			mammal [mæml̩]
*[kaləmn̩]			channel [tʃænl̩]
corn [kɔɹn],			peril [pɛɹl̩]
*[kɔɹn̩]			sale [seɪl], *[seɪl̩]

The table in (2) provides distinctive features to categorize natural classes depending on the manners of articulation.

(2)

	vowels	glides	liquids	nasals	obstruents
[syllabic]	+	−	−	−	−
[consonantal]	−	−	+	+	+
[approximant]	+	+	+	−	−
[sonorant]	+	+	+	+	−

Note 1 : '*' indicates a non-permissible form.

Note 2 : '~' indicates phonetic variation.

⊦ B ⊦

a. In the word-final position, /n/ is realized as a syllabic nasal when immediately preceded by _____ segments.

b. In the word-final position, /l/ is realized as a syllabic liquid when immediately preceded by _____ segments.

Based on the data in (1), fill in each blank in <B> with the ONE most appropriate feature in (2), respectively. Write your answers in the correct order. Then, identify the syllabic consonant that is always homorganic with the preceding consonant in the given data, and explain the reason.

_____

_____

_____

_____

_____

02 **Read the passage and follow the directions.** [2 points]

When two consonants appear word-initially, the sonority of the first consonant is lower than that of the second one except for '/s/ and voiceless obstruent' sequences such as [st] in *stop* and [sf] in *sphere*. Accordingly, the two liquids /l/ and /ɹ/ appear as the second consonant since they have relatively high sonority. However, it is not the case that all the combinations are possible as below.

[pl]	[bl]	[fl]	[kl]	[gl]
play	*bleed*	*fly*	*click*	*glass*
[pɹ]	[bɹ]	[fɹ]	[kɹ]	[gɹ]
pray	*breed*	*fry*	*crick*	*grass*

*[Θl]	*[tl]	*[dl]	[sl]	*[ʃl]
----	----	----	*slide*	----
[Θɹ]	[tɹ]	[dɹ]	*[sɹ]	[ʃɹ]
thrive	*try*	*dry*	----	*shrimp*

As presented above, some consonant clusters including a liquid as the second do not appear in word-initial positions except for a few loanwords. As a result, the contrast between the two liquids /l/ and /ɹ/ is neutralized after _____ obstruents in word-initial positions.

Note : '*' indicates a non-permissible form.

Fill in the blank with the ONE most appropriate word.

_____

03 Read the passage and follow the directions. [4 points]

┤ A ├

In a number of American English dialects, /oʊ/ is realized as a diphthong [oʊ] or a monophthong [o].

(1) /oʊ/ is realized as [oʊ].

a. Poe	[poʊ]
b. low	[loʊ]
c. hope	[hoʊp]
d. coat	[koʊt]
e. most	[moʊst]
f. flow	[floʊ]

(2) /oʊ/ is realized as [o].

a. pole	[pol]
b. Coletrane	[koltreɪn]
c. hole	[hol]
d. told	[told]
e. mole	[mol]
f. fold	[fold]

Observing the patterns in (1) and (2), one could make a generalization as in (3).

(3) /oʊ/ is realized as [o] when it is close to /l/.

However, the generalization in (3) does not always hold for the data above. Moreover, it cannot explain the contrast between (4) and (5) below.

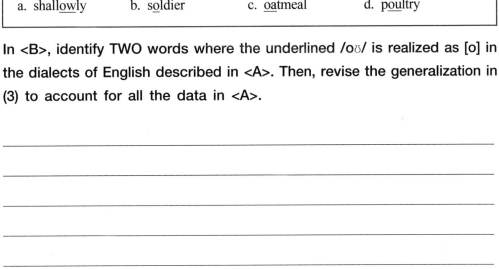

(4) /oʊ/ is realized as [oʊ].

    a. low-ly   [loʊli]

    b. slow-ly   [sloʊli]

    c. low-land-s [loʊləndz]

    d. toe-less   [toʊləs]

(5) /oʊ/ is realized as [o].

    a. goal-ie   [goli]

    b. roll-ing   [rolɪŋ]

    c. bowl-er   [bolər]

    d. hole-in-one [holɪnwʌn]

Note : '-' indicates a morpheme boundary.

─────────────────┤ B ├──────────────────

   a. shall<u>ow</u>ly   b. s<u>o</u>ldier   c. <u>oa</u>tmeal   d. p<u>ou</u>ltry

In <B>, identify TWO words where the underlined /oʊ/ is realized as [o] in the dialects of English described in <A>. Then, revise the generalization in (3) to account for all the data in <A>.

_____

_____

_____

_____

_____

04 **Read the passage and follow the directions.** [4 points]   2020년 B형 3번

Some morphemes in English are pronounced differently depending on their phonetic environments. These variants of the same morpheme are called *allomorphs*. An important question is how we know which allomorph appears for a given word.

Consider the following examples in (1), where the negative morphemes *il-* and *ir-* are added to a base:

(1) a. *il-* : i̲l̲legal, i̲l̲logical, i̲l̲literate, i̲l̲legible

   b. *ir-* : i̲r̲regular, i̲r̲rational, i̲r̲reducible, i̲r̲recoverable

Comparing the examples in (1a) with the ones in (1b), a simple distribution is observed for the two allomorphs [ɪl] and [ɪɹ]. That is, [ɪl] and [ɪɹ] are selectively combined with their bases conditioned by the initial sound of the base: when the base begins with /l/, the prefix *il-* is chosen, and when the base begins with /ɹ/, the prefix *ir-* is chosen.

There is another case where [l] and [ɹ] alternate between allomorphs. The adjectival suffix has two allomorphs: *-ar* [əɹ] and *-al* [əl], as shown in (2):

(2) a. *-ar* : singul̲a̲r̲, popul̲a̲r̲, sol̲a̲r̲, vel̲a̲r̲

   b. *-al* : rur̲a̲l̲, plur̲a̲l̲, vir̲a̲l̲, mor̲a̲l̲

These suffixes *-ar* [əɹ] and *-al* [əl] are attached to the base depending on the final consonant of the base. (1) and (2) are different in where the morpheme is attached: (1) precedes the base, which is a prefix, and (2) follows the base, which is a suffix. On the other hand, these two morphemes are similar in that the allomorphs for different morphemes show the same alternation between [l] and [ɹ]. It is interesting to find the two apparently different phonemes /l/ and /ɹ/ are involved in the alternation of the allomorphs *il-/ir-* and *-al/-ar*.

The two sounds /l/ and /ɹ/ share many phonetic properties such as voicing, the place of articulation, and the manner of articulation. They only differ in terms of the way air passes through the mouth. This characteristic difference can be made using the distinctive properties known as the distinctive feature [lateral].

Identify TWO phonological processes involved in (1) and (2) in the correct order. Then, using the distinctive feature [lateral] (i.e., [+lateral] or [−lateral]), generalize the distribution of the allomorphs *-al and -ar*.

05 Read the passage in <A> and the dialogue in <B>, and follow the directions. [4 points]

2020년 A형 7번

┤ A ├

One of the most effective ways of testing a learner's pronunciation is to observe and record repeated errors in a variety of situations. Speech contexts often change the way a given word is pronounced. Careful or emphasized speech is usually employed to show how to pronounce words clearly. In a connected or conversational speech, words are often contracted and the pronunciation of a word can change through the phenomena in (1) and sound rules in (2):

(1) a. That is nice > That's (Contraction)
    b. missed *[d], Ms. *[s] (Spelling pronunciation)

(2)

	Careful speech	Connected speech	Sound rules
a. can't you	[t j]	[tʃ]	Palatalization
b. because	[ə]	-	Vowel deletion
c. greater	[t]	[ɾ]	Tapping
d. advantage	[nt]	[n]	Consonant deletion

It is worth mentioning that spelling often influences learners' pronunciation of words. When spelling pronunciation errors are found in learners' pronunciation, they can sometimes be critical. For instance, if the plural form of *sea, seas*, is pronounced [sis] rather than [siz], it can be misunderstood as the word *cease* [sis] by listeners.

Note : '*' indicates incorrect pronunciation.

⊣ B ⊢

(Two students are talking about what they wrote during a dictation task without looking at each other's notes.)

S1 : Can you tell me what you got for the second sentence? I wrote down, 'Last [wɪnɚ] (winner) was colder,' and it does not make sense to me.

S2 : Why? It means what it says. 'Last [wɪntɚ] (winter) was colder.' How (i) <u>did you</u> understand it?

S1 : Oh, it is [wɪntɚ] (winter), the season! I thought it was winner. That is why the sentence did not make sense to me.

S2 : [wɪntɚ] (winter), [wɪnɚ] (winter), ... yes, when you say it quickly, it does sound the same.

S1 : Thanks! Wait, did you hear the last word in the fourth sentence? Can you tell me what it was?

S2 : 'My dog's skin is irritated by [fliz] (fleas).'

S1 : What is [fliz] (fleas)? Can you spell it for me?

S2 : F-L-E-A-S! Don't you know what fleas are?

S1 : Yeah, but isn't that pronounced as (ii) <u>[flis] (fleas)</u>? It is confusing.

S2 : Let's ask the teacher later why 's' sounds like 'z' here.

Note : S = student

Identify ONE phenomenon or sound rule from <A> that changes the pronunciation of (i) in <B> and explain how your answer applies to the given words. Then, identify ONE phenomenon or sound rule that causes S1's confusion in (ii) and explain how your answer applies to the given word based on the description in <A>.

_____

_____

_____

_____

_____

06 **Read the passages and follow the directions.** [4 points]

The alveolar lateral approximant /l/ presents appreciable differences among different varieties. In British English, we find the clear 'l,' which is articulated with the tongue tip in contact with the alveolar ridge, in words such as like, *law, leaf, light*, etc. On the other hand, /l/ is realized as the velarized dark 'l,' which has a quality similar to /u/ with raising of the back of the tongue toward the velum, in words such as *fall, file, belt, milk*, etc. In Welsh English, /l/ is always pronounced as the clear 'l.'

In some varieties of American English (AE), however, the clear 'l' may hardly be found; most commonly, the realizations differ in terms of shades of the dark 'l.' Thus, a dark 'l' is found in words given in (1a), a more velarized darker 'l' variety in words in (1b), and the darkest 'l' in words in (1c).

(1) Realizations of /l/ in some AE varieties
   a. dark 'l'
      lip, left, lash, leaf
   b. darker 'l'
      loose, low, lawn, lock
   c. darkest 'l'
      full, bolt, help, hill

In African American Vernacular English (AAVE), /l/ may vocalize to [ʊ] as in (2a) and may be deleted as in (2b).

(2) Realizations of /l/ in AAVE
   a. vocalization of /l/
      bell   [bɛl]   or   [bɛʊ]
      milk   [mɪlk]   or   [mɪʊk]
      football [fʊtbɔl]   or   [fʊtbɔʊ]
      children [tʃɪldɹən] or   [tʃɪʊdɹən]

b. deletion of /l/

help	[hɛlp]	or	[hɛp]
elm	[ɛlm]	or	[ɛm]
wolf	[wʊlf]	or	[wʊf]
twelve	[twɛlv]	or	[twɛv]

Based on the data given in (1a)-(1b), state the environment(s) for dark 'l' and darker 'l,' respectively, in some AE varieties. Then, based on the data given in (2a)-(2b), state the environment(s) for the vocalization of /l/ and the deletion of /l/, respectively, in AAVE.

07 Read the passage and fill in each blank with the ONE most appropriate word. Write your answers in the correct order. [2 points]   2019년 A형 4번

Across morpheme boundaries, obligatory nasal assimilation to bilabials or alveolars applies without restriction, as shown in (1).

(1) compose   composition

  symbol   symbolic

  sympathy   sympathetic

  condemn   condemnation

  intone   intonation

  indent   indentation

On the other hand, obligatory nasal assimilation to velars applies selectively, as shown in (2). (Note that optional nasal assimilation may apply postlexically to derive 'co[ŋ]cordance,' 'co[ŋ]gressional,' etc.)

(2) Nasal assimilation   No nasal assimilation

  co[ŋ]cord   co[n]cordance

  co[ŋ]gress   co[n]gressional

  co[ŋ]quer   co[n]cur

  co[ŋ]gruous   co[n]gruity

  sy[ŋ]chrony   sy[n]chronic

  i[ŋ]cubate   i[n]clude

The examples in (2) illustrate that obligatory nasal assimilation applies only when preceded by a(n) ① _____ vowel and followed by a(n) ② _____ vowel with a velar involved.

---

08 Read the passage and follow the directions. [4 points]

In a number of dialects of British English, a glide is inserted in certain environments, as shown in (1) and (2).

(1) /j/ insertion

being	/biɪŋ/	[bijɪŋ]
my other (car)	/maɪʌðə/	[maɪjʌðə]
free a (prisoner)	/friə/	[frijə]
enjoy ice cream	/ɛndʒɔɪaɪskɹim/	[ɛndʒɔɪjaɪskɹim]

(2) /w/ insertion

sewer	/suə/	[suwə]
few arrests	/fjuəɹɛsts/	[fjuwəɹɛsts]
now or never	/naʊɔnɛvə/	[naʊwɔnɛvə]
go away	/goʊəweɪ/	[goʊwəweɪ]

However, in such dialects, glide insertion is not attested in the examples in (3). Instead, /ɹ/ is inserted.

(3) No glide insertion

drawing	[dɹɔɹɪŋ]	*[dɹɔjɪŋ]	*[dɹɔwɪŋ]
ma and pa	[maɹənpɑ]	*[majənpɑ]	*[mawənpɑ]
law and order	[lɔɹənɔdə]	*[lɔjənɔdə]	*[lɔwənɔdə]
media event	[midiəɹɪvɛnt]	*[midiəjɪvɛnt]	*[midiəwɪvɛnt]

Note : * indicates a non-permissible form.

Based on the data given in (1)-(3), provide one single generalization for glide insertion. Then, state the condition(s) for /j/ insertion and the one(s) for /w/ insertion, respectively.

_____

_____

_____

09 Read the passage and follow the directions. [4 points]

The schwa vowel /ə/, which is a reduced or weak vowel in English, can be deleted in fast speech, as exemplified in (1).

(1) Schwa Deletion

	Careful Speech	**Fast Speech**
camera	[ˈkæməɹə]	[ˈkæmɹə]
veteran	[ˈvɛtəɹən]	[ˈvɛtɹən]

However, schwa deletion is not observed in fast speech for the following words.

(2) No Schwa Deletion

	Careful Speech	**Fast Speech**	
facilitate	[fəˈsɪləteɪt]	[fəˈsɪləteɪt]	*[fəˈsɪlteɪt]
famous	[ˈfeɪməs]	[ˈfeɪməs]	*[ˈfeɪms]

In the following examples of morphologically related words, schwa deletion may or may not be observed.

(3)

		Careful Speech	**Fast Speech**	
a.	principal	[ˈpɹɪnsəpəl]	[ˈpɹɪnspəl]	
	principality	[pɹɪnsəˈpæləti]	[pɹɪnsəˈpæləti]	*[pɹɪnˈspæləti]
b.	imaginative	[ɪˈmædʒənətɪv]	[ɪˈmædʒnətɪv]	
	imagination	[ɪmædʒəˈneɪʃən]	[ɪmædʒəˈneɪʃən]	*[ɪmædʒˈneɪʃən]

Note : * indicates a non-permissible form.

In the data given in (1) and (3), schwa deletion occurs in fast speech under two conditions related to a preceding and a following phonetic environment. State the two phonetic conditions for schwa deletion.

_____

_____

_____

10 **Read the passage and follow the directions.** [4 points]   2016년 B형 2번

┤ A ├

In American English, alveolar stops can be pronounced as a flap, which is caused by a single contraction of the muscles so that one articulator is thrown against another. It is often just a very rapid stop gesture. This sound can be written with the symbol [ɾ] so that *fatty* can be transcribed as [fǽɾi]. Alveolar stops become a flap when they are located between a stressed vowel and an unstressed vowel as in *water* and *header*. In addition to this rule, there are two other rules that account for the contexts where flapping occurs.

┤ B ├

autumn, riddle, monitor, saddle, humanity, daddy, battle, comedy, competing

Identify ALL the words from <B> that cannot be accounted for by the underlined rule in <A>. Then categorize them into TWO groups according to their occurrence contexts and state ONE rule for EACH group which accounts for each data set.

_____

_____

_____

_____

_____

11 Read the passage and follow the directions. [5 points]

Words such as *music* [mjuzɪk] and *cube* [kjub] are pronounced in the same way in both American English and British English. However, words such as *tuition*, *endure*, and *annuity* vary, as shown in (1a) and (1b).

(1a) British English

tuition [t̠juɪʃən]　　　　　　　duration [d̠jʊreɪʃən]

endure [ɪnd̠jʊə]　　　　　　　annuity [ən̠juəti]

perpetuity [pɜːpət̠juəti]　　　voluminous [vəl̠jumənəs]

(1b) American English

tuition [t̠uɪʃən]　　　　　　　duration [d̠ʊreɪʃən]

endure [ɪnd̠ʊr]　　　　　　　annuity [ən̠uəti]

perpetuity [pɜːpət̠uəti]　　　voluminous [vəl̠umənəs]

While in British English we see a /j/ after the underlined consonants /t/, /d/, /n/, and /l/ in the words given in (1a), the expected American English pronunciations are without a /j/ after the same underlined consonants, as shown in (1b). The same difference is observed after the underlined consonants /s/ and /z/ for the words in (2a) and (2b).

(2a) British English

assume [əs̠jum]　　　　　　　superb [s̠jupɜːb]

exude [ɪgz̠jud]　　　　　　　résumé [rɛz̠jʊmeɪ]

(2b) American English

assume [əs̠um]　　　　　　　superb [s̠upɝb]

exude [ɪgz̠ud]　　　　　　　résumé [rɛz̠ʊmeɪ]

However, the words given in (3) show that the underlined alveolars /n/ and /l/ are followed by a /j/ in American English as well as in British English.

(3) British English and American English

continue [kəntɪnju]   biannual [baɪænjuəl]

voluble [vɑljʊbəl]   valuation [væljueɪʃən]

Note : Vowel differences in some words between British English and American English are not represented in the data above.

Based on the data given in (1b), (2b), and (3), state the condition(s) when /j/ cannot follow alveolar consonants and the condition(s) when /j/ can in American English.

12 Read <A> and <B> and answer the question. [2.5점]   2013년 30번

┤ A ├

A phonological process commonly found in English is neutralization, whereby a phonemic contrast generally observed is not found in a given environment. For example, both /t/ and /d/ are realized as the flap [ɾ] between a stressed and an unstressed vowel in American English, as can be seen in *writer* [ɹaɪɾəɹ] and *rider* [ɹaɪɾəɹ]. By the flapping rule, the phonemic contrast between /t/ and /d/ is lost between a stressed and an unstressed vowel, resulting in the neutralization of the contrast in that position. As another example of neutralization, the vowel /i/ within syllables closed by /ɹ/ (e.g., b<u>ee</u>r) is produced somewhere between a tense /i/ and a lax vowel /ɪ/ in American English. That is, there is no contrast between a tense and a lax vowel before syllable final /ɹ/, even though this distinction exists elsewhere.

┤ B ├

a. At the beginning of a stressed syllable, an aspirated stop occurs, and an unaspirated stop does not (e.g., **p**ea, **t**ea, **k**ey).

b. In some accents of English, /p, t, k/ in syllable final position are realized as a glottal stop (e.g., ti**p**, pi<u>t</u>, ki**ck**).

c. In African American English, /ɪ/ and /ɛ/ are pronounced the same before nasal consonants (e.g., p<u>i</u>n, p<u>e</u>n).

Which of the following lists all and only the case(s) in <B> that show(s) the phonological process described in <A>?

① a   ② a, b   ③ a, b, c

④ b, c   ⑤ c

13 Read <A> and <B> and answer the question. 2012년 31번

A

When neighboring sounds mutually affect each other to merge into a third sound, the process is called coalescent assimilation, which can be found in palatalization in English. This coalescent assimilation or palatalization occurs when 'a morpheme-final or word-final alveolar obstruent' is followed by 'the palatal glide' in English, merging the two sounds into 'a palatalized fricative or affricate'. For example, within a word as in *architecture*, the underlying /t/ in the morpheme final position of *architect-* and the initial /j/ in the suffix *-ure* affect each other to merge into the palatalized affricate [ʧ]. This process can also be found across words as in the phrase *kiss you* in fast, casual speech of North American English.

B

a. You don't accept your failure easily, do you?

b. You seem to be under the delusion that he follows you.

c. The old class divisions had begun to melt down.

d. We should cut down on our spending next year.

e. He checked his yacht before his departure for Australia.

f. After six years, her gracious demeanor became known to everybody.

Which of the following lists all and only sentences that contain the expressions which can undergo the coalescent assimilation described in <A> both within a word and across words?

① a, c, d   ② a, d, e   ③ b, c, f

④ b, e, f   ⑤ c, d, e

14 **Read the description below and follow the directions.** [2 points]   2011년 33번

Phonological rules apply to phonemic strings and alter them in various ways to derive their phonetic pronunciations. The underlined parts in the following examples from native speakers of English show the application of the rules either diachronically or synchronically:

a. They may add nondistinctive features, which are predictable from the context.
   Key players on the ski team were sick.

b. They may change feature values to make two phonemes in a string more dissimilar.
   Are there any similar aspects among the spiritual groups?

c. They may insert segments that are not present in the phonemic string.
   The school has many kids from my neighborhood.

d. They may delete phonemic segments in a certain context.
   What's the difference between sign and signature?

Choose all and only the phonological rules that are shown with correct examples underlined.

① a, b   ② a, b, d   ③ a, c, d

④ b, c   ⑤ c, d

15 Read <A> and <B> and follow the directions. [2.5점]

┤ A ├

The following rules describe some characteristic features of Standard American English.

(1)

The lateral /l/ can be syllabic (i.e. standing as the nucleus of a syllable) following a sequence of a stressed vowel and an alveolar stop (an oral or a nasal stop).

(2)

A word-final /t/, /d/ or /n/ may assimilate in place of articulation to a following word-initial bilabial or velar stop, resulting in two identical consonants in some cases. But some features such as voicing and nasality of the consonant remain constant. When place assimilation results in two identical consonants, it is called total assimilation.

┤ B ├

Each sentence below may or may not contain a word/phrase to which rule (1) or (2) in <A> is applied.

a. Can you pass me the one in the middle?
b. He lost his pet cat yesterday.
c. You excel as a painter.
d. I like the blue soap dish.
e. I will cross the channel by boat.
f. Teachers extol the virtue of honesty.
g. You're a very good boy.
h. I heard that ten cooks went home.

Choose the correct match between each rule in <A> and the corresponding examples in <B>. For (2) in <A>, find ONLY the examples in which total assimilation occurs.

	(1)	(2)		(1)	(2)
①	a, c	d, h	②	a, e	b, d
③	a, e	b, g	④	c, f	d, h
⑤	e, f	b, g			

16 글 <A>를 읽고 <B>의 밑줄 친 부분에 각각 일어날 수 있는 음운현상을 <A>에서 찾아 번호를 쓰시오. (단, <A>에 제시된 조건만을 고려할 것.) [4점] 2008년 대전/충북/충남 17번

A

All languages modify complicated sequences in connected speech in order to simplify the articulation process. The main function of most of the adjustments in English is to promote the regularity of English rhythm—that is, to squeeze syllables between stressed elements and facilitate their articulation so that regular timing can be maintained. Specifically, the following optional phonological processes frequently occur in connected speech in North American English:

(1) Alveolar stops are assimilated in place of articulation to following bilabial or velar stops across word boundaries.

(2) Oral alveolar stops are pronounced as a flap after a stressed vowel and before an unstressed vowel.

(3) Oral alveolar stops are deleted if they are central in a sequence of three consonants.

B

(a) He has a <u>green car</u>.

(b) Please <u>send Susan</u> a box of chocolates.

(c) Would you care for a <u>bit of</u> cheese?

(d) I <u>met Bob</u> yesterday.

음운현상 번호

(a) green car   (   )

(b) send Susan   (   )

(c) bit of   (   )

(d) met Bob   (   )

17 <A>에서 설명하는 음운 현상이 나타나는 문장을 <B>에서 3개 찾아 쓰시오. [3점]

2007년 전국 12번

┤ A ├

In English we can find a type of assimilation where two segments assimilate to each other. The outcome of this assimilation is a third distinct segment which combines properties of the two assimilating segments. In careful speech, for example, *could you* would be realized as [kʊd juː]; but in normal conversation it is more likely to be realized as [kʊdʒə]. In the example, the alveolar stop [d] and following palatal approximant [j] fuse to give the voiced post-alveolar affricate [dʒ]. The voice, place, and manner of articulation of the two input segments are combined to form a third segment.

┤ B ├

(In the lobby of a library)

A : Hi, would you do me a favor?

B : Yes, what can I do for you?

A : I think I left my umbrella in the library yesterday.

B : Oh, did you? Any idea where you left it?

A : I don't know... But I sat by the window over there.

B : All right. Just a moment. I'll go and have a look.

A : Thanks.

(After some time)

B : I'm sorry. I couldn't find it anywhere. Why don't you come back tomorrow? I'll ask the janitor if he found it.

A : Okay, thanks. See you tomorrow.

MEN
TOR

Mentor Linguistics
**멘토영어학
기출분석**

Chapter 04

Syllables and Phonotactics

Preview & Review

 **Syllables**

1.1. Syllable Structure

Words are composed of one or more syllables. A syllable is a phonological unit composed of one or more phonemes. Every syllable has a nucleus, which is usually a vowel (but can be a syllabic liquid or nasal). The nucleus may be preceded and/or followed by one or more phonemes called the syllable onset and coda.

A syllable thus has a hierarchical structure. Using the IPA symbol σ (lowercase Greek letter 'sigma') for the phonological syllable, the hierarchical structure of the monosyllabic word *splints* can be shown:

(1)

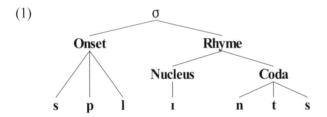

Beyond its relevance for the phonological rules, syllable has an important role with respect to the phonotactic constraints in languages. This refers to the system of arrangement of sounds and sound sequences.

It is on this basis that a speaker of English can judge some new form as possible or impossible word.

For example, both [blɪt] and [bmɪt] are non-existent as English words. If asked to choose between the two, a native speaker of English, without a moment's hesitation, would go for [blɪt].

The reason for this is that [bl] is a possible onset cluster in English, whereas [bm] is not.

This is not to say that no English word can have a [bm] sequence. Words such as submarine [sʌbməˌin] and submission [sʌbmɪʃən] are clear demonstrations of the fact that we can have /m/ after /b/ in English.

This, however, is possible only if these two sounds are in different syllables.

So the rejection of a word such as [bmɪt] is strictly based on a syllable-related generalization but not on a segment-related generalization.

(2)

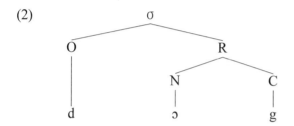

σ = syllable

O = onset

R = rhyme (or rime)

N = nucleus

C = coda

1.2. Sonority Hierarchy

We adopt the following 10-point scale suggested by Hogg and McCully (1987):

(3) Sounds	Sonority values	Examples
Low vowels	10	/ɑ, ʌ, æ/
Mid vowels	9	/e, o/
High vowels (and glides)	8	/i, u, (j, w)/
Retroflexes (and flaps)	7	/ɹ/
Laterals	6	/l/
Nasals	5	/m, n, ŋ/
Voiced fricatives	4	/v, ð, z, ʒ/
Voiceless fricatives	3	/f, θ, s, ʃ, h/
Voiced stops	2	/b, d, g/
Voiceless stops	1	/p, t, k/

(4)
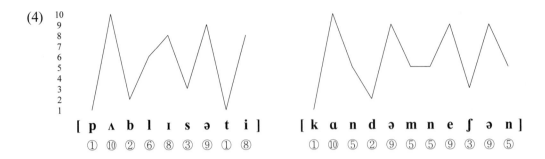

As we saw earlier, in English we can have syllables that do not contain a vowel. In these cases, the most sonorant consonant will be the syllable peak (i.e. syllabic consonant):

(5)

Although the principle of equating the sonority peaks to the number of syllables would hold for thousands of English words, it does not mean that it is without exceptions. We must acknowledge the fact that some English onset clusters with /s/ as the first consonant (e.g. stop [stɑp]), and coda clusters with /s/ as the last consonant (e.g. box [bɑks]), do violate this principle.

(6)
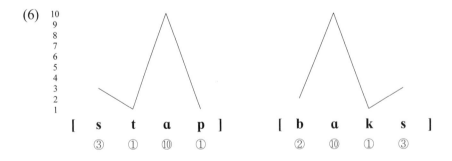

1.3. Syllabification

The principle on which we make the decision in these cases, which is known as the "**maximal onset principle**," simply assigns any series of intervocalic consonants to the syllable on the right as long as it does not violate language-specific onset patterns.

To demonstrate this, let us look at the word *publicity* again. This word, unambiguously, has four syllables and the nuclei are clearly identifiable vowels. First, we need to phonetically transcribe the word and identify the syllable nuclei.

(7) [p ʌ b l ɪ s ə t i]

Thus, the resulting syllabification of this word will be:

(8) [p ʌ . b l ɪ . s ə . t i]

Sometimes, we see the same sequences of sounds syllabified differently in different words. We will illustrate this phenomenon in the following two words, *complain* and *temptation*. The syllabifications of these two words are given in the following:

(9) a. [k ə m . p l e n]

b. [t ɛ m p . t e . ʃ ə n]

Our focus will be the [mp] sequence the two words share.

It is also useful to define the terms *ultimate* (the last syllable), *penultimate* (the syllable before the ultimate), and *antepenultimate* (the syllable before the penultimate), which will be used for the location of the syllables in a word. These can be shown in the following word, *probability*:

(10) [p ɹ ə . b ə . b ɪ .   l ə .   t i]
            antepenultimate   *penultimate*   *ultimate*

1.4. Syllable Weight

Syllable weight is an important factor in stress assignment in that heavy syllables attract stress. The weight of a syllable is determined by its rhyme structure. If the rhyme is non-branching (a short vowel, and no coda), **the syllable is light**. If, on the other hand, the rhyme is branching (has a short vowel, **except [ə], which is weightless and cannot carry stress**, followed by a coda (simple or complex), or has a long vowel or a diphthong with or without a following coda), **the syllable is heavy**.

02 Syllables and Phonotactics

The area which is concerned with the possible sequences of sounds in a language is **phonotactics**.

2.1. Single Onsets

The only consonant that is not allowed to take the onset position in English is /ŋ/.

Another sound, /ʒ/, does not start an English word (save for items such as *genre* [ʒɑnɹə], as well as some foreign names such as *Zhivago* [ʒɪvəgo]) but is capable of occurring in non-word-initial onsets, as in *vision* [vɪ.ʒən] and *measure* [mɛ.ʒɚ].

Finally, /ð/ deserves a mention for its restricted occurrence in word-initial position; this sound is found only in grammatical (function) words (e.g. *the, then, there,* etc.) word-initially. (cf. Lexical (content) words: *mother* [ma.ðɚ], *brother* [bɹa.ðɚ])

2.2. Single Codas

The only sound that cannot occur in English codas is /h/.

2.3. Double Onsets

Table 1 shows the occurring double onsets of English.

Table 1. English Double Onsets

C₁ \ C₂	p	t	k	f	m	n	l	ɹ	w	j
p	■						✓	✓		✓
b							✓	✓		✓
t		■						✓	✓	(✓)
d								✓	✓	(✓)
k			■				✓	✓	✓	✓
g							✓	✓	✓	
f				■			✓	✓		✓
v										✓
θ								✓	✓	
s	✓	✓	✓	✓	✓	✓	✓		✓	(✓)
ʃ								✓		
h										✓
m					■					✓
n						■				(✓)
l								■		(✓)

NOTE
✓ Double onsets that are allowed in English
(✓) Double onsets that are **not** found for **most speakers of American English**
■ Impossible combination

We can make the following observations. Affricates are the only class of consonants that do not appear in onset clusters. Besides this general statement, there are several other restrictions for two-member onset clusters:

(11) a. No voiced fricatives can serve as C₂. Only /v/ can be a C₁, and it can combine only with /j/ (e.g. *view*).

b. No non-lateral approximant (/ɹ, w, j/) can serve as C₁; the lateral can only precede /j/ (only for some speakers).

c. No voiced stop can serve as C₂.

d. No fricatives other than /f/ can serve as C₂, and this can only be preceded by a /s/ in rarely found vocabulary (e.g. *sphere*).

e. No stops and nasals are allowed as C_2, except after /s/ (e.g. *speak, small*).

f. /s/ and /ʃ/ are complementary: /s/ does not occur before /ɹ/, and /ʃ/ occurs only before /ɹ/ (e.g. *shrimp* [ʃɹɪmp]).

g. /h/ and /m/ can only occur before /j/ (e.g. *huge, music*).

h. /Θ/ can precede only /ɹ/ and /w/ (e.g. *three, thwart*).

i. Labials (C_1) do not cluster with a labial approximant.

j. No geminates (i.e. doubled consonant sounds) are allowed.

k. Alveolar stops (C_1) do not cluster with /l/.

We can summarize the situation in the following manners. In general, English double onsets are

(12) a. /s/ + C (where C = any consonant that can assume the position of C_2, except /ɹ/; /ʃ/ appears before /ɹ/), and

b. obstruent + approximant, with the limitations cited above.

2.4. Sonority Sequencing Principle

While the pattern of C_1 as an obstruent and C_2 as a sonorant is very common, we do not have any double onset in which the reverse (C_1 = sonorant and C_2 = obstruent) is true. We can make reference to sonority for the sequencing of sounds with respect to a syllable peak by the **Sonority Sequencing Principle (SSP)**. As given by Selkirk (1984: 116), SSP states that:

(13) In any syllable, there is a segment constituting a sonority peak that is preceded and/or followed by a sequence of segments with progressively decreasing sonority values.

Thus, the expected pattern is that, going from C_1 to C_2, the sonority level will rise. Such is the case in the overwhelming majority of English double onsets (e.g. *play* [ple], *cry* [kɹaɪ], *quick* [kwɪk]).

The violations of this principle are /s/ + stop clusters (/sp. st. sk/), in which the sonority level drops, instead rises, going from C_1 to C_2.

2.5. Triple Onsets

Triple onsets can be described as an addition of /s/ as C_1 to voiceless stop + approximant double onsets. Thus, we have:

(14) C_1 = /s/, C_2 = voiceless stop, C_3 = approximant.

Although the combinations can give us 12 logical possibilities, only seven of these occur:

(15) a.
           ɹ e.g. *spring*
           l e.g. *splash*
   s p
           j e.g. *spew*
           w e.g. *(excluded because /w/ cannot occur after labials)

b.
           ɹ e.g. *string*
           l e.g. *(excluded because no lateral after an alveolar stop)
   s t
           j e.g. *(/tj/ non-existent for most speakers)
           w e.g. *

c.
           ɹ e.g. *scrape*
           l e.g. *(very rare, *sclerosis* [sklɪəɹosɪs])
   s k
           j e.g. *skewer* ([skjuɚ])
           w e.g. *squeeze*

2.6. Double Codas

Double non-suffixed English codas can be generalized in the following fashion:

(16) a. C_1 is a nasal and C_2 is an obstruent (no voiced obstruent permitted except /d, z, dʒ/). Nasals (C_1) combining with stops (C_2) are invariably **homorganic**.

  b. If C_1 is /s/, then C_2 is a voiceless stop.

  c. C_1 is a liquid (/l, ɹ/), then C_2 is any consonant except for /z, ʒ, ð/. Also non-existent is the /lg/ cluster.

  d. If C_1 is a voiceless non-alveolar stop (/p, k/), then C_2 is a voiceless alveolar obstruent (/t, s/). Also permitted is the /ft/ cluster.

Possibilities increase considerably if we add to these the clusters created by the suffixes with /t, d, s, z, θ/ (past tense, plural, possessive, ordinals, etc.). Table 2 gives the actually occurring double codas.

Table 2. English Double Codas

C₁＼C₂	p	b	t	d	k	g	tʃ	dʒ	f	v	θ	s	z	ʃ	m	n	l
p	■		✓								✗	✓					
b		■		✗									✗				
t			■								✗	✗					
d				■							✗		✗				
k		✓		■								✓					
g			✗		■								✗				
tʃ		✗				■											
dʒ			✗				■										
f		✓						■			✗	✗					
v			✗						■				✗				
θ		✗								■		✗					
ð			✗										✗				
s	✓		✓		✓							■					
z			✗										■				
ʃ			✗											■			
ʒ			✗														
m	✓	✗	✗					✓					✗		■		
n		✓	✓			✓	✓				✓	✓	✓			■	
ŋ		✗	✓								✗		✗				
l	✓	✓	✓	✓	✓		✓	✓	✓	✓	✓	✓	✗	✓	✓	✓	■
ɹ	✓	✓	✓	✓	✓	✓	✓	✓	✓	✓	✓	✓	✗	✓	✓	✓	✓

NOTE
- ✓ Non-suffixed double codas
- ✗ Suffixed double codas
- ■ Impossible combination

The sonority sequencing principle (SSP) dictates the opposite of onset sequencing for codas. This means that optimal codas should have the sonority level dropping as we move from C_1 to C_2. Indeed, as Table 2 shows, this is the case for the double codas we find in non-suffixed (monomorphemic) forms in English (e.g. *arm* [ɑɹm], *sharp* [ʃɑɹp], *belt* [bɛlt]).

Exceptions are

(17) a. two-stop sequences, which are never homorganic (e.g. apt [æpt], act [ækt]), and

    b. stop + /s/, which always agree in voicing (e.g. lapse [læps], tax [tæks]).

2.7. Triple Codas

The triple codas of English do not lend themselves to the rather simple formula we gave for triple onsets. We can say, in more general terms, that with the exception of (18-1), below, which has three obstruents, all the other combinations consist of a liquid or a nasal (sonorant) followed by two obstruents. The following combinations are found in non-suffixed forms:

(18)		C_1	C_2	C_3	Examples
1		stop	fricative	stop	/dst/ **midst**, /kst/ next
2	(a)	nasal	stop	stop	/mpt/ exempt, /ŋkt/ sacrosanct
	(b)	nasal	stop	fricative	/mps/ mumps, /ŋks/ jinx
	(c)	nasal	fricative	stop	/nst/ **against**, /ŋst/ amongst
3	(a)	l	stop	stop	/lpt/ sculpt
	(b)	l	stop	fricative	/lts/ waltz
	(c)	l	fricative	stop	/lst/ **whilst**
4	(a)	ɹ	stop	stop	/ɹkt/ infarct, /ɹpt/ excerpt
	(b)	ɹ	stop	fricative	/ɹps/ corpse, /ɹts/ quartz
	(c)	ɹ	fricative	stop	/ɹst/ first
	(d)	ɹ	l	stop	/ɹld/ world
	(e)	ɹ	l	fricative	/ɹlz/ Charles

We have to acknowledge the fact that *midst* in (18-1), *against* in (18-2c), and *whilst* in (18-3c) are controversial and may be included in the suffixed category, as we encounter in some publications.

In addition to theses, a multiplicity of other triple codas is created via **suffixation**, the great majority of which are provided by /t, d/ of the simple past tense and by /s, z/ of the plural, the possessive, and the third person singular of the simple present. Also noteworthy are the possibilities created by /θ/, the "ordinal number morpheme" (e.g. *sixth* [sɪksθ]) and the ending deriving nouns from adjectives (deadjectival nominal morpheme) (e.g. *warmth* [wɔɹm θ]). The following list gives the possibilities of triple codas via suffixation in terms of general classes; thus, actually occurring clusters have many more combinations than the examples cited here:

(19)		C_1	C_2	C_3	Examples
1		nasal	obstruent	/t, d, s, z/	laments
2		/s/	stop	/t, d, s, z/	lisped
3	(a)	/l/	obstruent	/t, d, s, z/	gulped
	(b)	/l/	nasal	/d, z/	filmed
4	(a)	/ɹ/	obstruent	/t, d, s, z/	wharfs
	(b)	/ɹ/	/l/	/d, z/	curls
	(c)	/ɹ/	nasal	/d, z/	turned
5		obstruent	obstruent	obstruent (only /pts, kts, fts, pst, kst/)	lifts

While nasals and liquids serve frequently as C_1 in triple codas, and the sequences of /lk, mp, sk/ freely occur as double codas in English, triple codas combining these elements are very restricted. Thus, it is a noteworthy fact that English lacks /ɹlk, ɹmp, ɹsk, lmp, nsk/ as triple codas. Like double codas, clusters of obstruents in triple codas always agree in voicing (e.g. /spt/ *lisped*).

Unit 02 Questions

Answer Key p.505

01 Read the passage in <A> and the examples in <B>, and follow the directions. [4 points]

2023년 A형 6번

─────────────── A ───────────────

Native speakers' intuitions about possible and impossible words are heavily influenced by the phonological properties of sound sequences, represented by relative differences in sonority, i.e., how resonant one sound is compared to the other.

A group of English native speakers were asked to decide how each of the following nonsense words sounds to them, and to give each word a numerical rating, from '1' to '5', according to how confident the respondents are that those are English-like words. '1' meant that the word is definitely not English-like, and '5' meant that it can definitely be an English word. Their averaged ratings for the words are shown in (1).

(1)

Words	Mean scores
bod [bɑd]	4.66
timp [tɪmp]	4.30
rog [rɔg]	4.20
mbotto [mbato]	1.07

It appears that native speakers of English perceive words with simple onset to be more English-like than those with complex onset, and simply reject words that violate the phonotactics in English. However, the presence of onset clusters and legitimate phonotactics do not fully explain how the speakers' intuitions work. Another group of English native speakers were asked to do the same task for a different set of nonsense words, as illustrated in (2).

(2)

Words	Mean scores
shliz [ʃlɪz]	4.16
zloog [zlug]	3.76
nfape [nfeɪp]	1.98
mvupe [mvup]	1.76

```
┤ B ├
a. kneeb [knib]      b. rviss [rvɪs]
c. znape [zneɪp]     d. nkob [nkob]
```

Based on <A>, first, identify the TWO nonsense words in <B> that are likely to result in a low rating (closer to '1'). Then, state the ONE phonological generalization that can explain both why *bod, timp,* and *rog* are considered more English-like than *mbotto* in (1) and why *shliz* and *zloog* are considered more English-like than *nfape* and *mvupe* in (2).

_____

_____

_____

_____

_____

02 Read the passage and follow the directions. [2 points]

> It is well known in English that we get antepenultimate stress in nouns of at least three syllables when the penultimate syllable is light:
>
> (1) antepenultimate syllable stressed
>
> *cinema, asterisk, America, Canada, animal*
>
> When the penultimate syllable ends with a coda, or has a long vowel or a diphthong, stress, however, falls on that heavy penultimate syllable:
>
> (2) penultimate syllable stressed
>
> a. *utensil, agenda, synopsis*
> b. *aroma, horizon, arena*
>
> In the above examples in (2a), it is clear that a syllable boundary seats itself between word-internal consonantal sequences such as -ns- (in *utensil*), -nd- (in *agenda*), and -ps- (in *synopsis*), since English phonotactic constraint does not permit such consonantal sequences to occur as an onset cluster. However, the word-internal consonantal sequence -st- poses an interesting challenge for syllabification. Unlike the -ns-, -nd-, or -ps-, the -st- sequence could be an onset cluster (as in *student, stupid*) or a coda cluster (as in *list, mist*).

Fill in the blank with the ONE most appropriate word from the passage above.

> Considering the stress placement in the words given in (3) where -st- occurs, we can claim that the underlined s̲ is in _____ position.
>
> (3) antepenultimate syllable stressed
>
> *amne s̲ty, mini s̲ter, pede s̲tal*

03 **Read the passage and fill in the blank with ONE word.** [2 points] 2014년 A형 11번

In English, the lateral phoneme /l/ has two allophones: 'clear l', [l], and 'dark l', [ɫ], a velarized alveolar lateral. The articulatory difference between the two is that in the former the back of the tongue is lowered while in the latter it is raised toward the velum or retracted toward the uvula (without making contact in either case). Some examples with [l] and [ɫ] are:

(1) limb [lɪm], climb [klaɪm], lock [lɑk]

(2) miller [mɪlər], yellow [jɛlou], billow [bɪlou]

(3) mill [mɪɫ], fill [fɪɫ], pile [paɪɫ], milk [mɪɫk]

(4) middle [mɪdɫ], bubble [bʌbɫ], tunnel [tʌnɫ]

We can see that [l] and [ɫ] are in complementary distribution. [l] appears in an onset position as in (1) and (2), while [ɫ] appears in a coda position as in (3). The rule involved seems to be that velarization takes place whenever /l/ is in a coda position. However, the cases in (4) cannot be explained by this rule because [ɫ] is syllabic and constitutes the nucleus, which is usually occupied by a vowel. By minimally modifying the above rule, we can obtain a more accurate rule: /l/ is velarized if and only if it is part of the _____.

04 Read \<A\> and \<B\> and answer the question. [2점]

| A |

Although nearly everybody can identify individual syllables, it is difficult to define what is meant by a syllable. One possible theory of the syllable draws on the concept of sonority. The sonority of a sound is its loudness relative to that of other sounds with the same length, stress, and pitch. It is generally agreed that the sonority hierarchy is as follows:

The sonority theory of the syllable holds that a peak of sonority defines a syllable. That is, according to the theory, the peak of a syllable coincides with the peak of sonority. For example, in a sequence of sounds, [sænd], the vowel is more sonorous than [s] and [n], and [n] is more sonorous than [d]. This sequence of sounds forms one sonority peak on the vowel. Therefore, the theory correctly predicts that this word has one syllable.

| B |

| a. bright | b. speed | c. dance | d. sweet |

Which of the following lists all and only the examples in \<B\> that support the theory described in \<A\>?

① a, b, c   ② a, c, d   ③ b, c, d

④ b, d   ⑤ c, d

05 Read <A> and <B> and follow the directions. 2009년 31번

─────────────┤ A ├─────────────

Consider the following data in (1) and (2), which show certain restrictions on the sound combinations of English monosyllabic words:

(1) tip, lick, live, mess, limp, lint, sink, mend, mind, pie, wife, bike, sign, sea, leap, wreathe, league

(2) *[tɪ], *[lɪ], *[mɛ], *[lɪmk], *[mɛnb], *[maɪŋ], *[mɛmb], *[mɛŋg], *[maɪmb], *[maɪŋg]

The data in (1) are all legitimate English words, whereas those in (2) are not, as indicated by an asterisk '*'.

─────────────┤ B ├─────────────

a. A lax vowel (i.e. a short vowel) must be followed by at least one consonant.

b. When a consonant follows a tense vowel (i.e. a long vowel or diphthong), it must be a stop consonant.

c. When a sequence of a nasal and a stop follows a vowel, the two consonants are homorganic (i.e. having the same place of articulation).

d. When a sequence of a nasal and a voiced stop follows a vowel, the two sounds must be alveolar consonants.

e. When a sequence of a nasal and a stop follows a vowel, the two consonants all agree in voicing.

Choose all the correct statements about the data in <A> from the list in <B>.

① a, b, d   ② a, c, d   ③ a, c, e

④ b, c, d   ⑤ b, c, e

06 다음 글을 읽고, 빈칸 (1)과 (2)에 들어갈 수 있는 단어를 <보기>에서 각각 2개씩 찾아 그 기호를 쓰시오. [3점]

It is common that every syllable contains a vowel at its nucleus. However, certain consonants also act as the nucleus elements of syllables in English. Words such as ____(1)____, in which the nasal sound comes after stops or fricatives, show that the nasals are syllabic. But we can't say that nasals become syllabic whenever they occur at the end of a word after a consonant. Words such as ____(2)____, in which the nasal sound comes after a sonorant consonant, show that the nasals are not syllabic. Therefore, the key issue here appears to be the manner of articulation of the consonant preceding the nasal sound at the end of a word.

┤ 보기 ├

(a) charm	(b) chasm	(c) film
(d) seldom	(e) leaden	(f) salon

(1) _____

(2) _____

Mentor Linguistics
멘토영어학
기출분석

Chapter 05

Stress

Unit 01 Preview & Review

01 Stress: An Introduction

In many languages, certain syllables in a word are louder, slightly higher in pitch, and somewhat longer in duration than other syllables in the word. They are **stressed** syllables.

English is a "**stress-timed**" language. In general, at least one syllable is stressed in an English word. French is not a stress-timed language. The syllables have approximately the same loudness, length, and pitch. It is a "**syllable-timed**" language.

Stress is a cover term for **the prosodic features of** *duration*, *intensity*, **and** *pitch*; thus, the prominence of stressed syllables is generally manifested by their characteristics of being longer, louder, and higher in pitch than unstressed syllables. From the speaker's point of view, this corresponds to **the amount of effort expanded**, while from the hearer's point of view, it is **the perceptual prominence**.

Sentence and Phrase Stress

When words are combined into phrases and sentences, one syllable receives greater stress than all others. Just as there is only one primary stress in a word spoken in isolation, only one of the vowels in a phrase (or sentence) receives primary stress or accent. All of the other stressed vowels are demoted to secondary stress.

In English we place primary stress on the adjectival part of a **compound noun**, but we place the stress on the noun when the words are a **noun phrase** consisting of an adjective followed by a noun. The differences between the following pairs are therefore predictable:

(1) **Compound Noun**   **Adjective + Noun**

    tíghtrope ('a rope for acrobatics')   tight rópe ('a rope drawn taut')

    Rédcoat ('a British soldier')   red cóat ('a coat that is red')

    hótdog ('a frankfurter')   hot dóg ('an overheated dog')

    Whíte House ('the President's house') white hóuse ('a house painted white')

These pairs show that stress may be predictable from the morphology and syntax. The phonology interacts with the other components of the grammar. The stress differences between the noun and verb pairs (*subject* as noun or verb) are also predictable from the syntactic word category.

02 Lexical Categories and Stress

We will distinguish words of a lexical category from words of a non-lexical category. **Words of a lexical category** are nouns, verbs, adjectives and adverbs. Words of a non-lexical category include prepositions, determiners, pronouns and the conjunction. Words of a non-lexical category, often referred to as **function words**, are not normally stressed. Among the words of a lexical category, primary stress placement may vary, depending on the syntactic category of the word.

Monosyllabic words of a lexical category (such as *box, run, big*), are unproblematic: there is only one syllable for the primary stress to fall on. Let us therefore move on to morphologically simple **bisyllabic words**, and then proceed to morphologically simple **polysyllabic words** (words with three or more syllables).

2.1. Noun and Adjective Stress

There seem to be sufficient commonalities between the stress patterns of nouns and adjectives that they warrant a single grouping. <u>In **disyllabic words**</u>, the default stress is on the penult. **In a 20,000-monomorphemic-word sample**, both disyllabic nouns and adjectives reveal penult stress over 80 percent of the time. More precisely, 81.7 percent of **nouns** and 81 percent of disyllabic **adjectives** followed this pattern. Below are some examples from both categories:

(2) **Noun**   **Adjective**

ágent	cóokie	ábsent	sólid
bálance	cóuntry	árid	hónest
bállad	émpire	cómmon	réady
bóttom	dímple	flúent	súdden
bóttle	fáther	áctive	búsy
cábbage	húsband	éarly	ámple
cárrot	spínach	próper	vúlgar
chícken	zípper	pérfect	yéllow

The exceptions to the penult rule fall into two groups.

The first contains examples with weightless (unstressable) penults, because they have [ə] nucleus, and thus are stressed on the final syllable; for the reason, they might be considered exceptions:

(3) **Noun**   **Adjective**

appéal	giráffe	banál	compléte
ballóon	Japán	corrúpt	inténse
canóe	Tibét	corréct	seréne
Brazíl	machíne	precíse	secúre
canál	paráde	divíne	sincére
gazélle		alíve	

The second group constitutes the real exceptions because they are stressed in the final syllable despite the fact that they have stressable penults with branching rhymes:

(4) **Noun**   **Adjective**

typhóon   antíque   mundáne   robúst

sardíne   Julý   obscúre   obscéne

shampóo   okáy

In trisyllabic and longer **nouns**, we formulate the following: <u>stress penult if stressable (heavy/branching rhyme); if not stressable, then stress the next left syllable</u>. We show this with the following examples:

(5) **Three syllables**   **More than three syllables**

tomáto   ábdomen   barracúda

aróma   álgebra   aspáragus

diplóma   ánimal   apócalypse

horízon   búffalo   basílica

compúter   cómedy   thermómeter

bonánza   vítamin   harmónica

diréctor   áccident   expériment

agénda   África   astrónomy

Decémber   pólicy   cémetery

enígma   órigin   hippopótamus

The words in the leftmost group are stressed on the penultimate syllable because their penultimates are stressable (the first five quality for their long vowel or diphthong nuclei, and the last five because of the closed rhyme).

The words in the second trisyllabic group receive their stresses on the antepenultimate syllable because their penults are not stressable (**all with [ə] nuclei**).

The rightmost group consists of words that have more than three syllables, but the stress rule remains the same. The first word, *barracúda*, is stressed on the penult, as it contains a stressable penult, [u]. The remaining words (eight with four syllables, and the last one with five syllables) all have unstressable penults ([ə] nuclei) and thus are stressed on the antepenult.

2.2. Verb Stress

If **nouns and adjectives** have **the penult** as their pivot, **verb** focus is on **the ult**. The general tendency is as follows: stress ult if heavy (branching rhyme); if not, go to the next left syllable, as shown in the following:

(6) **Heavy ult stressed**   **Unstressable ult, thus penult stressed**

achíeve	inténd	bálance	púnish
admít	interfére	blóssom	fígure
agrée	impórt	bóther	súrface
annóunce	predíct	dístance	vísit
confíne	replý	fúrnish	díffer
digést		hárvest	

With the above generalization, we can account for over 99 percent of the stresses of disyllabic words. The few exceptions to the general tendency can be exemplified by the following, where penult is stressed **despite** the fact that the verb has **a heavy ult**:

(7) | | | | |
|---|---|---|---|
| cópy | [i] | réscue | [u] |
| díagram | [æm] | stúdy | [i] |
| wórry | [i] | énvy | [i] |
| árgue | [u] | | |

English has dozens of orthographically identical word-pairs differentiated by stress as **nouns (penult stress)** or **verbs (ult stress)**, as exemplified in the following:

(8) abstract   convict   insert   refuse
     address   discharge   insult   reject
     ally   escort   permit   retard
     combat   export   progress   subject
     compress   extract   project   suspect
     conduct   implant   protest   transfer
     conflict   import   rebel
     contrast   increase   refund

Although noun-verb shift is accomplished by a shift in stressed syllable in some of these (e.g. *import*, *insult*), in many others, the difference of stress is also accompanied by vowel reduction in the stressed syllable, and thus these noun-verb pairs, although **homographs**, are **not homophonous**. For example:

(9) abstract   N [ǽbstɹækt]   V [əbstɹǽkt]
     conveict   N [kɑ́nvɪkt]   V [kənvíkt]
     protest   N [pɹótɛst]   V [pɹətɛ́st]
     refuse   N [ɹɛ́fjus]   V [ɹəfjúz]

However, **not all** two-syllable words that are both nouns and verbs follow the stress-switch rule.

03 English Stress and Affixes

If the basic rules of stress looked rather untidy and replete with exceptions, **the rules accompanying affixes** can easily be said to overshadow the mono-morphemic roots.

Since the addition of prefixes does not change word stress, our presentation will be on the varying effects of suffixes on word stress. We can classify the suffixes as:

(10) a. stress-bearing suffixes

    b. stress-shifting suffixes

    c. stress-neutral suffixes

The common element between groups (10a) and (10b), when added to a root, is that they change the location of the stress from its original position. **Stress-bearing suffixes** attract the stress to themselves, while **stress-shifting suffixes** move the stress to some other syllable. Group (10b) and (10c) have the common element of not carrying stress.

3.1. Stress-bearing Suffixes

As stated above, these suffixes attract stress. Below are the **some** common **derivational suffixes**:

(11) -ade   lémon — lemonáde

    -aire   míllion — millionáire

    -ation   réalize — realizátion

    -ee   ábsent — absentée (exception: commíttee)

    -eer   móuntain — mountainéer

    -ese   Japán — Japanése

    -esque   pícture — picturésque

    -ette   kítchen — kitchenétte

    -itis   lárynx — laryngítis

    -ific   hónor — honorífic

Expectedly, these stress-bearing suffixes **always** constitute **heavy syllables**.

3.2. Stress-neutral Suffixes

These suffixes never make any difference to the stress pattern of the resulting word. Such suffixes include all eight **inflectional suffixes** (plural; possessive; third person singular present tense -**s**; progressive -**ing**; past -**ed**; past participle -**en**/-**ed**; comparative -**er**; and superlative -**est**), and **several derivational ones**:

(12)

-al	arríve — arríval	-ize	spécial — spécialize
-ant	ascénd — ascéndant	-less	bóttom — bóttomless
-cy	célibate — célibacy	-ly	fríend — fríendly
-dom	frée — fréedom	-ment	aménd — améndment
-er	pláy — pláyer	-ness	fránk — fránkness
-ess	líon — líoness	-ship	fríend — fríendship
-ful	gráce — gráceful	-some	búrden — búrdensome
-hood	nátion — nátionhood	-wise	clóck — clóckwise
-ish	gréen — gréenish	-th	grów — grówth
-ism	álcohol — álcoholism	-ty	cértain — cértainty
-ist	húman — húmanist	**-y**	**sílk — sílky**
-ive	submít — submíssive		

We should point out that the last item, **adjective-forming suffix** -*y*, should **not** be treated in the same way as the **noun-forming** -*y*, which shifts the stress to the antepenultimate, as in *hómophone — homóphony*, *phótograph — photógraphy*, etc.

3.3. Stress-shifting Suffixes

A multiplicity of derivational suffixes, when added to a root, shift the stress from its original position to the syllable immediately preceding the suffix. Below are some of the common ones in this group:

(13) -ian   Áristotle — Aristotélian

      -ial   súbstance — substánial

      -ian   líbrary — librárian

      -ical   geómetry — geométrical

      -icide   ínsect — insécticide

      -ic   périod — periódic (exceptions: Árabic, lúnatic)

      -ify   pérson — persónify

      -ious   lábor — labórious

      -ity   húmid — humídity

      -ometer   spéed — speedómeter

      -ual   cóntext — contéxtual

      -ous   móment — moméntous

      -y   hómonym — homónymy

If the original stress is on the last syllable of the root (the syllable immediately before the suffix), no change in location of the stress will result, because it is already where it should be (i.e.. *divérse — divérsity, absúrd — absúrdity, obése — obésity*).

04 Metrical Feet

Human beings speak *rhythmically*: they engage in the act of speaking by putting regular beats in the speech signal. You can hear those beats in an English utterance such as *The man went to the bar*. Here, the beats are on *man*, *went* and *bar*. In most varieties of English, we do not necessarily place a beat on every single syllable. In this utterance, no beat falls on the preposition *to*, or on the two occurrences of *the*. This is because English is *stress-timed*: the rhythmic beats fall only on *stressed* syllables.

Take the phrase *Chicken MacNuggets*, the name for a product sold by a well-known fast-food company. This is pronounced [ˌtʃɪkənməkˈnʌɡəts]. There are two stressed syllables in this sequence. (The second is more prominent than the first.) The sequences [ˈtʃɪkənmək] and [ˈnʌɡəts] form rhythmic units in the utterance. Those units are called ***metrical feet***.

A metrical foot in English consists of a stressed syllable followed by zero or more unstressed syllables. In our example, the first metrical foot contains a stressed syllable and two unstressed syllables: [ˌtʃɪkənmək]. The second metrical foot contains a stressed syllable and one unstressed syllable: [ˈnʌɡəts].

Notice that divisions between the metrical feet need not coincide with word boundaries: the word boundary falls between the words *Chicken* and the word *MacNuggets*. But the rhythmic boundary falls between [ˌtʃɪkənmək] and [ˈnʌɡəts]. We call these metrical feet ***trochaic***. This is an adjective derived from the noun *trochee*. A trochee is essentially a stressed-unstressed sequence, such as [ˈnʌɡəts].

The rhythm of English is *trochaic*: the basic rhythmic pattern consists of a stressed syllable followed by zero or more unstressed syllables. For instance, in the phrase *made in a factory*, the metrical structure is [ˈmeɪdɪnəˈfæktəɹi]. The two trochaic feet here are [ˈmeɪdɪnə] and [ˈfæktəɹi].

We assumed too that syllables with secondary stress also form trochaic metrical feet, as in the word *academic*: [ˌækəˈdɛmɪk]. The two trochaic metrical feet here are [ˌækə] and [ˈdɛmɪk]: the secondary stress in [ˌækə] forms a trochaic metrical foot with the following unstressed syllable, and the primary stress in [ˈdɛmɪk] forms a trochaic metrical foot with the following unstressed syllable.

Unit 02 Questions

Answer Key p.506

01 **Read the passages in <A> and <B>, and follow the directions.** [4 points]

2023년 B형 4번

─────────────┤ A ├─────────────

Many derivational suffixes in English share the same phonological forms, but serve different morphological functions. One example of this is the derivational suffix *-al*. Consider the following words ending in *-al* in (1). Some *-al* words are adjectives and others are nouns.

(1)

-al adjectives	*-al* nouns
annual	dismissal
natural	betrayal
gradual	reversal
federal	survival
floral	renewal
legal	referral

The noun-forming suffix *-al* imposes a morphological and a phonological requirement on the stems to which it attaches. From the morphological perspective, the noun-forming suffix *-al* must attach to a verb, as shown in *dismiss+al*, *betray+al*, *reverse+al*, etc. Not all verbs, however, can take the noun-forming suffix *-al*. Impossible *-al* nouns are shown in (2).

(2) *abandonal *fidgetal *investigatal *promisal *qualifial

English verbs and nouns exhibit a wide range of stress patterns. These are represented by the ultimate, penultimate, or antipenultimate stress, or by the trochaic or iambic foot structure, etc. The phonological requirement, in relation to stress and foot structure, for the noun-forming suffix -al can explain why the suffix sometimes creates unattested nouns. The attested -al nouns in (1) and the unattested ones in (2) differ markedly in their stress and foot patterns. The stress pattern shared in common among the attested -al nouns is also found in many underived nouns, as illustrated in (3).

(3) appendix   Chicago   veranda   avocado

     consensus   hiatus   Minnesota   arena

Note : '*' indicates an unattested word.

──────┤ B ├──────

The above data show that both attested -al nouns in (1) and underived nouns in (3) have the primary stress on the ① _____ syllable, creating a(n) ② _____ foot at the end.

Fill in the blanks ① and ② in <B> each with ONE word from <A>, in the correct order. Then, state the phonological generalization that determines which verb stem the noun-forming suffix -al can attach to.

_____

_____

_____

_____

_____

02 Read the passage and follow the directions. [4 points]

2022년 A형 6번

─┤ A ├─

In English, prosodic units such as syllable and foot are referred to in the phonological description. Here we are going to refer to foot, which is trochaic in English as in (1).

(1) a. di{'saster}   sy{'nopsis}   mi{'mosa}
    b. {'opportune}   {'insolent}   {'enmity}
    c. {ˌresur} {'rect} {ˌphoto} {'graphic} {ˌeco} {'nomical}

Now take a look at the data in (2). Voiceless stops are aspirated when they are followed by a stressed vowel, whether it is a primary stress as in (2a) or a secondary stress as in (2b). But even before a stressed vowel, they are not aspirated when it is preceded by /s/ as in (2c). Lastly, they are not aspirated when they are followed by an unstressed vowel as in (2d). So the phonological description of the aspiration phenomenon must be complicated without referring to foot.

(2) a. apartment [ə'pʰɑɹtmənt]
       maternal [mə'tʰɜɹnəl]
       academy [ə'kʰædəmi]
    b. personality [ˌpʰɜɹsə'næləti]
       Tennessee [ˌtʰɛnə'si]
       kangaroo [ˌkʰæŋgə'ɹu]
    c. asparagus [ə'spæɹəgəs]
       austerity [ɔ'stɛɹəti]
       mosquito [mə'skitoʊ]
    d. sympathy ['sɪmpəθi]
       sentimental [ˌsɛntə'mɛntəl]
       alcoholic [ˌælkə'hɔlɪk]

Note : '{   }' indicates foot boundaries.

| B |

a. op<u>e</u>ration   b. disen<u>t</u>angle   c. a<u>cc</u>ountability   d. subs<u>t</u>antial

In <B>, select TWO words where the underlined voiceless stop is realized as an aspirated stop. Then, state a rule which can account for all the aspirated stops in (2). Your answer must include 'foot.'

_____

_____

_____

_____

_____

03 Read the passage and follow the directions. [4 points]

2021년 A형 6번

┤ A ├

'Foot' is a prosodic unit above syllable, which consists of one obligatory strong syllable and optional weak syllables. Feet seem to have many different structures in English. For example, there are feet composed of a single stressed syllable (e.g., {'son}) and feet where a stressed syllable is followed by one stressless syllable (e.g., {'mother}) or by two or more stressless syllables (e.g., {'Canada}). Sometimes, a strong syllable appears in the second (e.g., {de'mand}, {ba'nana}).

Foot structure can change due to [ə]-deletion. First, the data in (1) show that [ə] in an initial stressless syllable can be deleted in fast speech.

(1) | | Normal speech | Fast speech |
|---|---|---|
| a. Toronto | [tʰə'rantoʊ] | ['ʈrantoʊ] |
| b. Marina | [mə'rinə] | ['mrinə] |

Second, the data in (2) demonstrate that [ə] in a medial stressless syllable can be deleted after a stressed and before a stressless syllable in fast speech.

(2) | | Normal speech | Fast speech |
|---|---|---|
| a. opera | ['apərə] | ['aprə] |
| b. general | ['dʒenərəl] | ['dʒenrəl] |

Third, the data in (3) tell us that when two stressless syllables occur between two stressed syllables, [ə] in either stressless syllable can be deleted in fast speech.

---

(3)   Normal speech   Fast speech
  a. respiratory ['rɛspərə,tʰɔri] ['rɛsprə,tʰɔri] or ['rɛspər,tʰɔri]
  b. glorification [,glɔrəfə'kʰeɪʃən] [,glɔrfə'kʰeɪʃən] or [,glɔrəf'kʰeɪʃən]

However, [ə]-deletion cannot occur even in fast speech when a stressless syllable occurs directly between two stressed syllables as in (4).

(4)   Normal speech   Fast speech
  a. operatic [,apə'ræɾɪk] [,apə'ræɾɪk], *[,ap'ræɾɪk]
  b. generality [,dʒɛnə'ræləri] [,dʒɛnə'ræləri], *[,dʒɛn'ræləri]

Note 1 : '*' indicates a non-permissible form.
Note 2 : '{ }' indicates foot boundaries.

	B
a. respirate ['rɛspə,reɪt]	b. chocolate ['ʧakəlɪt]
c. nationalize ['næʃənə,laɪz]	d. glorify ['glɔrə,faɪ]

Based on <A>, identify TWO words in <B> where [ə] can be deleted in fast speech. Then, describe the foot structure that is most preferred in fast speech, based on <A>.

_____

_____

_____

_____

_____

04 Read the passage and fill in the blanks. Write your answers in the correct order. [2 points]

2016년 A형 6번

English suffixes can be grouped into three different types when they are added to a root: stress-bearing, stress-shifting, and stress-neutral. Stress-bearing suffixes attract the primary stress to themselves as in (1a). Stress-shifting suffixes move the stress to some other syllables as in (1b). Stress-neutral suffixes do not make any difference to the stress of the root as in (1c). Meanwhile, the suffix -*y* is classified into two classes. Noun-forming suffix -*y* in (2) belongs to _____①_____ suffixes, while adjective-forming suffix -*y* in (2) belongs to _____②_____ suffixes.

(1) a. engine-engineer, attest-attestation, statue-statuesque

    b. public-publicity, commerce-commercial, library-librarian

    c. clever-cleverness, consult-consultant, parent-parenthood

(2) summer-summery, telephone-telephony,

    synonym-synonymy, frump-frumpy, advisor-advisory,

    photograph-photography, velvet-velvety

05 Read <A> and <B> and answer the question. [2.5점]

---| A |---

In English, some stress-shifting suffixes trigger a shift of stress in the base to which they are attached. In words with those suffixes, the assignment of stress depends on the syllabic internal structure of the base, as shown below:

(1) The primary stress falls on the syllable that is immediately before the suffix if that syllable is heavy (e.g., súbstance − substántial).

(2) If the syllable immediately before the suffix is light, the primary stress falls on the syllable immediately preceding that light syllable (e.g., admíre − ádmirable).

Note : A heavy syllable is defined as a syllable with a tense vowel, a diphthong, or a lax vowel followed by at least one coda segment. A light syllable, on the other hand, is an open syllable with one lax vowel, having no coda except when the vowel is /ə/.

---| B |---

The suffixes are given in parentheses.

a. homonym − homonymy (-y)

b. context − contextual (-ual)

c. navigate − navigation (-ion)

d. compete − competency (-ency)

e. insect − insecticide (-icide)

f. advantage − advantageous (-eous)

Which of the following is the correct grouping for the data in <B> based on the rules of (1) and (2)?

	(1)	(2)
①	a, c, d	b, e, f
②	a, d, e	b, c, f
③	b, c	a, d, e, f
④	b, c, f	a, d, e
⑤	b, c, e, f	a, d

06
글 <A>를 읽고 강세규칙 (1)−①, (1)−②, (2)−①, (2)−②에 해당하는 단어의 기호를 <B>에서 각각 두 개씩 찾아 쓰시오. (단, <A>에 제시된 강세규칙의 조건만을 고려할 것.)

[4점]

2008년 대전/충북/충남 14번

┤ A ├

The rules of word stress placement in English are complex and have exceptions, but some information such as the grammatical category of the word, the number of syllables the word has, and the phonological structure of those syllables is important in stress placement. Consider the following stress placement rules:

(1) In three-syllable verbs,
   ① if the final syllable is strong, then it is stressed;
   ② if the final syllable is weak, then it is unstressed, and stress is placed on the preceding syllable if that syllable is strong.

(2) In three-syllable nouns,
   ① if the final syllable is weak, or ends with [ə], then it is unstressed; if the syllable preceding this final syllable is strong, then that middle syllable is stressed;
   ② if the second and third syllables are both weak, then the first syllable is stressed.

Note : A strong syllable has a rhyme which either has a syllable peak which is a long vowel or diphthong, or a vowel followed by a coda (i.e., one or more consonants). Weak syllables have a syllable peak which is a short vowel, and no coda unless the syllable peak is [ə].

┤ B ├

(a) bonanza	(b) resurrect	(c) cinema	(d) remember
(e) embroider	(f) algebra	(g) entertain	(h) aroma

강세규칙	단어 기호
(1)−①	( ) ( )
(1)−②	( ) ( )
(2)−①	( ) ( )
(2)−②	( ) ( )

07 Read the passage and fill in each blank using phrases from it. [3점]

English has a set of principles or rules which allow native speakers to assign stress to the appropriate syllable of a word. The unit of a syllable may contain as its core a long vowel or a short vowel, a monophthong or a diphthong, or one or multiple consonants before or after the core.

Consider the following two-syllable verbs:

ball<u>ot</u>	exc<u>lude</u>	att<u>ract</u>	ann<u>oy</u>	div<u>ide</u>
abst<u>ract</u>	ent<u>er</u>	del<u>ight</u>	inc<u>line</u>	sal<u>ute</u>
cont<u>ain</u>	feat<u>ure</u>	prot<u>est</u>	port<u>ion</u>	sign<u>al</u>

We can see that the stress may fall on either the first or the second syllable. Since stress placement rules usually apply to the final syllable first, compare the underlined rhyme sections of the stressed second syllables with the rhymes of the unstressed counterparts. We notice that the final syllable is stressed when it contains ____①____, ____②____, or ____③____ in its rhyme section. That is, the final syllable is stressed when its rhyme is "heavy" in a sense.

① _____

② _____

③ _____

08 Read the passage and follow the directions. 2006년 서울/인천 11번

Words that contain salient information in a sentence are called content words. They include nouns, verbs, adjectives, and adverbs. The less prominent words in a sentence are called function words. Examples of function words are pronouns, articles, prepositions, and conjunctions. In connected speech, function words are pronounced differently than when they are spoken in isolation. Here are some examples:

Written Form	Spoken Form
Tom watched her last night.	['tɑm 'wɑʧt ər 'læst 'nayt]
A cup of tea.	[ə 'kʌp ə 'tiy]
Give them a break.	['gɪv əm ə 'breyk]
Now and then.	['naw ən 'ðɛn]

위 글의 예에 나타난 영어 기능어의 발음상 특징을 세 가지로 구분하여 각각 **10자 내외의 우리말로 쓰시오**(단, 발음기호의 사용은 가능하나 강세에 관한 내용은 제외). [4점]

(1) _____

(2) _____

(3) _____

09 다음 <A>를 읽고, <B>가 특별한 강조나 대조 없이 발음되었을 때, 몇 개의 음보(foot)로 이루어지는지 숫자로 쓰시오. [3점]

2005년 전국 18번

┤ A ├

Just as words have strong and weak parts, so do sentences have strong and weak parts. Function words are mostly unstressed in the sentence. English has stress-timed rhythm. There is nearly equal time between the sentence stresses. Stressed syllables will tend to occur at relatively regular intervals. Times from each stressed syllable to the next will tend to be the same, irrespective of the number of intervening unstressed syllables. To express the notion of such rhythm, the foot is used as a unit of rhythm. The foot begins with a stressed syllable and includes all following unstressed syllables up to (but not including) the following stressed syllable.

┤ B ├

Practice the sentences using natural rhythm and stress.

MEN TOR

Mentor Linguistics

멘토영어학
기출분석

Chapter 06

Intonation

Unit 01 Preview & Review

01 Pitch Contour, Tone Group, Tonic Accent, and Tonic Syllable

Intonation is variation of pitch that is not used to distinguish words. Languages that are not tone languages, such as English or French, are called intonation languages. The pitch contour of an utterance may affect the meaning of the whole sentence, so that *John is here* spoken with falling pitch at the end is interpreted as a statement, but with rising pitch at the end, a question.

We defined **intonation** as pitch variations that occur over a phrase or sentence. Intonation contours can be described in terms of **tone groups** or **intonational phrases**. **A tone group** is the part of a sentence over which an intonation contour extends. Within a tone group, each stressed syllable has a minor pitch increase, but there is one syllable in which this pitch increase is more significant. The syllable that carries the major pitch change is called the **tonic syllable**. For example, in the following sentence:

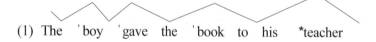

(1) The 'boy 'gave the 'book to his *teacher

the elements marked with a ' are stressed, but the major pitch increase is on *teacher*, which is marked with **an asterisk**.

Since in the usual cases in English, the **utterance-initial position** is reserved for **shared (old) information**, and the **new information** is placed in **utterance-final position**, the most common pattern is to put **the tonic accent** on **the last stressed lexical item** (noun, verb, adjective, adverb).

One should note, however, that this is merely a tendency, as we may easily find cases where the tonic accent is brought forward.

(2a) He   was   **some**what   *dis**cour**aged

(2b) He   was   *****some**what   dis**cour**aged

In (2b) the tonic accent on *somewhat* is a result of **emphasis (contrast)**.

Not all cases of placing the tonic accent earlier than the last stressed lexical item involve contrast/emphasis, as exemplified in (3):

(3) I have   *a **par**ty to plan
                *****let**ters to write

It is important to note that **a tone group** is **a unit of information** rather than a syntactically definable unit. Thus, the way the speaker shapes his or her utterance(s) depends on what he or she considers to be the important point(s) in the sentence. In (3), the speaker has the lexical item *party/letters* that has the greater importance.

02 Intonation Types and Sentences

2.1. Falling Intonation Contour

The sentences in general are examples of "**falling intonation contour**," which is quite typical of **utterances that express finality**.

It may be useful, to make a distinction between **"long" fall** versus **"short" fall**.

<1> A **full fall** is **unmarked for declaratives** where there is **clear finality in the statement** (i.e. there is nothing more to be said).

(4)   I am leaving the house right now.

This pattern is common in expressing emotional involvement:

(5)   I'm so glad.   (with genuine enthusiasm)

A falling contour is also typical of *wh*-questions (questions that start with a *wh*-word such as *what, which, where*):

(6)   Which way did she go?

<2> While a "long" fall shows a **definitive, involved** mood, **a "short" fall** is generally, an indication of a **detached** mood in the speaker. It displays a rather **neutral, perfunctory** attitude:

(7)   Whatever you say. (i.e. "I agree with it")

2.2. Rising Intonation Contour

If falling contour is indicative of "finality" or "completion," *rising* intonation represents "**non-definiteness**," "**lack of assurance**," or "**incompletion**." This pitch pattern is addressee-oriented, and the degree of "rise" is matched to the degree of **uncertainty** or **incompleteness**. Accordingly, we can describe this pattern as:

(a) "long" rise, or (b) "short" rise.

2.2.1. Long Rise

Long rise is a more marked pattern, which is indicative of an attitude of puzzlement or unbelieving:

In yes-no questions (typical order, or with statement order), such as:

(8a)   Is this a joke?   (8b)   This is a joke?

the speaker has the attitude of asking "are you sure you know what you are saying?" or "this is hard to believe."

2.2.2. Short Rise

A short rise, on the other hand, is more common and is used in a variety of situations:

<1> In **yes-no questions** (typical order or with statement order), such as:

    (9a)   Has your uncle left already?   (9b)   Your uncle has left already?

<2> **Echo questions**, such as:

    (10)   Where will I work? I haven't thought of that yet.

<3> **Repetition questions**, such as:

(11)　What are you doing? (I haven't heard you)

Note that this is different from (6), where the question in information-seeking.

<4> **Open-choice alternative questions**, such as: ❶

(12)　Would you like a paper or magazine? (something to read)

<5> **Certain tag questions** that signal **uncertainty**, such as:

(13)　She usually comes at ten, doesn't she?

<6> Items in a list prior to the last item, such as:

(14)　I need to buy a shirt, a jacket, and a tie.

<7> **Questions that display readiness to present some new information**, such as:

(15)　Do you know when the first kidney transplant was?

If this is uttered as **a neutral "information-seeking" question**, it will end in a falling pitch.

---

❶ Note the falling contour for the "closed choice" alternative:

Paper or magazine?

2.3. Falling-Rising Intonation Contour

Other than the falling and rising intonation discussed thus far, there are two other patterns that are combinatory. A *falling-rising* intonation is indicative of **an agreement with reservation**:

(16)   You can do it that way.

The speaker accepts that it can be done the way the hearer suggested and at the same time expresses some reservation or hesitation (i.e. "I don't think you should").

2.4. Rising-Falling Intonation Contour

The opposite, a *rising-falling* intonation, which is the dramatic equivalent of a simple "fall," reveals strong feelings of approval or disapproval:

(17a)   That's wonderful. (cf. "That's wonderful" with simple fall)

(17b)   You can't do that. (cf. "You can't do that" with simple fall)

2.5. Level Intonation

Finally, mention should be made of a *level* intonation, which marks a bored or sarcastic attitude:

(18)   A : John will be at the party.
       B : Great.

03 Overview

3.1. Intonation Patterns and Their Meaning

Intonation Patterns		Meaning		Markedness
Falling	long fall	finality or completion	clear finality in the statement (i.e. there is nothing more to be said) a definitive, involved mood	unmarked for declaratives
	short fall		a detached mood in the speaker a rather neutral, perfunctory attitude	
Rising	long rise	non-definiteness, lack of assurance, uncertainty, or incompletion	an attitude of puzzlement or unbelieving	more marked pattern
	short rise		used in a variety of situations	more common
Falling-Rising		an agreement with reservation		
Rising-Falling		strong feeling of approval or disapproval strong conviction, strength of feeling, certainty, exclamation		the dramatic equivalent of long fall, the emphatic kind of long fall
Level		a bored or sarcastic attitude		

Unit 02 Questions

Answer Key p.507

01 Read the following passage and answer the question. 2012년 36번

In English, a sequence of pitch levels can indicate the intonation pattern of an intonational phrase. In the following data, the numbers in parentheses at the end of each intonational phrase correspond to the pitch level as follows: 1 indicates a low pitch, 2 a normal pitch, and 3 a high pitch. Thus, the 2-3-1 pattern is what is known as rising-falling intonation, and 2-3 represents rising intonation. This kind of pitch change takes place around the tonic syllable depending on factors such as the pattern of a sentence and the intention of the speaker. Importantly, sentences that are ambiguous in writing may be unambiguous when spoken with different intonation patterns as in the following examples:

(a) A : Do you know him?
  B : Do I KNOW him? (2-3-2) He's my BROther. (2-3-1)

(b) A : Let's go back to the classroom.
  B : It's time for class to START? (2-3)

(c) A : Let's go somewhere this summer!
  B : Where do you want to GO? (2-3-1)
    Do you want to go to LONdon, (2-3) or PAris? (2-3)

(d) A : We might need to go that way to escape from this hazard.
  B : Are you CERtain? (2-3-2)

(e) A : What time is it now?
  B : What TIME is it now? (2-3)

(CAPITAL letters indicate tonic syllables. Intonation is marked only for B's utterances.)

Given that each dialog is produced in a common and neutral context in North American English, which of the following is the most plausible?

① In dialog (a), B is asking A to repeat what A said.

② In dialog (b), B states that the class will resume very soon.

③ In dialog (c), B wants A to choose between London and Paris to visit.

④ In dialog (d), B does not think that A is certain at all.

⑤ In dialog (e), B is asking A the correct time.

02 다음 글을 읽고, 지시에 따르시오. [4점]

2008년 서울/인천 6번

Intonation in questions functions to differentiate normal information from contrastive or expressive intentions. In other words, intonation performs an important conversation management function, with the speaker being able to subtly signal to the interlocutor to respond in a particular fashion, or to pay particular attention to a piece of highlighted information.

There are two syntactic options for making yes/no questions. The first option, which is general or unmarked, involves the inversion of the subject and the auxiliary verb, as in (1).

(1) Did Tom cook | DINer?

This unmarked option is accompanied by rising intonation. In this pattern, the speaker is asking about the truth of what he or she is saying.

The second option, which is less general or marked, takes the form of a statement with no subject-auxiliary inversion, as in (2).

(2) Tom cooked | DINer?

In this marked pattern with rising intonation, the speaker is either asking the interlocutor to repeat or is making an assumption and wants the interlocutor to confirm it (i.e., the speaker has good reason to expect a *yes* answer).

Another prosodic pattern for the uninverted question has emphatic stress, high pitch, and exaggerated intonation on one or two of the constituents that lend themselves to focus, as in (3).

(3) Tom | cooked | DINer?

In this pattern, the speaker is reacting with surprise or disbelief to certain information just received.

For learners of English, it does not make sense to practice the unmarked and marked versions of *Tom cooked dinner* in isolation and out of context. Learners must understand early on that one version is appropriate in one context, whereas the other is appropriate in another context.

아래 대화의 빈칸 ①에 들어갈 Kelly의 발화를 위 글 (1)~(3)에서 찾아 번호를 쓰고, 대화의 내용에 근거하여 그 이유를 50자 내외의 우리말로 쓰시오.

(Kelly is a friend of Lisa's family.)

Lisa : The guys kept doing nice things for me because it was Mother's Day. Bob washed the car, Joe ironed the shirts, and Tom cooked dinner.

Kelly : (① _____)

Lisa : It was quite amazing to me, too. He's never even boiled an egg before.

• ① : (_____)

• 이유 : _____

_____

_____

03

다음 <A>를 읽고, <B>가 나타내고자 하는 의미를 "as well as"를 사용하여 한 문장의 영어로 쓰시오. (문장에서 진한 글씨체로 된 부분은 억양구에서 액센트(tonic accent)를 받는 곳임) [3점]

2005년 전국 23번

┤ A ├

The position of a tonic accent is closely connected with information type. A focused constituent usually receives the tonic accent, while a non-focused constituent, which is understood to be old information or is presupposed, is unaccented. Consider the following sentence:

Peter met Jennifer in his office, too.

The meaning of *too* is to indicate that what has been said previously with the use of one word or term applies as well with the use of another word of the same form-class. For example, if *Jennifer* and *too* are accented in this sentence (/ Peter met **Jennifer** in his office, // **too.** /), it is presupposed that Peter met some other person in his office and the presupposed part is unaccented. Thus, the sentence means that Peter met Jennifer as well as some other person.

┤ B ├

/ **Peter** met Jennifer in his office, // **too.** /

04 다음 발음에 관한 (A)와 (B)를 읽고, (B)의 밑줄 그은 부분에 알맞은 말을 쓰시오. [3점]

2004년 전국 9번

┤ A ├

대화 상황:

A foreign student is applying for a library card at a university library. He is handed a form by an overworked male assistant, who is a native speaker of English, but after looking at it, he realizes it is the wrong one.

대화:

Foreign student : Excuse ＼ME. You have ＼GIVEn me the ＼＼WRONG form.

Library assistant : Sorry. I gave you what you ＼ASKed for [irritated, appeals to others in the queue for support].

Foreign student : ＼＼NO. It ＼IS the ＼＼WRONG form.

Library assistant : OK. There's no need to be rude.

Key

＼ means falling intonation.

＼＼ means extra emphasis on stressed syllables.

Capital letters mean stressed syllables.

┤ B ├

Instead of the underlined section of the conversation, a native speaker of English might say the following:

"Ex＼CUSE me. You've given me the wrong ＼FORM."

Compared to the native speaker's utterance, the foreign student's pronunciation appears to give the impression of being _____.

MEMO

MEN
TOR

Mentor Linguistics

멘토영어학
기출분석

Part 04

Morphology

Chapter 01
Morphology

Mentor Linguistics

멘토영어학
기출분석

Morphology

Unit 01 Preview & Review

01 Words and Morphemes

The study of **word-formation** and **word-structure** is called **morphology**. Morphological theory provides a general theory of word-structure in all the languages of the world. Its task is to characterize the kinds of things that speakers need to know about the structure of the words of their language in order to be able to use them to produce and to understand speech.

1.1. Words

Word is the smallest linguistic unit capable of standing meaningfully on its own in the grammar of a language.

According to Leonard Bloomfield, 'a minimum free form is a word'. By this, he meant that the word is the smallest meaningful linguistic unit that can be used on its own.

1.1.1. Word Knowledge

Depth of word knowledge refers to a learner's knowledge of the different aspects of a given word. This knowledge has to do with extent of knowledge of the following categories:

(1) a. pronunciation and orthography;
b. morphological properties;
c. syntactic properties and collocations;
d. semantic properties including connotations, polysemy, antonymy, and synonymy;
e. register;
f. and frequency.

A key concept in this notion of vocabulary depth is that as the word is known in a deeper manner, then the more words that are associated with that word are also known. It is also congruent with the view that lexical depth is incremental and there are degrees of word knowing. Knowledge of vocabulary is multidimensional, encompassing various types of knowledge. The relationships between words are connected on different dimensions. Words may be related

(2) a. thematically (*book-journal-manuscript*),

    b. phonologically (*dock-sock-rock*),

    c. morphologically (*indemnification-notification-intensification*),

    d. conceptually (*pan-pot-steamer*), and

    e. sociolinguistically (*dude-guy-man*)

among others.

The number of relations that are established between words is in part a function of the number of exposures to a word providing a variety of information about the item. Understanding the richness of these connections represents the depth of knowledge of a particular word.

1.1.2. Content Words and Function Words

Languages make an important distinction between two kinds of words—**content words** and **function words**.

Nouns, verbs, adjectives, and adverbs are the **content words**. These words denote concepts such as objects, actions, attributes, and ideas that we can think about like *children, build, beautiful,* and *seldom.* **Content words** are sometimes called the **open class words** because we can and regularly do add new words to these classes, such as *Facebook* (noun), *blog* (noun, verb), *frack* (verb), *online* (adjective, adverb), and *blingy* (adjective).

Other classes of words do not have clear lexical meanings or obvious concepts associated with them, including

(3) **conjunctions** such as *and, or,* and *but*;
   prepositions such as *in* and *of*;
   the **articles** *the* and *a/an*, and
   pronouns such as *it*.

These kinds of words are called **function words** because they specify grammatical relations and have little or no semantic content.

Function words are sometimes called **closed class words**. This is because it is difficult to think of any conjunctions, prepositions, or pronouns that have recently entered the language.

1.1.3. Onomatopoeic Words

There is some **sound symbolism** in language—that is, words whose pronunciation suggests their meanings. Most languages contain **onomatopoeic words** like *buzz* or *murmur* that imitate the sounds associated with the objects or actions they refer to.

1.2. Morphemes

The linguistic term for the most elemental unit of grammatical form is **morpheme**.

The study of the internal structure of words, and of the rules by which words are formed, is **morphology**.

A single word may be composed of one or more morphemes:

(4) One morpheme   boy
                        desire
                        meditate
    two morphemes   boy + ish
                        desire + able
                        meditate + tion

three morphemes	boy + ish + ness
	desire + able + ity
four morphemes	gentle + man + li + ness
	un + desire + able + ity
more than four	un + gentle + man + li + ness
	anti + dis + establish + ment + ari + an + ism

A **morpheme**—the minimal linguistic unit—is thus an arbitrary union of a sound and a meaning (or grammatical function) that cannot be further analyzed.

Bound and Free Morphemes

Our morphological knowledge has two components: knowledge of the individual morphemes and knowledge of the rules that combine them. One of the things we know about particular morphemes is whether they can **stand alone** or whether they must be attached to a base morpheme.

Some morphemes like *boy, desire, gentle,* and *man* may constitute words by themselves. These are **free morphemes**.

Other morphemes like *-ish, -ness, -ly, pre-, trans-,* and *un-* are never words by themselves but are always parts of words. These affixes are **bound morphemes** and they may attach at the beginning, the end, or both at the beginning and end of a word.

1.3. Affixes

Affixes like *-ing* or *-y* are called **bound morphemes** because they cannot stand alone. They always have to be attached to the stem or root of a word in order to be used. There are two types of affixes: **derivational** and **inflectional**.

1.3.1. Derivational and Inflectional Affixes

Derivational affixes are added to a stem or root to form a new stem or word, possibly, but not necessarily, resulting in a change in syntactic category or meaning. For example, the derivational affix *-er* is added to a verb like *kick* to give the noun *kicker*.

On the other hand, by the addition of **inflectional affixes**, forms with different grammatical functions are created as in *cats*. That is, **inflectional affixes** have a strictly grammatical function, marking properties such as tense and number.

English has eight inflectional suffixes:

(5) -s (third per. sing. present)   "she look**s** here"

  -s (plural)   "two cat**s**"

  -s (possessive)   "cat**'s** tail"

  -ed (past tense)   "she look**ed** here"

  -en, -ed (past participle)   "she has eat**en**"

  -ing (progressive)   "she is eat**ing**"

  -er (comparative)   "she is short**er** than you"

  -est (superlative)   "she is the short**est**"

1.3.2. Prefixes and Suffixes

We know whether an affix precedes or follows other morphemes, for example that *un-, pre-* (*premeditate, prejudge*), and *bi-* (*bipolar, bisexual*) are **prefixes**. They occur before other morphemes.

Some morphemes occur only as **suffixes**, following other morphemes. English examples of suffix morphemes are *-ing* (*sleeping, eating, running, climbing*), *-er* (*singer, performer, reader*), *-ist* (*typist, pianist, novelist, linguist*), and *-ly* (*manly, sickly, friendly*), to mention only a few.

1.3.3. Suffixes and Word Stress

If the basic rules of stress looked rather untidy and replete with exceptions, **the rules accompanying affixes** can easily be said to overshadow the mono-morphemic roots.

Since the addition of prefixes does not change word stress, our presentation will be on the varying effects of suffixes on word stress. We can classify the suffixes as:

(6) a. stress-bearing suffixes

   b. stress-shifting suffixes

   c. stress-neutral suffixes

1.3.3.1. Stress-bearing Suffixes

These suffixes attract stress. Below are the **some** common **derivational suffixes**:

(7)
-ade	lémon — lemonáde
-aire	míllion — millionáire
-ation	réalize — realizátion
-ee	ábsent — absentée (exception: commíttee)
-eer	móuntain — mountainéer
-ese	Japán — Japanése
-esque	pícture — picturésque
-ette	kítchen — kitchenétte
-itis	lárynx — laryngítis
-ific	hónor — honorífic

1.3.3.2. Stress-neutral Suffixes

These suffixes never make any difference to the stress pattern of the resulting word. Such suffixes include all **inflectional suffixes**, and **several derivational ones**:

(8)
-al	arríve — arríval	-ize	spécial — spécialize
-ant	ascénd — ascéndant	-less	bóttom — bóttomless
-cy	célibate — célibacy	-ly	fríend — fríendly
-dom	frée — fréedom	-ment	aménd — améndment
-er	pláy — pláyer	-ness	fránk — fránkness
-ess	líon — líoness	-ship	fríend — fríendship
-ful	gráce — gráceful	-some	búrden — búrdensome
-hood	nátion — nátionhood	-wise	clóck — clóckwise
-ish	gréen — gréenish	-th	grów — grówth
-ism	álcohol — álcoholism	-ty	cértain — cértainty
-ist	húman — húmanist	**-y**	**sílk — sílky**
-ive	submít — submíssive		

1.3.3.3. Stress-shifting Suffixes

A multiplicity of derivational suffixes, when added to a root, shift the stress from its original position to the syllable immediately preceding the suffix. Below are some of the common ones in this group:

(9) -ian   Áristotle − Aristotélian

    -ial   súbstance − substánial

    -ian   líbrary − librárian

    -ical   geómetry − geométrical

    -icide   ínsect − insécticide

    -ic   périod − periódic (exceptions: Árabic, lúnatic)

    -ify   pérson − persónify

    -ious   lábor − labórious

    -ity   húmid − humídity

    -ometer   spéed − speedómeter

    -ual   cóntext − contéxtual

    -ous   móment − moméntous

    -y   hómonym − homónymy

1.4. Roots and Stems

Morphologically complex words consist of a morpheme root and one or more affixes. Some examples of English roots are *paint* in *painter*, *read* in *reread*, *ceive* in *conceive*, and *ling* in *linguist*. A **root** may or may not stand alone as a word (*paint* and *read* do; *ceive* and *ling* don't).

When a root morpheme is combined with an affix, it forms a stem. Other affixes can be added to a stem to form a more complex stem, as shown in the following:

(10) **root** Chomsky (proper) noun
 stem Chomsky + ite noun + suffix
 word Chomsky + ite + s noun + suffix + suffix

 root believe verb
 stem believe + able verb + suffix
 word un + believe + able prefix + verb + suffix

 root system noun
 stem system + atic noun + suffix
 stem un + system + atic prefix + noun + suffix
 stem un + system + atic + al prefix + noun + suffix + suffix
 word un + system + atic + al + ly prefix + noun + suffix + suffix + suffix

Linguists sometimes use the word **base** to mean any root or stem to which an affix is attached. In the preceding example, *system, systematic, unsystematic,* and *unsystematical* are bases.

Bound Roots

Bound roots do not occur in isolation and they acquire meaning only in combination with other morphemes. For example, words of Latin origin such as *receive, conceive, perceive,* and *deceive* share a common root, *-ceive*; and the words *remit, permit, commit, submit, transmit,* and *admit* share the root *-mit*. For the original Latin speakers, the morphemes corresponding to *ceive* and *mit* had clear meanings, but for modern English speakers, Latinate morphemes such as *ceive* and *mit* have no independent meaning. Their meaning depends on the entire word in which they occur.

02 Word Formation Rules and Word Structure

2.1. Derivational Morphology

A characteristic of all human languages is the potential to create new words. The categories of noun, verb, adjective, and adverb are open in the sense that new members are constantly being added. One of the most common types of formation is **derivation**, which creates new words from already existing morphemes.

Derivation is the process by which a new word is built from a base, usually through the addition of an **affix**. However, derivation does not always apply freely to the members of a given category. Sometimes, for instance, a particular derivational affix is able to attach only to stems with particular phonological properties.

The Suffix -*en*

A good example of this involves the English suffix -*en*, which combines with adjectives to create verbs with a causative meaning. However, there are many adjectives with which -*en* cannot combine, since the suffix -*en* is subject to a phonological constraint. In particular, it can only combine with a monosyllabic stem that ends in an obstruent.

The Suffix -*able* and the Prefix *un-*

Words with more than one affix are formed by means of several steps. For example, consider the word *unusable*, which is composed of a prefix *un-*, a stem *use*, and a suffix -*able*. The prefix *un-*, meaning 'not', attaches only to adjectives and creates new words that are also adjectives such as *unkind*. The suffix -*able*, on the other hand, attaches to verbs and forms adjectives such as *countable*. Since *un-* cannot attach to *use*, the suffix -*able* attaches first to the stem *use*, creating *usable*. The prefix *un-* is then allowed to combine with *usable* to form *unusable*.

The Suffix -*al*

There are two types of derivational suffix -*al* : the type that attaches to **nouns** and forms **adjectives** as in (11a), and the type that attaches to **verbs** and forms **nouns** as in (11b).

(11) a. central, coastal, musical

　　　b. refusal, proposal, recital

The second type, called a deverbal suffix, can derive well-formed nouns if a requirement are satisfied. The requirement is that the final syllable of the verb it attaches to has stress, and based on this requirement, English lacks nouns like *fidgetal, *promisal, and *abandonal.

2.2. Inflectional Morphology

Consider the forms of the verb in the following sentences:

(12) a. I sail the ocean blue.

    b. He sails the ocean blue.

    c. John sailed the ocean blue.

    d. John has sailed the ocean blue.

    e. John is sailing the ocean blue.

In sentence (12b) the -s at the end of the verb is an agreement marker; it signifies that the subject of the verb is third-person and is singular, and that the verb is in the present tense. It doesn't add lexical meaning. The suffix -ed indicates past tense, and is also required by the syntactic rules of the language when verbs are used with *have*, just as -ing is required when verbs are used with forms of *be*.

Inflectional morphemes represent relationships between different parts of a sentence. For example, -s expresses the relationship between the verb and the third-person singular subject; -ed expresses the relationship between the time the utterance is spoken (e.g., now) and the time of the event (past). If you say "John danced," the -ed affix places the activity before the utterance time. **Inflectional morphology** is closely connected to the syntax and semantics of the sentence.

Inflectional morphemes in English follow the derivational morphemes in a word. Thus, to the derivationally complex word *commit + ment* one can add a plural ending to form *commit + ment + s*, but the order of affixes may not be reversed to derive the impossible *commit + s + ment = *commitsment*.

In distinguishing inflectional from derivational morphemes in Modern English we may summarize in the table below:

Table 1. Characteristics of Derivational and Inflectional Affixes in English

Derivational	Inflectional
Lexical function	Grammatical function
May cause word class change	No word class change
Some meaning change	Small or no meaning change
Never required by rules of grammar	Often required by rules of grammar
Precede inflectional morphemes in a word	Follow derivational morphemes in a word
Some productive, many nonproductive	Productive

2.3. Morphological Structure: Hierarchical Structure of Words

A word is not a simple sequence of morphemes. It has an internal structure. For example, the word *unsystematic* is composed of three morphemes: *un-*, *system*, and *-atic*. The root is *system*, a noun, to which we add the suffix *-atic* resulting in an adjective, *systematic*. To this adjective, we add the prefix *un-* forming a new adjective, *unsystematic*.

(13)

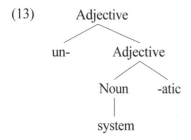

This tree represents the application of two morphological rules:

(14) Noun + atic   →   Adjective
(15) un + Adjective   →   Adjective

Inflectional morphemes are equally well represented. The following tree shows that the inflectional agreement morpheme *-s* follows the derivational morphemes *-ize* and *re-* in *refinalizes*:

(16)

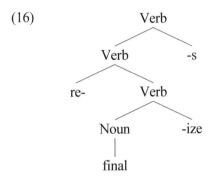

The tree also shows that *re-* applies to *finalize*, which is correct as **refinal* is not a word, and that the inflectional morpheme follows the derivational morpheme.

2.4. Structurally Ambiguous Words

The hierarchical organization of words is most clearly shown by structurally ambiguous words. Consider the word *unbuttonable*. The two meanings of the word correspond to different structures, as follows:

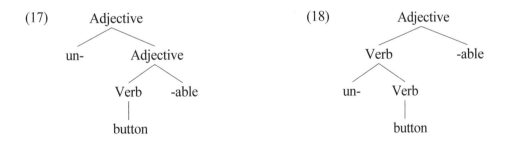

The ambiguity of this word arises because the prefix *un-* can combine with different grammatical categories.

MENTOR LINGUISTICS

In the first structure the verb *button* combines with the deverbal adjective-forming suffix *-able* to form an adjective *buttonable* ('able to be locked'). Then the prefix *un-*, meaning 'not,' combines with the derived adjective to form a new adjective *unbuttonable* ('not able to be buttoned'). In the second case, the prefix *un-* combines with the verb *button* to form a derived verb *unbutton*. Then the derived verb combines with the suffix *-able* to form *unbuttonable*, 'able to be unbuttoned.'

An entire class of words in English follows this pattern: *unlockable, unzippable,* and *unlatchable,* among others. The ambiguity arises because the prefix *un-* can combine with an adjective, as illustrated in the rule (19a), or it can combine with a verb, as illustrated in the rule (19b), as in *undo, unstaple, unearth, and unloosen.*

(19) a. un- + Adjective   →   Adjective
     b. un- + Verb   →   Verb

03 Morphological Processes

3.1. Compounding

A **compound** is formed by combining two bases, which may be words in their own right, to form a new lexical item. This is shown in (20) where the two bases are separated by a hyphen:

(20) shop-steward   ink-pot

     room-mate   road-show

     moon-light   shoe-string

Compounds differ in their structure. The majority of English compounds are nouns. Common types of **noun compounds** include the following:

(21)

Noun		*Noun*		*Noun*	
Adj.	*Noun*	*Noun*	*Noun*	*Adj.*	*Noun* (agent/instrument)
red	tape	bathroom		schoolteacher	
High	Court	ball-point		head-hunter	
blackberry		briefcase		housekeeper	
hothouse		bulldog		firefighter	
White	House	ashtray		matchmaker	
soft-ball		desktop		gamekeeper	
easychair		inkwell		door-keeper	

Let us now turn to examples of **adjectiveal compounds**. Some are listed in (22):

(22)

N + Ven	*Adj. + Ving*	*Adj. + Ven*
crestfallen	hard-working	clear-sighted
waterlogged	good-looking	hard-featured
heartbroken	easygoing	soft-hearted
frost-bitten	fast-growing	new-born

NOTE *Ven* is the past participial form of the verb. It is the verb form that ends *-en* or *-ed* after has in, e.g. *It has eaten* or in *It has wounded.*

An interesting property of most compounds is that they are headed. This means that one of the words that make up the compound is syntactically dominant. In English the head is normally the item on the right hand of the compound. The syntactic properties of the head are passed on to the entire compound. Thus in our examples above, if we have a compound like *easychair* which is made up of the adjective *easy* and the noun *chair*, syntactically the entire word is a noun. This applies to all the words in the left-hand column in (21).

3.2. Back-Formation

A new word may be formed from an existing word by "subtracting" an affix thought to be part of the old word; that is, ignorance sometimes can be creative. Thus, *peddle*, was derived from *peddler* on the mistaken assumption that *-er* was the "agentive" suffix. Such a word is called a **back-formation**. The verbs *hawk, stoke, swindle,* and *edit* all came into the language by this word-formation process.

3.3. Conversion, Function Shift, Zero Derivation

In English very often lexical items are created not affixation but by **conversion** or **zero derivation**, i.e. without any alternation being made to the shape of the input base. The word-form remains the same, but it realizes a different lexical item.

Conversion of verbs into nouns and nouns into verbs is extremely productive in English. Usually the same word-form can be used as a verb or a noun, with only the grammatical context enabling us to know which category it belongs to. Thus, *jump* in the two sentences below is exactly the same in form but it belongs to two different lexemes. In (23a) *jump* is the non-finite form of the verb 'jump' while in (23b) it is the singular form of the noun *jump*.

(23) a. The pig will jump over the stile!
     b. What a jump!

In *what a jump!* the verb is converted into a noun by 'zero derivation', i.e. without using any affix. What enables us to know whether the word is a noun or a verb is the position that it occupies in the sentence. If we see the subject *the pig* and the auxiliary verb *will* before the word *jump*, we know it must be a verb. But when *jump* occurs after the indefinite article *a* we know it must be a noun.

3.4. Affixation

Adding affixes to an existing word is very common way of creating new words. English exploits this possibility by adding the agentive *-er* to the prepositions *up* and *down* to create the nouns *upper* and *downer*, which were invented in connection with drugs but have extended their meaning to anything that lifts or dampens one's spirits. More commonly, *-er* is suffixed to verbs (V) and means 'one who Vs' as in *runner* 'one who runs,' *campaigner*, and *designer*.

English takes advantage of two kinds of affixation: **prefixing** and **suffixing**. Prefixes like *un-*, *pre-*, and *dis-* serve to change the meaning of words, though not usually their lexical category. Thus the prefix *un-* added to an adjective creates a new adjective with the opposite meaning, as in *untrue, unpopular, unsuccessful,* and *unfavorable.* The prefix *dis-* added to a verb derives a verb with the opposite meaning, as in *disobey, disappear, dishonor,* and *displace. Pre-* serves as a prefix to several categories of words. It can be prefixed to verbs (*preaffirm, preallot, preplan, prewash,* and *premix*), adjectives (*pre-Copernican, precollegiate, precultural, presurgical*), or nouns (*preantiquity, preaffirmation, preplacement*).

3.5. Clipping

Clipping is the abbreviation of longer words into shorter ones, such as *fax* for *facsimile*, the British word *telly* for *television, prof* for *professor, piano* for *pianoforte,* and *gym* for *gymnasium.* Once considered slang, these words have now become lexicalized, that is, full words in their own right. These are only a few examples of such clipped forms that are now used as whole words. Other examples are *ad, bike, math, gas, phone, bus,* and *van* (from *advertisement, bicycle, mathematics, gasoline, telephone, omnibus,* and *caravan*).

3.6. Blending

Blends are similar to compounds in that they are produced by combining two words, but parts of the words that are combined are deleted. *Smog*, from *smoke* + *fog*; *brunch*, from *breakfast* and *lunch*; *motel*, from *motor* + *hotel*; *infomercial*, from *info* + *commercial*; and *urinalysis*, from *urine* + *analysis* are examples of blends that have attained full lexical status in English.

3.7. Acronym and Abbreviation

Acronyms are words derived from the initials of several words. Such words are pronounced as the spelling indicates: *NASA* [næsə] from National Aeronautics and Space Administration, *UNESCO* [yunɛsko] from United Nations Educational, Scientific, and Cultural Organization, and *UNICEF* [yunisɛf] from United Nations International Children's Emergency Fund. *Radar* from "radio detecting and ranging," *laser* from "light amplification by stimulated emission of radiation," and *scuba* from "self-contained underwater breathing apparatus."

When the string of letters is not easily pronounced as a word, the "acronym" is produced by sounding out each letter, as in *NFL* [ɛ̃nɛfɛl] for National Football League, *UCLA* [yusiɛle] for University of California, Los Angeles, and *MRI* [ɛ̃maraɪ] for magnetic resonance imaging. These special kinds of acronyms are sometimes called **alphabetic abbreviations**.

3.8. Word Coinage

Words may be created outright to fit some purpose. The advertising industry has added many words to English, such as *Kodak, nylon, Orlon,* and *Dacron.* Specific brand names such as *Xerox, Band-Aid, Kleenex, Jell-O, Brillo,* and *Vaseline* are now sometimes used as the generic name for different brands of these types of products. Some of these words were actually created from existing words (e.g., *Kleenex* from the word *clean* and *Jell-O* from *gel*).

Unit 02 Questions

Answer Key p.508

01 **Read the passage and follow the directions.** [2 points]   2021년 A형 2번

┤ A ├

There are many ways to make new words or word forms in English as listed in (1).

(1) Morphological process	Example
a. blending	spoon + fork → spork
b. clipping	celebrity → celeb
c. compounding	ice + cream → icecream
d. conversion	microwave (noun) → microwave (verb)
e. derivation	divine + ity → divinity
f. inflection	want + ed → wanted
g. initialism	automatic teller machine → ATM

Sometimes multiple morphological processes serially apply to a morpheme to create a new word or word form. Take a look at (2).

(2) a. Marie <u>revisited</u> Korea for her concert in December.
   b. Ted <u>babysits</u> for his neighbor to make money.

Revisited in (2a) goes through derivation (re+visit) and inflection (revisit+ed), and babysits in (2b) goes through compounding (baby+sit) and inflection (babysit+s).

┤ B ├

Assuming that box is a noun, unboxing is created in the order of ① _____, ② _____, and inflection.

Based on <A>, fill in each blank in <B> with an appropriate morphological process from (1). Write your answers in the correct order.

---

02 Read the passage and fill in the blank with ONE word. [2 points]

2017년 A형 4번

Trisyllabic laxing is a rule which changes a tense vowel into a lax vowel. This rule applies when the target vowel is pushed into the ante-penultimate syllable (i.e., the third syllable from the end) due to the attachment of a suffix, as exemplified below.

supreme — supremacy
apply — application
sane — sanity
divine — divinity
opaque — opacity

The tense vowels in words like 'nightingale' and 'ivory' do not undergo trisyllabic laxing although these words contain the minimum of three syllables required by the trisyllabic laxing rule. The explanation is that these forms are exempt from trisyllabic laxing since they do not have any _____.

03 Read <A> and <B> and answer the question. [1.5 points]   2013년 31번

────────────┤ A ├────────────

Affixes like *-ing* or *-y* are called bound morphemes because they cannot stand alone. They always have to be attached to the stem or root of a word in order to be used. There are two types of affixes: derivational and inflectional. Derivational affixes are added to a stem or root to form a new stem or word, possibly, but not necessarily, resulting in a change in syntactic category or meaning. For example, the derivational affix *-er* is added to a verb like *kick* to give the noun *kicker*. On the other hand, by the addition of inflectional affixes, forms with different grammatical functions are created as in *cats*. That is, inflectional affixes have a strictly grammatical function, marking properties such as tense and number.

────────────┤ B ├────────────

a. In *condemnation*, *-ation* is an inflectional affix.

b. In *nonrefundable*, *non-*, *re-*, and *-able* are all derivational affixes.

c. In *governments*, *-ment* is a derivational affix, and *-s* is an inflectional affix.

d. In *insincerity*, *in-* and *-ity* are both inflectional affixes.

e. In *lovelier*, *-ly* is a derivational affix, and *-er* is an inflectional affix.

Based on <A>, which of the following lists all and only the correct statements in <B>?

① a, b, c   ② a, b, d   ③ b, c, d

④ b, c, e   ⑤ c, d, e

04 Read <A> and <B> and follow the directions. [2 points]

─────┤ A ├─────

Century after century, English speakers have added thousands of new words, borrowing many of them from other languages and constructing others from elements already available. The following are some common word-formation processes:

(1) Coinage   (2) Clipping

(3) Compounding   (4) Back formation

─────┤ B ├─────

a. Can I get a <u>raincheck</u> for this?

b. Who will <u>typewrite</u> this article for me?

c. This is great. Can I have a <u>xerox</u>?

d. I usually have <u>brunch</u> on Sundays.

e. Could you <u>empty</u> the box for me?

f. Will Ms. Brown be our <u>sub</u> again today?

Match each word-formation process in <A> with an underlined example in one of the sentences in <B>.

	(1)	(2)	(3)	(4)
①	c	b	d	f
②	c	b	e	f
③	c	f	a	b
④	d	b	e	f
⑤	d	f	a	b

05 Read the passage and follow the directions. [4점]

Depth of word knowledge refers to a learner's knowledge of the different aspects of a given word. This knowledge has to do with extent of knowledge of the following categories: pronunciation and orthography; morphological properties; syntactic properties and collocations; (①) including connotations, polysemy, antonymy, and synonymy; register; and frequency. A key concept in this notion of vocabulary depth is that as the word is known in a deeper manner, then the more words that are associated with that word are also known. It is also congruent with the view that lexical depth is incremental and there are degrees of word knowing. Knowledge of vocabulary is multidimensional, encompassing various types of knowledge. The relationships between words are connected on different dimensions. Words may be related thematically (book-journal-manuscript), phonologically (②), morphologically (indemnification-notification-intensification), conceptually (③), and sociolinguistically (④) among others. The number of relations that are established between words is in part a function of the number of exposures to a word providing a variety of information about the item. Understanding the richness of these connections represents the depth of knowledge of a particular word.

Fill in blank ① with the most appropriate word, and blanks ②, ③, and ④ with the letter of the most appropriate example from the box below.

(a) dude-guy-man   (b) dock-sock-rock   (c) pan-pot-steamer

① _____

② (   )

③ (   )

④ (   )

06 다음 글을 읽고 지시에 따라 답하시오. [4점]   2008년 대전/충북/충남 18번

> A word is not a simple sequence of morphemes. It has an internal structure. For example, the word *unsystematic* is composed of three morphemes: *un-*, *system*, and *-atic*. The root is *system*, a noun, to which we add the suffix *-atic* resulting in an adjective, *systematic*. To this adjective, we add the prefix *un-* forming a new adjective, *unsystematic*.
>
> The hierarchical organization of words is most clearly shown by structurally ambiguous words. Consider the word *unbuttonable*. The two meanings of the word correspond to different structures, as follows:
>
>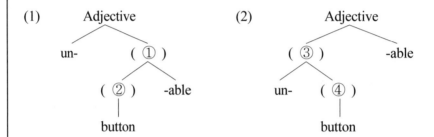
>
> The ambiguity of this word arises because the prefix *un-* can combine with different grammatical categories.

위 수형도의 빈칸 ①~④에 들어갈 문법범주(품사)를 쓰고, (1)과 (2)에 해당하는 단어 'unbuttonable'의 의미를 각각 쓰시오.

(1) 문법범주 : ① _____   ② _____

　　단어의 의미 : _____

(2) 문법범주 : ③ _____   ④ _____

　　단어의 의미 : _____

07 다음 (1), (2), (3)은 단어 형성 유형에 대한 설명이다. 각 유형에 해당하는 예를 <보기>에서 하나씩 찾아 그 기호를 쓰시오. [3점] 2007년 전국 3번

---

(1) Blending is formed by combining parts of existing words.

(2) Acronyms are formed from the first letter(s) of each word in a phrase and pronounced as a word.

(3) Functional Shift is formed by converting a word belonging to one category to another without any changes to the form of the word.

┤ 보기 ├

(a) waterbed : water + bed

(b) NYU : New York University

(c) water (Verb) : water (Noun)

(d) netizen : Internet + citizen

(e) national (Adjective) : nation (Noun)

(f) NASA : National Aeronautics and Space Administration

---

(1) _____

(2) _____

(3) _____

Part

04

08 다음에서 설명하는 음운론적 제약으로 인해 생성될 수 없는 파생어를 <보기>에서 모두 찾아 쓰시오. [3점]

2006년 전국 11번

A characteristic of all human languages is the potential to create new words. The categories of noun, verb, adjective, and adverb are open in the sense that new members are constantly being added. One of the most common types of formation is derivation, which creates new words from already existing morphemes.

Derivation is the process by which a new word is built from a base, usually through the addition of an affix. However, derivation does not always apply freely to the members of a given category. Sometimes, for instance, a particular derivational affix is able to attach only to stems with particular phonological properties. A good example of this involves the English suffix -*en*, which combines with adjectives to create verbs with a causative meaning. However, there are many adjectives with which -*en* cannot combine, since the suffix -*en* is subject to a phonological constraint. In particular, it can only combine with a monosyllabic stem that ends in an obstruent.

┤ 보기 ├

abstracten	olden	quicken	greenen
liven	bluen	louden	stouten

• 생성될 수 없는 파생어 : _____

09 **Read the passage and follow the directions.** 2006년 서울/인천 5번

Words with more than one affix are formed by means of several steps. For example, consider the word *unusable*, which is composed of a prefix *un-*, a stem *use*, and a suffix *-able*. The prefix *un-*, meaning 'not', attaches only to adjectives and creates new words that are also adjectives such as *unkind*. The suffix *-able*, on the other hand, attaches to verbs and forms adjectives such as *countable*. Since *un-* cannot attach to *use*, the suffix *-able* attaches first to the stem *use*, creating *usable*. The prefix *un-* is then allowed to combine with *usable* to form *unusable*.

Now consider the word *reusable*, in which the prefix *re-* attaching only to verbs is used. Our understanding of how the affixes combine with other morphemes enables us to state the formation of *reusable* as a two-step process whereby _____(1)_____ attaches to _____(2)_____ first, and then _____(3)_____ is added to _____(4)_____.

Fill in each blank with an affix or a word. [3점]

(1) _____

(2) _____

(3) _____

(4) _____

10 다음 예문을 읽고, 물음에 답하시오. [총 3점]   2002년 전국 16번

- Why don't you <u>email</u> me this evening?
- The employer <u>peopled</u> the house with ten adults.

---

(1) 위의 밑줄 친 단어들과 관련된 어형성(word-formation) 방법을 쓰시오. [1점]

_____

(2) 단어 water를 위의 email과 동일한 품사로 사용하여 다음 문장을 완성하시오. [2점]

My mother _____

MEMO

Mentor Linguistics

멘토영어학
기출분석

Part 05

Semantics and Pragmatics

MEN
TOR

Mentor Linguistics

멘토영어학
기출분석

Chapter 01

Semantics

Preview & Review

01 Sentential Semantics

Linguistic knowledge permits you to determine <1> whether a sentence is true or false, <2> when one sentence implies the truth or falseness of another, and <3> whether a sentence has multiple meanings. One way to account for this knowledge is by formulating semantic rules that build the meaning of a sentence from the meanings of its words and the way the words combine syntactically. This is often called **truth-conditional semantics** because it takes **speakers' knowledge of truth conditions** as basic. It is also called **compositional semantics** because it calculates the truth value of a sentence by **composing, or putting together, the meanings of smaller units**.

1.1. Meaning Relations in Truth-Conditional Semantics

Truth conditional semantics studies lexical relations by comparing predications that can be made about the same referring expression. Its task is to account for the meaning relations between different expressions in a language. Three of such relations are **entailment**, **paraphrase** and **contradiction**.

Entailment is the relation between two propositions—let's label them 'p' and 'q'—such that if p is true, q must also be true, but if q is true, it does not necessarily follow that p is true.

Paraphrase is the relation between two propositions, p and q, such that if either is true, the other is necessarily true also, and if either is false, the other is false.

Contradiction is the relation between two propositions such that if either is true, the other is necessarily false.

Semantic relations may hold between sentences of a language. Sometimes these relations are the result of particular words in the sentences, but in other cases the relations are the result of syntactic structure. We will look at an approach to meaning based on the notion of **truth**, which has grown out of the study of logic. In particular we examine how successfully **a truth-based approach** is in characterizing the semantic relations of **entailment** and **presupposition**.

What kind of knowledge about the meaning of a language does the native speaker have? For sentence meaning, a semantic theory should reflect an English speaker's knowledge:

(1) That a and b below are **synonymous**:

    a. My brother is a bachelor.

    b. My brother has never married.

(2) That a below **entails** b:

    a. The anarchist assassinated the emperor.

    b. The emperor is dead.

(3) That a below **contradicts** b:

    a. My brother Sebastian has just come from Rome.

    b. My brother Sebastian has never been to Rome.

(4) That a below **presupposes** b, as c does d:

    a. The Major of Manchester is a woman.

    b. There is a Major of Manchester.

    c. I regret eating your sandwich.

    d. I ate your sandwich.

(5) That a and b are necessarily true, i.e. **tautologies**:

    a. Ireland is Ireland.

    b. Rich people are rich.

(6) That a and b are necessarily false, i.e. **contractions**:

    a. ?He is murderer but he's never killed anyone.

    b. ?Now is not now.

We can give a rough characterization of each, as follows:

(7) A is **synonymous** with B: A has the same meaning as B.

(8) A **entails** B: we know that if A then automatically B.

(9) A **contradicts** B: A is inconsistent with B.

(10) A **presupposes** B: B is part of the assumed background against which A is said.

(11) A is a **tautology**: A is automatically true by virtue of its own meaning, but informationally empty.

(12) A is a **contradiction**: A is inconsistent with itself, i.e. asserts and denies the same thing.

1.2. Factive Predicates

The term '**factive verb**' is due to a pioneering study by Paul and Carol Kiparsky (1968). An illustrative sample of these verbs is provided in (13).

(13) Factive Verbs: be significant, be tragic, be relevant, be odd, regret, ignore, resent, know, realize, bear in mind, take into account, make clear, find out

What is common to them is that any simple assertion with a **factive predicate**, such as (14a), commits the speaker to the belief that the complement sentence, just by itself, is also true.

(14) a. It is odd that Bill is alone.

    b. Bill is alone.

    c. It is possible that Bill is alone.

It would be insincere for anyone to assert (14a) if he did not believe that (14b) is true. Intuitively, in uttering (14a) the speaker must take it for granted that Bill is alone; he is making a comment about that fact. The same relation holds between (15a) and (15b).

(15) a. Mary realized that it was raining.

    b. It was raining.

    c. Mary believed that it was raining.

Notice that these relations break down if we replace *odd* by *possible* and *realized* by *believed*. (14c) and (15c) do not carry a commitment to the truth of the complement sentence.

With factive verbs, it does not make a difference whether the main sentence is affirmative or negative. The negations of (14a) and (15a), which you find in (16), also obligate the speaker to accept the complement as true.

(16) a. It isn't odd that Bill is alone.

    b. Mary didn't realize that it was raining.

Even the illocutionary force of the main sentence is irrelevant. The question in (17) carries along the same commitment as (13a) and (16a).

(17) Is it odd that Bill is alone?

These facts about negation and questions become important when we have to distinguish between factive and implicative verbs.

1.3. Implicative Predicates

Some predicates do not presuppose the truth of a proposition that occurs as one of their arguments but carry some implication about the truth or non-truth of the proposition. We find an interesting variety of implications and can recognize different kinds of **implicative predicates**, first sketched by Karttunen (1971)[2] and sometimes called '**conditional factives**.' Consider first:

(18) a. I managed to catch my bus, and I caught it.

b. I managed to catch my bus, but I didn't catch it.

Sentence (18a) is as **redundant** as *I caught my bus, and I caught it*. Sentence (18b) is as **contradictory** as *I caught my bus, and I didn't catch it*.

If you hear someone say "I managed to catch my bus," you will no doubt **infer** that the speaker did catch th bus in question. Hearing the negative equivalent, "I didn't manage to catch my bus," you **infer** that the speaker did not catch the bus.

The verb *manage*, like some other verbs followed by a reduced clause, has a certain **implicative value**.

Different predicates have different implicative values, and we recognize **six groups of predicates** according to what they imply about the truth value of the included clause.

In our **first group**, which includes manage, if the predicate is affirmative, it implies that the following proposition is true, and if the predicate is negative, there is an implication that the following proposition is false. (The symbol '→' below should be read 'implies.')

(19) a. I managed to catch my bus. → I caught my bus.

b. I didn't manage to catch my bus. → I didn't catch my bus.

[2] Laurie Karttunen (1971) "Implicative Verbs," *Language* 47: 340-58.

More examples:

(20) a. We happened/chanced to see your brother. → We saw your brother.

   b. We didn't happen/chanced to see your brother. → We didn't see your brother.

(21) a. He chose/condescended to wait for us. → He waited for us.

   b. He didn't choose/condescend to wait for us. → He didn't wait for us.

(22) a. She remembered to stop at the post office.

   → She stoped at the post office.

   b. She didn't remember to stop at the post office.

   → She didn't stop at the post office.

With these verbs, Group 1, affirmative implies affirmative and negative implies negative.

(23) $+ \rightarrow +$ $- \rightarrow -$

Group 2 verbs occur in these sentences:

(24) a. We neglected/failed to make reservations. → We didn't make reservations.

   b. We didn't neglect/fail to make reservations. → We made reservations.

(25) a. I avoided/missed/escaped attending that party. → I didn't attend that party.

   b. I didn't avoid/miss/escape attending that party. → I attended that party.

With these verbs affirmative implies negative, that the embedded proposition is not true, and negative has an affirmative implication, that the embedded proposition is true.

(26) $+ \rightarrow -$ $- \rightarrow +$

Both Group 1 and Group 2 verbs are followed only by clauses with tacit subject; the subject of the embedded proposition is the same as the subject of the main clause.

Verbs in some of the groups below are followed by clauses with tacit or overt subjects. When both kinds exists, both are illustrated here.

Group 3:
(27) a. Henry acknowledged/admitted starting the fire. → Henry started the fire.
      b. Henry didn't acknowledge/admit starting the fire. → ?

(28) a. Circumstance forced us to cancel our plans. → We canceled our plans.
      b. Circumstance didn't force us to cancel our plans. → ?

We recognize that Henry's failure to admit starting the fire does not inform us whether he did or did not actually start the fire.

For Group 3 implicative verbs, affirmative implies affirmative but negative has no implication.

(29) $+ \rightarrow +$ $- \rightarrow 0$

Group 4:
(30) a. Mary pretended to be asleep. → Mary was not asleep.
      b. Mary didn't pretend to be asleep. → ?

(31) a. A sudden storm prevented the men from completing the job.
          → The men didn't complete the job.
      b. A sudden storm didn't prevent the men from completing the job. → ?

(32) a. We forgot to make reservations. → We didn't make reservations.
      b. We didn't forget to make reservations. → ?

In Group 4, affirmative implies negative but negative has no implication.

(33) $+ \rightarrow -$ $- \rightarrow 0$

Group 5:

(34) a. We tried to answer. → ?

   b. We didn't try to answer. → We didn't answer.

Affirmative has no implication, while the negative implies negative.

(35) $+ \to 0$ $- \to -$

Group 6:

(36) a. We hesitated to accept the offer. → ?

   b. We didn't hesitate to accept the offer. → We accepted the offer.

Affirmative has nothing, negative implies affirmative.

(37) $+ \to 0$ $- \to +$

02 Lexical Semantics

The meaning of a phrase or sentence is partially a function of the meanings of the words it contains. Similarly, the meaning of a morphologically complex word is a function of its component morphemes.

However, there is a fundamental difference between word meaning—or lexical semantics—and sentence meaning. The meaning of entries in the mental lexicon—be they morphemes, words, or idioms—is conventional; that is, speakers of a language implicitly agree on their meaning, and children acquiring the language must simply learn those meanings outright.

2.1. Lexical Semantic Relations

Lexical relations include synonymy, antonymy, hyponymy, and meronymy.

2.1.1. Synonymy

Synonyms are words or expressions that have the same meaning in some or all contexts. There are dictionaries of synonyms that contain many hundreds of entries, such as:

(38) apathetic/phlegmatic/passive/sluggish/indifferent
    pedigree/ancestry/genealogy/descent/lineage

2.1.2. Antonymy

Words that are opposite in meaning are **antonyms**.

Words are related in various kinds of antonyms such as complementary pairs, gradable pairs, relational opposites, and reversive pairs.

2.1.2.1. Complementary Pairs

Complementary pairs:

(39) alive/dead, present/absent, awake/asleep

They are complementary in that *alive = not dead* and *dead = not alive*, and so on.

2.1.2.2. Gradable Pairs

Gradable pairs of antonyms:

(40) big/small, hot/cold, fast/slow, happy/sad

The meaning of adjectives in gradable pairs is related to the objects they modify. The words do not provide an absolute scale. For example, we know that "a small elephant" is much bigger than "a large mouse." *Fast* is faster when applied to an airplane than to a car.

Another characteristic of certain pairs of gradable antonyms is that one is **marked** and the other **unmarked**.

The unmarked member is the one used in questions of degree. We ask, ordinarily, "How high is the mountain?" (not "How low is it?"). We answer "Ten thousand feet high" but never "Ten thousand feet low," except humorously or ironically.

Thus *high* is the unmarked member of *high/low*. Similarly, *tall* is the unmarked member of *tall/short*, *fast* the unmarked member of *fast/slow*, and so on.

2.1.2.3. Relational Opposites or Converse Antonyms

Relational opposites:

(41) give/receive, buy/sell, teacher/pupil

They display symmetry in their meanings. If X gives Y to Z, then Z receives Y from X. If X is Y's *teacher*, then Y is X's *pupil*. Pairs of words ending in *-er* and *-ee* are usually relational opposites. If Mary is Bill's *employer*, then Bill is Mary's *employee*.

The following sentences contain **converse predicates**, which necessarily have a valency of 2 or more.

(42) a. The map is above the chalkboard.
     b. The chalkboard is below the map.

(43) a. Sally is Jerry's wife. (Sally is the wife of Jerry.)
     b. Jerry is Sally's husband. (Jerry is the husband of Sally.)

Converseness is a kind of antonymy between two terms. For any two converse relational terms X and Y, if [a] is the X of [b], then [b] is the X of [a]. In (42a) *map* has the role of Theme and *chalkboard* the role of Associate; in (42b) the roles are reversed. The same is applies to *Sally* and *Jerry* in (43a) and (43b).

Common **converse pairs** include kinship and social roles (*husband-of/wife-of; employer-of/employee-of*) and directional opposites (*above/below; in front of/behind; left-of/right-of; before/after; north-of/south-of; outside/inside*).

There are a few pairs of converse 3-argument predicates: give-to/receive-from; sell-to/buy-from; lend-to/borrow-from.

(44) a. Dad lent me a little money.
     b. I borrowed a little money from Dad.

If A gives X to B, B receives X from A. All three of these pairs of predicates are built around the relationship of **source** and **goal**.

Some conjunctions, or clause connector, like *before* and *after* form converse pairs.

(45) a. Herbert left the party before Jean (left the party).

b. Jean left the party after Herbert (left the party).

In all these examples of sentences with converse pairs, (a) and (b) are paraphrases.

Consider these paraphrastic sentences:

(46) a. The dictionary is heavier than the novel.

b. The novel is lighter than the dictionary.

Although *heavy* and *light* are non-binary (gradable) antonyms, the comparative forms are converse: more heavy = less light; more light = less heavy.

(47) a. The dictionary is more expensive than the novel.

b. The novel is less expensive than the dictionary.

Factoring out the common term, *more* and *less* are converse.

There are practical **constraints on converseness**. Though we can say (48), it would be unusual to speak of the Grand Hotel as being behind a newspaper kiosk.

(48) #A newspaper kiosk is in front of the Grand Hotel.

Converseness requires the two arguments, theme and associate, to be of about the same size, rank, or importance. Talmy (1975) uses the terms **figure** and **ground** for entities of unequal rank like these. The figure, the newspaper kiosk in (48), is located with respect to the ground, the Grand Hotel in (48), but not the ground with respect to the figure.

A special kind of converseness is the use of a single term in a **symmetrical relationship**, as in (49):

(49) a. Line AB is parallel to Line CD.

　　 b. Line CD is parallel to Line AB.

This relationship can also be expressed as:

(49) c. Line AB and Line CD are parallel to each other.

or simply as:

(49) d. Line AB and Line CD are parallel.

To generalize, if X is a **symmetrical predicate**, the relationship *a X b* can also be expressed as *b X a* and *a and b X (each other)*. Here 'a' and 'b' interchange the roles of These and Associate. The features [sibling] and [spouse] are each symmetrical (C sibling-of D → D sibling-of C; E spouse-of F → F spouse-of E).

Other examples of symmetrical predicates appear in these sentences:

(50) a. The truck is similar to the bus.

　　 b. Line AB intersects Line CD.

　　 c. Hampton Road converges with Broad Street.

　　 d. Oil doesn't mix with water.

2.1.2.4. Reversive Pairs

Reversives includes pairs of verbs such as *fold/unfold*. As *unfold* depicts the reverse process of *fold*, and vice versa, one member of a reversive pair describes the reverse process of the other member. Other examples of reversives are *tie/untie, enter/exit*.

Unit 02 Questions

01 Read the passage and follow the directions. [4 points]   2018년 A형 9번

There are expressions that are ambiguous because of scope interaction between a quantifier and another quantifier or between a quantifier and a negative expression. Consider the following sentences.

(1) a. Every boy likes a girl.
　　b. Every student respects a professor.

Sentence (1a) and sentence (1b) are ambiguous because *every boy* and *every student* can have a wide scope over *a girl* and *a professor*, and *a girl* and *a professor* can have a wide scope over *every boy* and *every student*, respectively.

(2) a. Every student has not done their assignment.
　　b. I have not eaten all the cookies.

In (2a) and (2b), *every student* and *all the cookies* can have a wide scope over *not*, and *not* can have a wide scope over *every student* and *all the cookies*.

Sentence (3) below is ambiguous. Write TWO possible meanings of the sentence and state how its ambiguity can be explained in terms of scope interaction.

---

(3) Mary refused to visit every city that Tom visited.

_____

_____

_____

02 Read the passage in <A> and the sentences in <B>, and follow the directions. [4 points]

2016년 A형 10번

─┤ A ├─

There are two kinds of events or situations that predicates describe in sentences: One is telic and the other atelic. A telic event is the kind of event that has a natural finishing point and once it is completed, it cannot go on any further as shown in (1). In contrast, an atelic event does not have a natural finishing point and it can go on and on as shown in (2).

(1) a. They built the barn.
    b. They reached the summit.

(2) a. The room was sunny.
    b. The choir sang.

One of the tests for telicity is modification of the event duration by an adverbial led by *in* or *for*. Telic predicates take *in* adverbials; atelic predicates take *for* adverbials, as shown in (3-5) below. In the sentences describing a telic event in (3-4), *in* adverbials have either the event duration interpretation as in (3a) or the event delay interpretation as in (4a). In the latter interpretation, the time which elapses prior to the event is specified by *in* adverbials, and the event occurs at the end of the stated interval. Meanwhile, in the sentences describing an atelic event as in (5), *for* adverbials have the event duration interpretation only.

(3) a. They built the barn in two days.
    b. #They built the barn for two days.

(4) a. They reached the summit in half an hour.
    b. #They reached the summit for half an hour.

(5) a. #The room was sunny in an hour.
    b. The room was sunny for an hour.

It is essential to use simple past tense sentences when we do the above adverbial test; if *in* adverbials occur in future tense sentences, they can modify any type of predicate, including atelic predicates, and produce the event delay interpretation, as shown in (6a). This in turn leads to the following; certain unambiguous sentences with *in* adverbials may become ambiguous in the future tense as in (6b).

(6) a. The room will be sunny in an hour.

    b. They will build the barn in two days.

Note : # indicates that the sentence is anomalous.

B

(i) a. John walked to the park.

    b. John walked in the park.

(ii) a. John will arrive at the station in five minutes.

    b. John will eat the pizza in five minutes.

    c. John will play football in five minutes.

Based on the description in <A>, identify the type of event, telic or atelic, that each sentence of (i) in <B> describes. Then choose ONE ambiguous sentence in (ii) in <B> and explain why it is ambiguous.

03 Read the following and answer the question. [2점] 2011년 32번

Typical examples of antonymy include complementary pairs and gradable pairs. The difference between them is whether there is a scale containing the "opposites" at either end, with a midpoint between them. There are other types of antonymy as well: relational opposites and reversives. Consider *husband/wife*. The relation between *husband* and *wife* is symmetrical in the respect that if X is Y's *husband*, then Y is X's *wife*. Pairs of words displaying such a symmetrical relationship are relational opposites, and _____(1)_____ is another good example. Reversives, meanwhile, include pairs of verbs such as *fold/unfold*. As *unfold* depicts the reverse process of *fold*, and vice versa, one member of a reversive pair describes the reverse process of the other member. Another example of reversives is _____(2)_____.

Which of the following best fits in the blanks?

	(1)	(2)
①	income/outcome	tie/untie
②	teacher/student	cover/undercover
③	nominator/nominee	place/misplace
④	parent/offspring	like/dislike
⑤	trainer/trainee	enter/exit

04 The use of corpora has ever been increasing in the areas of language study and language education. This reflects the belief that language learning is essentially probabilistic and the learner's accumulated experiences with actual usage in various social contexts are essential. The data in [A], obtained from a concordance program, is particularly useful in precisely characterizing language patterns, and corpus-based dictionaries prove more helpful to language learners than traditional dictionaries.

[A]

Concordance lines for *for two weeks*

I'm planning to stay here	for two weeks,	or maybe longer. If I
at this. Try this plan	for two weeks	and see how you feel.
After you've dieted and exercised	for two weeks,	you're going to start feeling

Concordance lines for *in two weeks*

The doctor cured his pneumonia	in two weeks	using conventional treatments. His patient
diet. She lost four pounds	in two weeks	simply by cutting down on
deadline. He wrote the article	in two weeks	and went on a trip

Clauses can express different types of situations such as activities and accomplishments as exemplified below.

(1) a. John walked in the park.
    b. Mary danced in the party.

    [activities]

(2) a. John ate an apple.
    b. Mary built the house last year.

    [accomplishments]

The situations described by the sentences in (2) have an inherent terminal point beyond which they cannot continue, but those expressed by the sentences in (1) have no such terminal point. In one paragraph, first, analyze the usages of *for two weeks* and *in two weeks* in [A] above, with reference to the situation types described by the sentences they are part of, and second, explain why (3a) is grammatical but (3b) is not and how the meaning of the verb *painted* in (3c) is different from the one in (3d). [15 points]

2011년 2차 논술 4번

(3) a. John painted for two weeks.

b. *John painted in two weeks.

c. John painted the wall for two weeks.

d. John painted the wall in two weeks.

05 Read <A> and <B> and follow the directions.

A

The two sentences below stand in a semantic relation.

(1) Mary sings arias beautifully.

(2) Mary sings arias.

Whenever sentence (1) is true, sentence (2) is also true; whenever sentence (2) is false, (1) is also false. This relation is called entailment: sentence (1) entails sentence (2).

B

(a) X : John met with some of the delegates.

　　Y : John did not meet with all of the delegates.

(b) X : John does not eat vegetables.

　　Y : John does not eat broccoli.

(c) X : John regretted telling a lie.

　　Y : John told a lie.

(d) X : John was not present at the reception.

　　Y : John was absent from the reception.

(e) X : John bought a fake leather jacket.

　　Y : John bought a leather jacket.

Based on <A>, choose all the pairs in <B> in which X entails Y.

① a, b　　　　　　② a, b, d　　　　　　③ b, c, d

④ b, d　　　　　　⑤ c, d, e

06 다음 문장 (a)와 (b)에서 밑줄 친 long과 short을 유표성(markedness)과 관련하여 30자 내외의 우리말로 설명하시오.　　　　　　　　　　　　　2007년 전국 21번

(a) How <u>long</u> is the train?

(b) How <u>short</u> is the train?

---

07 다음 (a)~(f) 중에서 종속절의 의미가 사실로 전제되어 있는 문장을 모두 찾아 기호를 쓰고, 전제(presupposition)를 암시해주는 단어를 쓰시오. [4점]　　　　2006년 전국 9번

(a) Mary is angry that Jeff failed the exam.

(b) Mary is sure that Jeff failed the exam.

(c) Mary was hopeful that she convinced the principal.

(d) Mary was surprised that she convinced the principal.

(e) It is significant that Mary defended her dissertation successfully.

(f) It is possible that Mary defended her dissertation successfully.

• 기호 : _____

• 전제를 암시해 주는 단어 : _____

08 Read the passage and follow the directions.

2006년 서울/인천 6번

> The meanings of words change over time. There are some general directions in which word meanings change. They may undergo extensions in meaning when their denotation covers more than it did. For example, the word *barn* used to denote a storage place for barley but its denotation generalized to cover any kind of farm-based storage shed. Semantic reductions, on the other hand, occur when the denotation of a word shrinks. The word *starve* used to denote dying in general but now denotes dying of hunger.
>
> The connotations of words can also change. Degradations in meaning occur when a word acquires a worse connotation, while semantic elevations come about when a word takes on somewhat grander connotations over time. *Lewd* started out meaning those who were lay people as opposed to clergy. It then narrowed to mean those who were ignorant, and from there narrowed to obscene. *Chivalrous*, by contrast, was at one time synonymous with warlike; it now refers to more refined properties such as fairness, generosity, and honor.

The table below shows how the meanings of *villain, ledger,* and *manufacture* have changed over time. Fill in each cell with ONE word from the passage. [3점]

Words	Meaning Changes	Types of Change
villain	Middle English : a humble serf Current English : a scoundrel	(1)
ledger	Middle English : any book Current English : an account book	(2)
manufacture	Latin : to make by hand Current English : to make by hand or by machinery	(3)

(1) _____

(2) _____

(3) _____

09 **Read the passage and follow the directions.** 2006년 서울/인천 9번

The following two sentences have different meanings or implications:

(1) Jane managed to talk with the Dean.
(2) Jane tried to talk with the Dean.

To observe the meaning difference, we can add some expressions to the sentences:

(3) Jane managed to talk with the Dean, *but couldn't talk with him.*
(4) Jane tried to talk with the Dean, *but couldn't talk with him.*

Sentence (3) is contradictory in meaning, but sentence (4) is not. The reason for the contradiction is that the first clause implies that the complement proposition (i.e., Jane's talking with the Dean) is true, but the second clause denies it.

위 글의 내용에 근거하여 아래 문장이 의미상 자연스럽지 않은 이유를 25자 내외의 우리말로 쓰시오. [4점]

Laura managed to answer the question, and finally she answered it.

MEMO

Mentor Linguistics

멘토영어학
기출분석

Chapter 02

Pragmatics

Unit 01

Preview & Review

01 Deixis

The study of the linguistic meaning of morphemes, words, phrases, and sentences is called **semantics**. The study of **how context affects meaning**—for example, how the sentence *It's cold in here* comes to be interpreted as 'close the windows' in certain situations—is called **pragmatics**.

Pragmatics is the study of the <u>use of language in communication</u>, particularly the <u>relationships between sentences</u> and the **contexts** and **situations** in which they are used.

1.1. Pronouns and Other Deictic Expressions

One way (in which **context** can supplement a less-than-explicit sentence meaning) is through <u>words that receive part of their meaning via context and the orientation of the speaker</u>. Such words are called **deictic** and include pronouns (*she, it, I*), demonstratives (*this, that*), adverbs (*here, there, now, today*), prepositions (*behind, before*) and complex expressions involving such words (*those towers over there*).

Imagine both sets of sentences in (1) being spoken by Arnold Schwarzenegger in Venice on December 11, 2012.

(1) a. <u>Arnold Schwarzenegger</u> really likes it in Venice. <u>On December 11, 2012</u>, there was a boat parade in the canals <u>in Venice</u>. <u>On December 12, 2012</u>, an art festival will be held. <u>The art festival on December 12, 2012</u> will be extremely fun.

    b. <u>I</u> really like it in Venice. <u>Today</u>, there was a boat parade in the canals <u>here</u>. <u>Tomorrow</u> an art festival will be held. <u>It</u> will be extremely fun.

Even though <u>the referent of a pronoun</u> is lexically restricted, we need to look to <u>the context in which the pronoun is uttered</u> to determine the referent. This process is called **reference resolution**.

There are two types of context relevant for the resolution of a pronoun: **linguistic** and **situational**. <u>Linguistic context</u> is anything that has been uttered in the discourse prior to or along with the pronoun. <u>Situational context</u> is anything non-linguistic.

1.2. Pronouns and Situational Context

<u>Situational context</u> is anything non-linguistic.

Next week has a different reference when uttered <u>today</u> than <u>a month from today</u>.

Directional terms such as (2) are deictic insofar as you need to know the orientation in space of the conversational participants to know their reference.

(2) before/behind   left/right   front/back

The verbs *come* and *go* have a deictic aspect to their meaning. If someone says *A thief came into the house* versus *A thief went into the house*, you would assume the speaker to have been in the house in the first case, and not in the house in the second.

1.3. Pronouns and Linguistic Context

<u>Linguistic context</u> is anything that has been uttered in the discourse prior to or along with the pronoun.

A reflexive pronoun is a sort of pronoun that needs to receive its reference via linguistic context, and more specifically by sentence-internal linguistic context. In other words, it requires that the sentence contain another NP—an antecedent—that it can co-refer with. In English, reflexive pronouns end with -self or -selves, like himself or themselves. (3a) shows that a reflexive pronoun requires an antecedent in the sentence. (3b) shows that a reflexive pronoun must match the person, gender, and number of its antecedent.

(3) a. *Herself left.

    b. *John wrote herself a letter.

(4) a. *Himself washed John.

    b. *Jane said the boy bit herself.

Non-reflexive pronouns (which we'll refer to simply as pronouns) such as *he, she, him, her, it,* etc. also have their reference resolved via linguistic context.

(5) Sue likes pizza. She thinks it is the perfect food.

(6) Sue : I just got back from Rome.

    Mary : I've always wanted to go there!

(7) John : It seems that the man loves the woman.

    Bill : Many people think he loves her.

02 Maxims of Conversation

2.1. Grice's Maxims

Paul Grice (1975) proposes that conversations are governed by what he calls the **Cooperative Principle**: the assumption that participants in a conversation are cooperating with each other. This Cooperative Principle, in turn, consists of four conversational maxims:

(8) Maxim of Quality: Truth
- Do not say what you believe to be false.
- Do not say that for which you lack adequate evidence.

(9) Maxim of Quantity: Information
- Make your contribution as informative as is required for the current purposes of the exchange.
- Do not make your contribution more informative than is required.

(10) Maxim of Relation: Relevance
- Be relevant.

(11) Maxim of Manner: Clarity
- Avoid obscurity of expression.
- Avoid ambiguity.
- Avoid unnecessary wordiness.
- Be orderly.

Maxim of Quality states that each participant's contribution should be truthful and based on sufficient evidence. **Maxim of Quantity** states that each participant's contribution to a conversation should be no more or less informative than required. **Maxim of Relation** states that each participant's contribution should be relevant to the subject of the conversation. **Maxim of Manner** states that each participant's contribution should be expressed in a reasonably clear fashion; that is, it should not be vague, ambiguous, or excessively wordy.

These are not prescriptive rules but rather part of a strategy used by the community of language users to enable the use of **conversational implicature**. They tend to be violated only by uncooperative people.

So if John stops Mary on the street and asks her for directions to the library, and she responds "Walk up three streets and take a left," it's a successful discourse only because Mary is being cooperative (and John assumes Mary is being cooperative). In particular, John assumes that Mary is following the **Maxim of Quality**.

2.2. Implicature

2.2.1. Maxims of Conversation and Implicature

Grice pointed out that an utterance can imply a proposition (i.e., a statement) that is not part of the utterance and that does not follow as a necessary consequence of the utterance. He called such an implied statement an **implicature**.

Let us start with the following two examples of conversational implicatures:

(12) Sue : Does Mary have a boyfriend?

　　 Bill : She's been driving to Santa Barbara every weekend.

(13) John : Do you know how to change a tire?

　　 Jane : I know how to call a tow truck.

In (12), Bill asserts that Mary has been driving to Santa Barbara every weekend. But he implicates that Mary has a boyfriend (and that the boyfriend lives in Santa Barbara). In (13), Jane asserts that she knows how to call a tow truck. But she implicates that she doesn't know how to change a tire.

When one listens to everyday conversations, **implicatures** appear everywhere. It is often enough for a speaker to just hint at a certain piece of information; the addressee will interpret that information as relevant to the ongoing interaction and will infer the speaker's intention. This facilitates processing for the listener. It probably also does so for the speaker. Speakers manage to select just the relevant information for expression.

Consider the following example. John says to his wife, Mary, and she responds:

(14) John : Uncle Chester is coming over for dinner tonight.
   Mary : *I guess I'd better hide the liquor.*

Someone hearing this interchange might draw the inference that Uncle Chester has a drinking problem. In Grice's terms, we might say that Mary's utterance raises the implicature that Uncle Chester has a drinking problem.

There are three important points to note about this example. First, the implicature is not part of Mary's utterance. Second, the implicature does not follow as a necessary consequence of Mary's utterance. (A necessary consequence of an utterance is called an entailment and will be covered in the chapter on semantics.) Third, it is possible for an utterance to raise more than one implicature, or to raise different implicatures if uttered in different contexts. Thus, implicatures are heavily dependent upon the context of an utterance, including the participants.

A maxim is violated when a speaker chooses to be uncooperative for whatever reason. A maxim is obeyed in a literal discourse devoid of implicature, as in (15).

(15) Dad : Very nice girl. What do you think, Hon?
   Mom : Not really.

Implicatures can arise when a maxim is flouted. To flout a maxim is to choose not to follow that maxim in order to implicate something.

On the other hand, the discourse in (16) is an example of the **Maxim of Relevance** being **flout**ed.

(16) Dad : Very nice girl. What do you think, Hon?
　　　Mom : The turkey sure was moist.

Because Mom knows that the quality of the turkey isn't relevant to being a "very nice girl"—and because Dad is assuming that Mom knows it, too—Dad can pick up on the fact that Mom is implicating that she doesn't like the girl.

03 Speech Acts

Austin (1962, 1975) claimed that all utterances, in addition to meaning whatever they mean, perform specific acts via the communicative force of an utterance. Furthermore, he introduced a threefold distinction among the acts one simultaneously performs when saying something.

(17) **Three facets of a speech act**
   a. Locutionary act : the production of a meaningful linguistic expression.
   b. Illocutionary act : the action intended to be performed by a speaker in uttering a linguistic expression, by virtue of the conventional force associated with it, either explicitly or implicitly.
   c. Perlocutionary act : the bringing about of consequences or effects on the audience through the uttering of a linguistic expression, such consequences or effects being special to the circumstances of the utterance.

A **locutionary act** is the basic act of speaking, which itself consists of three related subacts. They are (i) a **phonic act** of producing an utterance-inscription, (ii) a **phatic act** of composing a particular linguistic expression in a particular language, and (iii) a **rhetic act** of contextualizing the utterance-inscription.

In other words, the first of these three subacts is concerned with the physical act of making a certain sequence of vocal sounds (in the case of spoken language) or a set of written symbols (in the case written language). The second refers to the act of constructing a well-formed string of sounds/symbols, be it a word, phrase or sentence, in a particular language. The third subact is responsible for tasks such as assigning reference, resolving deixis, and disambiguating the utterance-inscription lexically and/or grammatically. These three subacts correspond broadly to the three distinct levels and modes of explanation in linguistic theory, namely, phonetics/phonology, morphology/syntax, and semantics/pragmatics.

When we say something, we usually say it with some purpose in mind. This is the **illocutionary act**. In other words, an illocutionary act refers to the type of function the speaker intends to fulfil, or the type of action the speaker intends to accomplish in the course of producing an utterance. It is an act defined within a system of social conventions. In short, it is an act accomplished in speaking.

Examples of illocutionary acts include accusing, apologizing, blaming, congratulating, giving permission, joking, nagging, naming, promising, ordering, refusing, swearing, and thanking. The functions or actions just mentioned are also commonly referred to as the **illocutionary force** or **point** of the utterance. Indeed, the term 'speech act' in its narrow sense is often taken to refer specifically to illocutionary acts.

The same linguistic expression can be used to carry out a wide variety of different speech acts, so that the same locutionary act can count as having different illocutionary forced in different contexts. Depending on the circumstances, one may utter (18) below to make a threat, to issue a warning or to give an explanation.

(18) The gun is loaded.

Conversely, the same speech act can be performed by different linguistic expressions, or the same illocutionary force can be realized by means of different locutionary acts. The utterance in (19), for example, illustrate different ways of carrying out the same speech act of requiring.

(19) (At ticket office in railway station)
    a. A day return ticket to Oxford, please.
    b. Can I have a day return ticket to Oxford, please?
    c. I'd like a day return ticket to Oxford.

Finally, a **perlocutionary act** concerns the effect an utterance may have on the addressee. A perlocution is the act by which the illocution produces a certain effect in or exerts a certain influence on the addressee. A perlocutionary act represents a consequence or by-product of speaking, whether intentional or not. It is therefore an act of performed by speaking.

For example, in an armed bank robbery, a robber may utter (18) to get the cashier to open the safe. This effect of the act performed by speaking is also generally known as the **perlocutionary effect**.

While there are unclear cases, the main differences between illocutions and perlocutions can be summed up as follows. In the first place, illocutionary acts are intended by the speaker, while perlocutionary effects are not always intended by him or her. Secondly, illocutionary acts are under the speaker's full control, while perlocutionary effects are not under his or her control. Thirdly, if illocutionary acts are evident, they become evident as the utterance is made, while perlocutionary effects are usually not evident until after the utterance has been made. Fourthly, illocutionary acts are more, while perlocutionary effects are less conventionally tied to linguistics forms.

Part

05

04 Overview

4.1. Grice's Maxims

(1) Maxim of Quality: Truth
- Do not say what you believe to be false.
- Do not say that for which you lack adequate evidence.

(2) Maxim of Quantity: Information
- Make your contribution as informative as is required for the current purposes of the exchange.
- Do not make your contribution more informative than is required.

(3) Maxim of Relation: Relevance
- Be relevant.

(4) Maxim of Manner: Clarity
- Avoid obscurity of expression.
- Avoid ambiguity.
- Avoid unnecessary wordiness.
- Be orderly.

4.2. Implicature

Grice (1972) pointed out that an utterance can imply a proposition (i.e., a statement) that is not part of the utterance and that does not follow as a necessary consequence of the utterance. He called such an implied statement an **implicature**.

4.3. Three Facets of a Speech Act

a. **Locutionary act** : the production of a meaningful linguistic expression.

b. **Illocutionary act** : the action intended to be performed by a speaker in uttering a linguistic expression, by virtue of the conventional force associated with it, either explicitly or implicitly.

c. **Perlocutionary act** : the bringing about of consequences or effects on the audience through the uttering of a linguistic expression, such consequences or effects being special to the circumstances of the utterance.

4.4. Main Differences Between Illocutions and Perlocutions

1) Illocutionary acts are intended by the speaker, while perlocutionary effects are not always intended by him or her.

2) Illocutionary acts are under the speaker's full control, while perlocutionary effects are not under his or her control.

3) If illocutionary acts are evident, they become evident as the utterance is made, while perlocutionary effects are usually not evident until after the utterance has been made.

4) Illocutionary acts are more, while perlocutionary effects are less conventionally tied to linguistics forms.

Unit 02 Questions

Answer Key p.511

01 Read the passage in <A> and the interaction in <B>, and follow the directions. [4 points]

2020년 A형 5번

┤ A ├

Different words and phrases can be used to organize the structure and manage the flow of ongoing conversations. Language elements of this function include different types such as conjunctions, cataphoric words, hedges, and back channel cues. Conjunctions join words, phrases, or clauses together. Cataphoric words refer forward to other words which will be used later in the conversation. Hedges are words or phrases employed not to express the truth of a statement categorically, and back channel cues indicate that one is paying attention to his or her interlocutor's speech. As using these types of language is associated with discourse and strategic competence, the ability to use them in an effective way constitutes part of communicative competence.

┤ B ├

(Two students are doing a task on finding differences between each other's pictures without showing them to each other.)

S1 : Do you see any people in your picture?

S2 : I have a man. He is tall.

S1 : Is he the only person?

S2 : I also have a woman in my picture.

S1 : There are two in mine, too. What are they doing?

S2 : They are sitting together.

S1 : That's one difference. They are standing in mine.

S2 : What is the woman wearing?

S1 : She is wearing a jacket.

S2 : What color is it?

S1 : It's black.

S2 : That is the same in my picture.

S1 : Oh, wait, on her jacket, I found this. There is a letter P on it.

S2 : I also see a P on her jacket in my picture.

S1 : What about the man? What is he wearing?

S2 : He is in a blue coat. It is sort of neat.

S1 : The man's coat is brown in mine. That's another difference.

Note : S = student

Identify TWO types among those mentioned in <A> that are used in <B>. Then, provide evidence for each identified type from <B>.

_____

_____

_____

_____

_____

02 Read the passages and follow the directions. [2 points]

---| A |---

Non-verbal communication is an important aspect of intercultural communication. It includes the following categories, which also apply to cultural norms in public space. First, there is kinesics, which is the use of gestures or body language. A second category is oculesics, which refers to eye contact and eye movement. Eyes can provide signals as to one's mood, such as being interested, bored, empathetic, or annoyed. Third, there is proxemics, which relates to physical distance between interlocutors (and other people in public spaces). A fourth category is kinesthetics (also called haptics), meaning touching or making physical contact with someone. Across cultures, norms relating to these categories can vary significantly, which can lead to misunderstandings or inappropriate behavior in cross-cultural situations.

---| B |---

A group of students in Ms. Lee's school won a regional English contest and they received an all-expense-paid trip to Seattle as a reward. In preparation, Ms. Lee tutored them on how to be polite, which included lessons comparing cultural norms and non-verbal communication in Korea and America. However, the following event occurred.

After arriving in Seattle, they were hungry, so they asked their shuttle bus driver to stop at the nearest fast food restaurant, but it was busy and the line was long. A student, Gyumin, led the group through the line. As the line moved, so did Gyumin, inching ever so closer to the front. He was excited—this was his first time in a restaurant abroad—and he was eager to order his meal. However, Ms. Lee noticed something recurring. Gyumin was closely following a middle-aged American man in line, and as the line moved forward, Ms. Lee saw that the man frequently turned his head to the side and, with a scrunched forehead, gazed down at Gyumin for a moment as if to tell him something. Ms. Lee quietly pulled Gyumin aside and the following exchange occurred:

T : Gyumin, do you remember what I taught you about lining up?

S : You mean not to bump into anyone? I didn't!

T : No, no, not that. Rather, do you remember the arm's length rule?

S : Oh, that!

T : It's okay. Just remember it for next time. We want to be polite while we are here.

S : Okay. I got it.

Note : T = teacher, S = student

Given the information in <A>, write the ONE most appropriate category that Gyumin violated in <B> in regards to cultural norms in America.

03 Read the conversation between a teacher and a student and follow the directions. [2 points]

2016년 A형 8번

(*Sujin, who is in an exchange programme in England, is having a conversation with her teacher, Ms. Connor.*)

Sujin : Hi, how're you doing?

Ms. Connor : I'm doing well. Are you alright?

Sujin : Yes. Um ... I have fun ... but still intimidated by talking to people in English.

Ms. Connor : What's the problem?

Sujin : I have my British friend Kate in my class. Yesterday, she told me, "I like your jacket! Really unusual. Great on you." So I said, "Really? I don't think so." I felt she was rather embarrassed and something was wrong.

Ms. Connor : Oh, you should just say, "Thank you" in that situation. Remember, cultural norms involving language use differ from country to country. Don't worry, you're on the right track. It's a normal process of learning in a new culture.

Sujin : Oh, I see. I should have understood her and said, "Thanks." OK, thank you very much.

Complete the comments by filling in ① with TWO words and by filling in ② with ONE word. Write your answers in the correct order.

Sujin experienced misunderstanding as she performed a ___①___ of compliment response in an interaction with her British friend. Since cultures differ from one another and language is inextricably interwoven with culture, cultural knowledge of language use in context plays a crucial role in cross-cultural communication. This entails the concept of ___②___ competence, one of the core components of communicative competence, which enables learners to use the L2 in socioculturally appropriate ways.

---

04 Read <A> and <B> and answer the question.

┤ A ├

The Maxim of Informativeness, also called the Maxim of Quantity, has two clauses: "Make your contribution as informative as is required (for the current purposes of the exchange)," and "Do not make your contribution more informative than is required." The first clause, requiring the speaker to give enough information, is identified as the basis of a wide range of implicatures, known as **scalar implicatures**. Scalar implicatures typically arise with terms denoting quantities or degrees of attributes which can be graded on some scale of informative strength. With a scalar implicature, it is assumed that the speaker obeys the Maxim of Informativeness and makes the strongest statement consistent with what he or she knows or believes to be the case. The speaker's use of an expression on an information strength scale implicates the negation of any higher term on the same scale.

┤ B ├

Cases	Implicatures
a. The light in Peter's office is on.	Peter is in his office.
b. Two or three did very well.	Not more than two or three did very well.
c. Some of the faculty left yesterday's guest lecture before it ended.	The lecture didn't go well.
d. It's fairly warm outside.	It isn't hot outside.

Which of the following lists all and only the cases in <B> that correctly show the scalar implicatures described in <A>?

① a, b   ② a, d   ③ b, c

④ b, d   ⑤ c, d

05 Read \<A\> and \<B\> and answer the question.　　　2012년 34번

---| A |---

If I utter the clause *Tom has arrived* with the intention of thereby committing myself to the truth of the proposition "Tom has arrived," I have uttered it with illocutionary force of statement. If I say *Sit down* with the intention of telling you to sit down, my utterance has the illocutionary force of a directive.

A natural utterance of (1) would be both a statement and a promise, though the promise is of course more important, more salient than the statement.

(1) I promise to return the key tomorrow.

The promise force is called primary, and the statement second. Making the statement can be regarded as simply the means of making the promise. I make a promise by stating that I do, and the statement is true simply by virtue of my uttering the clause with the intention of making a promise.

Illocutionary force is very often conveyed indirectly rather than directly. Consider (2).

(2) Do you know what time it is?

A likely context for this (not the only possible one of course) is where I don't know the time, want to know the time, and believe you may well be able to tell me. In this context it would indirectly convey "What time is it?" This is why it would be thoroughly uncooperative in such a context for you to respond merely with *Yes*. *Yes* would answer the question that is actually asked, but not the one that I in fact want to have answered.

---| B |---

a. I declare the meeting open. (uttered to people present in the meeting)
b. I'll declare the meeting open soon. (uttered to people chatting before the meeting begins)
c. Can you turn the light on? (uttered to someone who is close to the light)
d. Get well soon. (uttered to someone who is in the hospital)

Which of the following lists all and only utterances in \<B\> that most probably have primary, indirect illocutionary force?

① a, b, d　　　② a, c　　　③ b, c　　　④ b, c, d　　　⑤ c, d

06 Read <A> and <B> and follow the directions.

| A |

The reference of certain expressions relies entirely on the context of the utterance and can only be understood in light of these circumstances. This aspect is known as deixis. The first and second person pronouns are always deictic because their reference is entirely dependent on context. You must know who the speaker and listener are to interpret them. Time and place adverbials can also serve as deictic expressions. They should sometimes undergo deictic shifting to fit into the speaker and listener perspective under a new situation.

| B |

The sentences in (2) are John's utterances. At 3 p.m. on the same day, you as the speaker are reporting to a third party what John said.

(1) This morning on the other side of the street, John told me that

_____.

(2) a. Mary met the man right here.

 b. There was a big sale yesterday.

 c. The car was parked on the other side of the street.

 d. Tom met Mary five years ago.

 e. Mary will come in an hour.

 f. I met Mary several days ago.

Choose all the sentences in (2) that should undergo deictic shifting when they are put verbatim in the blank.

① a, c, e, f

② a, e, d

③ b, c, d, f

④ b, d, e

⑤ c, d, f

07 Read the following and answer the question. [1.5점]

It has been argued that there are three kinds of speech acts: locutionary act, illocutionary act, and perlocutionary act. A(n) ___(1)___ act is performed to convey the speaker's intent in uttering a sentence (e.g. to praise, to criticize, to warn, to threaten, etc.). In the dialog below, the speaker can express his/her intention in the given situation without manifesting it literally.

W : Isn't it too cold in here?
M : (Near the stove) I'll turn on the stove.
W : Thank you.
M : A pleasure of mine.

Information that is conveyed implicitly in a conversation is referred to as conversational implicature. This can be accounted for in terms of a conversational principle called the Co-operative Principle. In relation to this principle, there are maxims assumed to ensure the facilitation of conversational interactions between hearer and speaker: the maxim of quantity, the maxim of quality, the maxim of relation, and the maxim of manner. In the above dialogue the woman didn't make a request explicitly, but the man understood her words as a request and turned on the stove. How this was possible can be accounted for in terms of the maxim of ___(2)___.

Which of the following best fits in the blanks above?

(1)	(2)
① illocutionary	quantity
② illocutionary	relation
③ locutionary	manner
④ perlocutionary	quality
⑤ perlocutionary	manner

08 Read the passage and follow the directions. [4점]

2008년 서울/인천 18번

The problem posed by indirect speech acts is the problem of how it is possible for the speaker to say one thing and mean that but also to mean something else. The problem is made more complicated by the fact that some sentences seem almost to be conventionally used as indirect requests. For a sentence like *Can you pass me the salt?*, it takes some ingenuity to imagine a situation in which its utterance would not be a (①).

Here is a short list of some of the sentences that could quite standardly be used to make requests and other directives such as orders. These sentences naturally tend to group themselves into certain categories.

Group 1 Sentences concerning the hearer's ability to do something:

Can you pass me the salt?

Are you able to reach the book on the top shelf?

Group 2 Sentences concerning the speaker's wish or want that the hearer will do something:

I would like you to go now.

I would appreciate it if you would get off my foot.

Group 3 Sentences concerning the (②) doing something:

Would you kindly get off my foot?

Aren't you going to eat your cereal?

Group 4 Sentences concerning the hearer's desire or willingness to do something:

Would you be willing to do this for me?

(③ _____)

Group 5 Sentences concerning reasons for doing something:

It might help if you shut up.

It would be a good idea if you left town.

Fill in blanks ① and ② with the most appropriate word from the passage. Change the word form if necessary. For blank ③, write one example sentence that includes *be convenient*.

09 Read passage <A> and <B>. Given the rough characterization of speech acts in passage <B>, fill in the blanks with the most appropriate information taken from passage <A>. [4점]　　2007년 서울/인천 18번

A

Suppose that I am an American soldier in the Second World War and that I am captured by Italian troops. And suppose that I wish to get these troops to believe that I am a German officer in order to get them to release me. What I would like to do is to tell them in German or Italian that I am a German officer. But let us suppose I don't know enough German or Italian to do that. So I, as it were, attempt to put on a show of telling them that I am a German officer by reciting those few bits of German that I know, trusting that they don't know enough German to see through my plan. Let us suppose I know only one line of German, which I remember from a poem I had to memorize in a high-school German course. Therefore I, a captured American, address my Italian captors with the following sentence: 'Kennst du das Land, wo die Zitromen blühen?' In saying this sentence, I intend my captors to believe that what I mean is 'I am a German officer.' and I intend to produce this effect by means of their recognition of my intention. Nonetheless, the words I utter mean 'Do you know the land where the lemon tree bloom?'

B

An utterance act is simply an act of uttering sounds, syllables, words, phrases, and sentences from a language. A locutionary act is an act of saying the propositional content of an utterance, while an illocutionary act is characterized as an act performed in saying something.

Utterance Act:　　The author utters to his Italian captors, "Kennst du das Land, wo die Zitromen blühen?"

Locutionary Act:　He says to them, "＿＿＿＿＿＿＿①＿＿＿＿＿＿＿"

Illocutionary Act:　He suggests that ＿＿＿＿＿＿＿②＿＿＿＿＿＿＿.

① ＿＿＿＿＿＿＿＿＿＿＿＿＿＿＿＿＿＿＿＿＿＿＿＿＿＿＿＿＿＿＿＿＿＿

② ＿＿＿＿＿＿＿＿＿＿＿＿＿＿＿＿＿＿＿＿＿＿＿＿＿＿＿＿＿＿＿＿＿＿

10 Read the passage and follow the directions.

The following text is superficially cohesive but makes no sense and is therefore not _____(1)_____:

A puppy is sitting on a stool. A stool is often made of wood. Carpenters work with wood. A piece of wood can be bought from a lumber store.

In this text, the relationships between propositions are overtly signalled by means of _____(2)_____ repetition, yet the propositions are not logically connected in terms of how we perceive the world. On the other hand, we can provide a good example of a short text that seemingly has no overt cohesive devices yet makes perfect sense:

The picnic was ruined. No one remembered to bring a corkscrew.

This text is not _____(3)_____ but it is coherent. Coherence is created due to the fact that the writer and the reader share the knowledge that relates corkscrews to wine bottles and wine to picnics. The _____(4)_____ knowledge in this case is imperative for the perception of coherence in the text.

Fill in each blank with the most suitable word from the box below. [4점]

propositional	extratextuen	coherent	creative
lexical	imperative	cohesive	

(1) _____

(2) _____

(3) _____

(4) _____

11 <A>의 밑줄 친 부분에 해당하는 발화(utterance)의 예를 <B>의 밑줄 친 ①~④에서 모두 찾아 번호를 쓰시오. [2점] 2006년 전국 5번

─┤ A ├─

An organizational pattern recurrent in conversation is that of two adjacent utterances, which are produced by different speakers, and are related to each other in such a way that they form a pair type. They are called an adjacency pair. 'Question-answer', 'greeting-greeting', and 'offer-acceptance/refusal' are some examples of adjacency pairs. In adjacency pairs, utterances are related so that a particular first pair part sets up the expectation of a particular second pair part. For example, a 'question' expects a 'reply' and they form a pair type; an 'offer' expects an 'accept' or a 'decline', and each of the latter forms a pair type with the former. So strong is this expectation that if the second pair part does not occur, its absence will be noticeable and noticed by participants.

─┤ B ├─

(1) Woman : Hi, Annie.

Mother : Annie, ① didn't you hear someone say hello to you?

Woman : Oh, that's okay, she smiled hello.

Mother : You know you're supposed to greet someone, don't you, Annie?

Annie : (hangs head) Hello.

(2) Jack : Well, I really must go now.

Amy: Where are you going?

Jack: Oh, I have to check out a book from the library.

Amy: ② That's nice. I'll come with you.

Jack: (looks a bit uncomfortable) ③ Oh, er... well, actually, I have to go to the post office, first.

(3) Wife : My mother wants us to visit her this weekend.

Husband: (reading the newspaper) England is going to the World Cup!

Wife : ④ Did you hear me?

Husband : Sorry, Dear. What was that?

Wife : You never listen to me!

12 Read the passage and follow the directions. [3점] 2004년 서울/인천 3번

When one listens to everyday conversations, implicatures appear everywhere. It is often enough for a speaker to just hint at a certain piece of information; the addressee will interpret that information as relevant to the ongoing interaction and will infer the speaker's intention. This facilitates processing for the listener. It probably also does so for the speaker. Speakers manage to select just the relevant information for expression.

A blatant failure to respect a conversational maxim can convey some intention in a marked way. Here is an example of such exploitation: Arnold and Betty jointly attend a harpsichord performance. When it is over, the following conversation ensues.

Arnold : How did you like it?

Betty : It was a nice piano recital.

Betty's answer violates the maxim of quality, since she knows perfectly well that the instrument was a harpsichord. This is in fact mutually known. Arnold therefore infers that Betty is flouting a maxim, and, on the assumption that Betty is cooperative, Arnold will try to find out what Betty intended to convey. The most likely interpretation here is that the performer played the harpsichord as if it were a piano—i.e., without real feel for the instrument. A less likely but possible interpretation is that the harpsichord was such an awful make that it sounded like a piano. Which interpretation _____. There is no standard or conversational way to infer the intention in this case of flouting a maxim. A speaker who exploits a maxim, for instance, to produce irony, as in the above example, must estimate whether enough contextual conditions are fulfilled in order for the addressed interlocutor to make the inference. It should further be noticed that Betty's remark does not convey the same information that would have been conveyed if she had said *The performer played without real feel for the instrument.* That would not have been ironical; the breaking of the maxim creates the special effect of irony.

Fill in the blank with ALL AND ONLY the words and phrases in the box.

Arnold, the, mutually, context, depends, infer from, will, Betty's answer, upon, known

13 Read the passage and follow the directions. [3점]   2004년 서울/인천 5번

Indirectness itself does not reflect powerlessness. It is easy to think of situations where indirectness is the prerogative of those in power. For example, a wealthy couple who know that their servants will do their bidding need not give direct orders, but can simply state wishes: The woman of the house says, "It's chilly in here," and the servant sets about raising the temperature. The man of the house says, "It's dinner time," and the servant sees about having dinner served. Perhaps the ultimate indirectness is _____: The hostess rings a bell and the maid brings the next course; or a parent enters the room where children are misbehaving and stands with hands on hips, and the children immediately stop what they're doing.

Fill in the blank in 10 words or so, including ALL the words in the box. You may change their forms, if necessary.

all, something, anything, someone, get, without, say

14 다음 대화와 글을 읽고, 밑줄 그은 부분에 알맞은 단어를 쓰시오.

(during a coffee break at work)

Tony : I have two tickets for the theater tonight.
Susan : Good for you. What are you going to see?
Tony : *Measure for Measure.*
Susan : Interesting play. Hope you enjoy it.
Tony : Oh, so you're busy tonight.

 In this conversation, Susan, deliberately or otherwise, takes Tony's utterance as a statement of fact, rather than a(n) _____(1)_____ . The interlocutors are either native speakers of English or competent users of the language. It is not at the level of grammar or vocabulary that they are not able to achieve their intention or purpose of communication, but at the _____(2)_____ level. Susan misunderstood the _____(3)_____ force of the utterance within the context. It is clear from this example that interpreting discourse, and thus establishing _____(4)_____ , is a matter of readers and listeners using their linguistic knowledge to relate the discourse world to entities, events, and states of affairs beyond the text itself.

(1) _____

(2) _____

(3) _____

(4) _____

MEN
TOR

Mentor Linguistics

멘토영어학
기출분석

MEN
TOR

Mentor Linguistics

멘토영어학
기출분석

Chapter 01

Sociolinguistics

Preview & Review

01 Language in Use

1.1. An Introduction to Socioliguistics

Sociolinguists study the relationship between language and society. They are interested in explaining why we speak differently in different social contexts, and they are concerned with identifying the social functions of language and the ways it is used to convey social meaning.

1.2. Styles or Registers

Most speakers of a language speak one way with friends, another on a job interview or presenting a report in class, another talking to small children, another with their parents, and so on. These "situation dialects" are called **styles**, or **registers**.

Nearly everybody has at least an **informal** and a **formal style**. In an **informal style**, the rules of contraction are used more often, the syntactic rules of negation and agreement may be altered, and many words are used that do not occur in the **formal style**.

The use of **styles** is often a means of identification with a particular group (e.g., family, gang, church, team), or a means of excluding groups believed to be hostile or undesirable (cops, teachers, parents).

1.3. Slang

One mark of an **informal style** is the frequent occurrence of **slang**. **Slang** is something that nearly everyone uses and recognizes, but nobody can define precisely. It is more metaphorical, playful, elliptical, vivid, and shorter-lived than **ordinary language**.

The use of slang has introduced many new words into the language by recombining old words into new meanings. *Spaced out*, *right on*, *hang-up*, *drill down*, and *rip-off* have all gained a degree of acceptance.

Slang also introduces entirely new words such as *barf*, *flub*, *hoodie*, and *dis*.

Finally, slang often consists of ascribing entirely new meanings to old words. *Rave* has broadened its meaning to 'an all-night dance party,' where *ecstasy* (slang for a kind of drug) is taken to provoke wakefulness; *crib* refers to one's home and *posse* to one's cohorts. *Weed* and *pot* widened their meaning to 'marijuana'; *pig* and *fuzz* are derogatory terms for 'police officer'; *rap*, *cool*, *dig*, *stoned*, *split*, and *suck* have all extended their semantic domains.

1.4. Jargon and Argot

Practically every conceivable science, profession, trade, and occupation uses specific slang terms called **jargon**, or **argot**.

Linguistic jargon, some of which is used in this book, consists of terms such as *phoneme*, *morpheme*, *case*, *lexicon*, *phrase structure rule*, *X-bar schema*, and so on.

Part of the reason for specialized terminology is for clarity of communication, but part is also for speakers to identify themselves with persons with whom they share interests.

1.5. Taboo

How can language be filthy? In fact, how can it be clean? The filth or beauty of language must be in the ear of the listener, or in the collective ear of society.

Nothing about a particular string of sounds makes it intrinsically clean or dirty, ugly or beautiful. If you say that you pricked your finger when sewing, no one would raise an eyebrow, but if you refer to your professor as a prick, the judge quoted previously would undoubtedly censure this "dirty" word.

Part

06

You know the obscene words of your language, and you know the social situations in which they are desirable, acceptable, forbidden, and downright dangerous to utter. This is true of all speakers of all languages. All societies have their taboo words. (Taboo is a Tongan word meaning 'forbidden.') People everywhere seem to have a need for undeleted expletives to express their emotions or attitudes.

1.6. Euphemisms

The existence of taboo words and ideas motivates the creation of euphemisms. A euphemism is a word or phrase that replaces a taboo word or serves to avoid frightening or unpleasant subjects. In many societies, because death is feared, there are many euphemisms related to this subject. People are less apt to die and more apt to pass on or pass away. Those who take care of your loved ones who have passed away are more likely to be funeral directors than morticians or undertakers. And then there's feminine protection.

02 Language and Sexism

It's clear that language reflects sexism. It reflects any societal attitude, positive or negative; languages are infinitely flexible and expressive. But is language itself amoral and neutral? Or is there something about language, or a particular language, that abets sexism? Before we attempt to answer that question, let's look more deeply into the subject, using English as the illustrative language.

Marked and Unmarked Forms

There is an asymmetry between male and female terms in many languages in which there are male/female pairs of words. The male form is generally unmarked and the female term is created by adding a bound morpheme. We have many such examples in English:

(1) **Male**   **Female**

    heir   heir**ess**

    major   major**ette**

    hero   hero**ine**

    Robert   Robert**a**

    equestrian   equestri**enne**

    aviator   aviat**rix**

When referring in general to the profession of acting, or flying, or riding horseback, the unmarked terms *actor, aviator,* and *equestrian* are used. The marked terms are used to emphasize the female gender. (A rare exception to this is the unmarked word *widow* for a woman with a deceased husband but *widower* for a man with a deceased wife.)

Moreover, the unmarked third person pronoun in English is male (*he, him, his*). *Everybody had better pay **his** fee next time* allows for the clients to be male or female, but *Everybody had better pay **her** fee next time* presupposes a female client. While there has been some attempt to neutralize the pronoun by using *they*, as in *Every teenager loves **their** first car*, most teachers find this objectionable and it is unlikely to become the standard. Other attempts to find a suitable genderless third person pronoun have produced such attempts as *e, hesh, po, tey, co, jhe, ve, xe, he'er, thon,* and *na,* none of which speakers have the least inclination to adopt, and it appears likely that *he* and *she* are going to be with us for a while.

With women occupying more and varied roles in society (from combat military to "Wichita Linemen"), many of the marked female forms have been replaced by the male forms, which are used to refer to either sex. Thus women, as well as men, are authors, actors, poets, heroes, heirs, postal carriers, firefighters, and police officers. Women, however, remain countesses, duchesses, and princesses, if they are among this small group of female aristocrats.

Unit

02

Questions

Answer Key p.513

01 Read the dialogue and fill in both blanks with the ONE most appropriate word. (Use the SAME word in both blanks.) [2 points]　　2018년 A형 8번

S : Ms. Lee, can I ask you a question?

T : Sure, go ahead.

S : I went over your feedback on my essay, and I really appreciate it. You pointed out the expression "die" could be revised to "pass away."

T : Yes, I did.

S : I don't understand the difference between the two expressions. As far as I understand, they have the same meaning.

T : Oh, I see. That's actually an example of a(n) _____.

S : Hmm ....

T : Let me make it clearer with another example. How do you think someone would feel if they were called "poor"?

S : Well, they may feel bad.

T : Okay, what about "less privileged"?

S : Oh, I understand your point. Two words or expressions may mean the same thing, but we may have different feelings and attitudes about them.

T : That's the point. A(n) _____ is a polite word or expression that you use instead of a more direct one, to avoid shocking or upsetting someone.

S : Interesting!

T : Good.

S : Thank you, Ms. Lee. Your feedback is always helpful.

Note : T＝teacher, S＝student

02 Read the passage and follow the directions.

2005년 서울/인천 14~15번

Trying to avoid using the pronoun *he* for both sexes, we can wear ourselves and our readers out writing *he or she* (or *she or he*) all the time. Some reference books use *s/he*, which is clumsy and cannot be read aloud. Other writers see as the way ahead using *they, them,* and *their* as unisex words. The grammatical objection is that the singular *nobody* conflicts with the plural *they*. In spite of this, *they* and *their* are taking on a plural or singular sense as required. This is not new. It dates back to the nineteenth century, when Thackeray was writing "Nobody prevents you, do *they*?"

At the same time, this elastic attitude towards singular and plural upsets some people a great deal. It may be possible to recast a sentence to avoid it: the example "Nobody has taken *their* seat yet" could be rewritten "_____," although the meaning is not quite the same.

There is no universally acceptable way out of this dilemma. But probably the most popular choice among speakers of English is to use the plural forms *they, them,* and *their* as singular unisex words. In a conversation on the BBC, Antonia Byatt, a Booker prizewinner, and Bryan Magee agreed this is the best solution to the problem. <u>So you will be in good company.</u>

---

(1) Fill in the blank with a sentence beginning with "People." [2점]

People _____

_____

(2) Paraphrase So you will be in good company using approximately 25 words. Include "because" in your paraphrase. [3점]

_____

_____

_____

Mentor Linguistics
멘토영어학
기출분석

Answer Key

Chapter **01** Raising & Control Constructions

01 boring, pleasant, tough

---

02 **Version 1** In the case of 'sure', subject to subject raising is possible: *John is sure to pass the test.*; however, in the case of 'probable' the raising is not possible: **John is probable to pass the test.*

Version 2 In the sentence with the predicative adjective 'sure', subject to subject raising is permissible: *John is sure to pass the test.* In contrast, subject raising is not allowed with the adjective 'probable': **John is probable to pass the test.*

---

03 (1) non-finite clause
(2) Bill is believed to be taller than him.
(3) Believed in (6) and (7) cannot allow an NP like Bill to immediately follow it.

---

04 ①

---

05 ⑤

---

06 The sentences containing an unaccusative verb are (iii) and (v) since they allow *there*-inversion as follows: (iii) *There remained several students in the school library* / (v) *There arose several complications in the medical experiment.*

---

07 First, PRO in (ia) is non-arbitrary and it is obligatory control. PRO (ib) is arbitrary. Second, in (ii), control constructions are sentence (a) and sentence (c). (iia) is object control and (iic) is subject control.

Chapter 02 Complements & Adjuncts

01

(1) (A) complement
   (B) adjunct
(2) • the modifier : on the stool
   • the modified heads : read, book

02

• 비문법적인 문장의 기호 : (c)
• 비문법적인 이유 :
  Version 1 A complement and an adjunct cannot be conjoined.
  Version 2 Complements cannot conjoin with adjuncts (in terms of parallelism in coordination).

---

03 ②

---

04 ④

05

NPs, the NP with a Complement + an Adjunct in (ia) is grammatical but the NP with an Adjunct + a Complement in (ib) is ungrammatical.
(i) a. a contender for the PGA title with a knee injury.
   b. *a contender with a knee injury for the PGA title.
As for a pair of wh-questions, the wh-phrase within the PP Adjunct in (iia) cannot be preposed; in contrast, the wh-phrase within the PP Complement in (iib) can.
(ii) a. *What part (kind) of injury is he a contender with?
   b. What title is he a contender for?

---

06 complement

Chapter 03 Constituency

01

Version 1

In (B1), the underlined sequence cannot move as a unit: *The sculpture into the museum, the people can move. By contrast, the underlined sequence in (B2) moves as a unit in forming the construction: The sculpture from the museum, the people can see.

Version 2

In ① the NP 'the sculpture' and the PP 'into the museum' are separate constituents, and then they can move independently. But the whole phrase 'the sculpture into the museum' is not a constituent, and it cannot move.

Ex) a. Into the museum, the people can move the sculpture.

b. The sculpture, the people can move into the museum.

c. *The sculpture into the museum, the people can move.

In contrast, in ② the whole phrase 'the sculpture from the museum' is a syntactic unit, and it can move together. But the NP and the PP cannot move separately.

Ex) a. *From the museum, the people can see the sculpture.

b. *The sculpture, the people can see from the museum.

c. The sculpture from the museum, the people can see.

 POINT

Movement Test

If we can move a particular string of words in a sentence from one position to another, then it behaves as a constituent.

Substitution Test (Replacement)

(1) A particular string of words is a constituent if it can be substituted by a suitable proform.

(2) If you can replace a group of words with a single word then we know that group forms a constituent.

02

⑤

03   The underlined part the reviewers of Bill's new book in (2) qualifies as a constituent. It is an NP. In (2), the underlined part can be replaced by the pronoun *them,* as in 'Call them in a week'. The underlined part also can be moved in passivization: 'Let the viewers of Bill's new book be called in a week'. And the underlined part in (3), *young composers of jazz* is a syntactic constituent which is an N-bar because it can be substituted by the pro-form *one*: The music festival was crowded with the ones from Asia.

04   First, the extraposed CP in (ii) in \<B\> is adjoined to TP. Second, the preposing in (iii) is ungrammatical. In (ii) 'work with John' is a VP constituent and the extraposed CP 'who knew him' from the Subject position is adjoined to TP; in (iii) the preposed phrase 'Work with John who knew him' is not a (single) constituent. Therefore, preposing the whole phrase in (iii) results in ungrammaticality.

05   specifier

06   Sentence (i) is ungrammatical. The AdvP 'persuasively' and CP 'that their offer should be rejected' cannot be coordinated by the conjunction 'or' because only constituents which belong to the same phrasal category can be coordinated. Sentence (iii) is grammatical because CP 'that he was insulted' can be in the focus position of a *wh*-cleft sentence.

07   'Korean' in (i) should be interpreted as language and 'Korean' in (ii) as nationality. In (i) 'linguistics' is a complement and it can be conjoined by another complement 'Korean'; coordination is possible when two constituents share the same type of syntactic function. In (ii) the noun 'professor' can be replaced by 'one' when it is modified by an adjunct; 'Korean' is an adjunct.

08   ① VP-ellipsis ② Head Movement

09   noun

Sentence (ii) is ungrammatical. It violates Subjacency because the *wh*-phrase 'which actress' crosses over two bounding nodes, the NP node 'a picture of ' and the TP node in the main clause. Crossing over more than one bounding node in one cycle of movement would result in ungrammaticality.

10   First, in <B> the structurally unavailable reading is (3b) and the ungrammatical sentence is (4a). Second, in (4a), in tree diagrams the sentence adverb 'surely' which adjoins to the S node cannot occur between the word 'not' which merges at SpecVP and the V-bar 'break his promise'; the adverb 'surely' ends up crossing the VP branch to adjoin to the S node, violating the NCB constraint.

11   ① preposition ② adverb

Chapter **04** Verb Complements

01
(1) agreement

(2) The NP object following the verb 'tell' should carry a [+human] ([+animal]) feature.

(3) The verb 'believe' takes one complement (NP+*to*-infinitive) and the non-referential 'there' occurs in the subject position of the *to*-infinitive clause. On the other hand, the verb 'tell' takes two complements: one NP and the other *to*-infinitive clause. The NP complement should be [+animal] object of the main verb 'tell'. In (6) the nonreferential 'there' which should be in the subject position occurs in the object position, which leads to an ungrammaticality.

---

02 ②

---

03 ②

Chapter 05 Binding Theory / Relative Clauses / Complementizers

01   ③

---

02   clause

---

03   If the VP structure (4) in <A> fits (ii) in <B>, '*each other*' occurs in the specifier position of VP and '*the boys*' appears in the complement position of the V'. In this case, according to the definition of the c-command in <A>, the antecedent '*the boys*' cannot c-command its anaphor '*each other*'. This fact can explain the ungrammaticality of the sentence (ii) in <B>. On the other hand, if the VP structure (3) is chosen, '*the boys*' can c-command '*each other*' and then the ungrammaticality of the sentence (ii) in <B> cannot be explained.

---

04   **Version 1**
In (1), the that-clause functions as a noun complement. The complementizer 'that' has no function in its own clause, and the embedded clause is complete without 'that'. In (2), however, the that-clause functions as an adjectival adjunct. The relative 'that' has the function of direct object in its own clause, and hence the embedded clause is not complete without the relative. (The relative pronoun 'which' can substitute for 'that' in this case but not in the sentences in (1).)

Version 2
The that clause in (1) is a noun complement. The complementizer *that* cannot be omitted. However, the *that* clause in (2) is an adjectival (relative clause) adjunct. Also the complementizer that can be omitted.

05

Restrictive and nonrestrictive relative clauses differ from each other in terms of punctuation and prosodic features. **First of all**, while restrictive relative clauses must not be separated from their head noun (antecedent) by commas, nonrestrictive relative clauses have commas around them, being separated from their head noun. With the respect of prosodic features, they show different intonation pattern. To be specific, restrictive relative clauses do not have a special intonation pattern. On the other hand, nonrestrictive relative clauses are marked by pauses and reflect a rising and falling intonation pattern at the antecedent noun.

Second, the two pictures A and B of (2) can be described with a sentence as follows: "The girls, who are wearing a skirt, are dancing" refers to Picture-A and "The girls who are wearing a skirt are dancing" indicates Picture-B. In Picture-A, the girls who are dancing do not need to be identified by a restrictive relative clause because all the girls (five girls) are dancing. However, a restrictive relative clause is needed to identify its head noun (which girls (three girls) the speaker refers to) in Picture-B.

Third, in <B>, 1, 2, 5, 6 (and 8) are nonrestrictive modifications for the following reasons. First, 1 is nonrestrictive because the antecedent "Ted Baker" is a proper noun. Restrictive relative clauses cannot modify a proper head noun. 2, 5, and 6 can be proven to be nonrestrictive in that they provide additional information about their antecedent noun which have already been identified and do not play any role in identifying their head noun reference. (Last, in 8, "the chief of the island" is supposed to be the only one in the island, so it also functions to add information.)

06

① the object of the omitted preposition
② the object of the verb

07

(1) Ungrammatical sentence(s) : (b), (d), (f), (h), (j)

	whether	if
(2) Grammatical Category	a wh-phrase	complementizer
(3) Syntactic Evidence	It can appear with a to-infinitive. The conjunction 'or (not)' can follow it. It can be the object of preposition.	It cannot occur with a to-infinitive, or with a preposition. The conjunction 'or (not)' cannot immediately follow it.

08   Sentence (4) and sentence (5) can be conjoined with the coordinate conjunction but as in sentence (6). Sentence (4) has the status of CP because main clauses lacking an overt complementizer are CP constituents. Sentence (5) has also the status of CP because main clauses containing an inverted auxiliary (here should) are CP constituents. Therefore, the given two sentences can be conjoined because they belong to the same grammatical category, CP.

Chapter 06 Case Theory / Theta Roles / Ambiguity

01
- Ungrammatical sentences : (a), (d)
- Reason:

  Version 1 In <B>, the sentences (a) and (d) are ungrammatical because they violate the case filter.

  Version 2 In (a) the NP Mary is not case-assigned, and in (d) the NP John is not case-assigned.

02   ③

03   ① Instrument
            ② Theme

04   Sentence (5) in <B> is syntactically well-formed. The matrix subject 'Tom' originates in the subject position of the lowest embedded clause and is assigned a theta role by the verb phrase brag about 'himself' (or the verb brag). In this position, the reflexive pronoun (or the anaphor) 'himself' can be bound by its antecedent 'Tom' in its binding domain, the smallest clause; thus, it does not violate the binding condition. Then 'Tom' in the subject of the lowest embedded clause moves to the matrix subject position. This movement does not violate any movement constraint because 'Tom' does not cross any subject.

05   (1) d
            (2) b

06   ①

07

Version 1

The sources of the ambiguity of the sentence in <B> are due to different structures and homonymy. First, the word "ring" is homonymy and has two different meanings. As a noun, it means a piece of jewelry and as a (intransitive) verb, 'to ring'. Second, the structural ambiguity occurs along with this homonymy. Two constructions are as follows: (1) a verb (saw) + NP (John's nose's ring), and (2) a verb (saw) + NP (John's nose) + bare-infinitive (ring). These lead to two interpretations. One reading is "Mary saw John, wearing a nose ring", and the other reading is "Mary saw John's nose ring like a bell."

Version 2

The sources of the ambiguity are differing structures and homonymy. In the structure ambiguity, 'John's nose ring' can be a noun object of the main verb 'saw' and the one reading is 'Mary saw the nose ring which John wore'. And the other reading is 'Mary saw John, and 'John's nose was ringing.' Because 'John's nose' and 'ring' can be divided into a noun and a verb. In terms of homonymy, 'ring' as a noun can be interpreted as a piece of jewelry and as a verb, 'to ring'.

08

(i) has the embedded reading. The locational adverbial 'in any room' can modify only the embedded predicate 'sing' because the NPI 'any' must be c-commanded by the negation 'not'. (If it modifies the matrix predicate 'said', 'any' can not be c-commanded by the negation 'not'.) (ii) has both readings. The adverbial 'in any room' can modify either the matrix predicate 'say' or the embedded predicate 'sang' because sentence (ii) observes the c-command condition in both readings.

Part 02 Grammar

본문 p.198

Chapter 01 School Grammar

01 **Version 1** The sentences (2) and (3) are ungrammatical. The stem in (2) contains the auxiliary verb 'had'. In the corresponding tag question, the same auxiliary verb is placed in the tag but in its negative form (hadn't). In contrast, the stem in (3) the verb 'had' is a main verb. If the stem in a tag question contains a main verb, then 'do' appears in the tag but in its negative form (didn't).

Version 2 (2) and (3) are ungrammatical because the wrong auxiliary is used in the tag. In (1) and (2) the auxiliary is 'had' and the auxiliary 'had' should be used in the tag. In contrast, in (3) and (4) the verb 'had' is a main verb and the auxiliary 'do' should be used in the tag.

02 (1) ① ④ ⑦ → prefer NP to NP
(2) ② ⑥ ⑧ → prefer gerundive clause to gerundive clause
(3) ③ ⑤ ⑨ → prefer to-infinitive clause rather than bare infinitive clause

03

Ungrammatical Parts	Your Corrections
will you catch a cold	you will catch a cold
should listen	should have listened

04 (1) 비문법적인 문장: (c)
(2) 문법적인 문장: The doctor examined the patient, and then she picked up the telephone.

05 (1) arrived → arriving
(2) asking → asked
(3) arranging → arranged

06
    (1) widely → wide
    (2) highly → high
    (3) late → lately

07
    ① There's (There is) a lot of (lots of) selfish people who(m)
    ② converse with
    ③ a lot of (lots of) selfish people you'd hesitate to talk with
    ④ a lot of (lots of) selfish guys you'd hesitate to talk with

08
    ① to
    ② Dr. Manning's
    ③ the existence of bacteria

09
    ⑤

10
Stative verbs and dynamic verbs are different from each other with respect to their meaning. Stative verbs like *know* have stative senses when they refer to a single unbroken state of affairs. Dynamic verbs like *learn*, on the other hand, are related to action, activity, and to temporary or changeable conditions. They also behave differently in terms of manner adverbs, progressives and imperatives. First, dynamic verbs can be used with manner adverbs such as *carefully*, but stative verbs cannot. For example, stative verb like *know* cannot be used with manner verb: **I know the man carefully*. In contrast, dynamic verb such as learn can be used with a manner adverb: *John learned the topic very carefully*. Second, Stative verbs generally cannot occur in the imperative and progressive, but dynamic verb senses can. For example, **Know how to swim* and **I am knowing how to swim* are not permissible, but *Learn how to swim* and *I am learning how to swim* are acceptable. All these phenomena are based on the semantic difference and usage between stative and dynamic verbs.

11 ②

12 The two types of verbs differ in terms of the possibility of a resultative reading. Verbs like *fall* and *drop* in the above extract are possible in resultative constructions: *Mary dropped dead* and *John fell sick*. The resultative words *dead* and *sick* denote the state achieved by the human referents *Mary* and *John* as a result of the action denoted by the verbs *dropped* and *fell*. In contrast, verbs like *work* and *swim* cannot have such resultative sentences: **Mary worked sick* and **John swam tired*.

Student B's utterance *It was dropped* in the extract above is not possible if we assume that it is a passive sentence derived from the transitive verb *drop*. The reason is as follows: if the sentence *It was dropped* is a passive sentence derived from its active counterpart sentence *Someone dropped it*, then the object pronoun *it* refers to *the birth rate in Korea*, which means that *someone dropped the birth rate in Korea*. In this sentence, the birth rate cannot be dropped by someone or an agent. Birth rate cannot rise or drop by someone's action. The Noun Phrase *birth rate* must be used as a subject in a purely intransitive sentence not in a passivized sentence. So the sentence *The birth rate dropped* is acceptable but its passivized one *The birth rate (It) was dropped* is not.

13 ①

14 ⑤

15 Version 1

In (3a) and (3b), the verb 'painted' (paint) belongs to activities and this verb does not have an inherent terminal point. For-phrases are most natural in situations in which such endpoints do not exist. By contrast, in-phrases are most acceptable in situations in which natural endpoints exist. <u>On the other hand, the verb 'painted' in (3c) and (3d) comes together with both 'for two weeks' and 'in two weeks'. In this case,</u> in (3c), when the activity verb 'painted' is used with 'for two weeks', the completion of painting is not assumed because the verb has no terminal point. However, in (3d), the action of painting is completed when the verb takes in-adverbial such as 'in two weeks'.

Paraphrasing the underlined part

The meaning is different between (3c) and (3d) when the given verb is used with for-adverbials and in-adverbials.

Version 2

'Paint' means that the agent's drawing activity when used as an intransitive verb, so 'for two weeks' is acceptable, but 'in two weeks' is not, since it has no terminal point. In other words, the activity does not show change of state. On the other hand, paint of (3c) and (3d) comes together with both 'for two weeks' and 'in two weeks'. In (3c) when the verb is used with 'for two weeks' the completion of painting is not assumed (assured). On the other hand, in (3d) when it is used with 'in two weeks' the action of painting is completed.

16　　　①

17　　　③

18　　　The ungrammatical sentence found in this dialogue is, 'I know it is tough that other players defeat her.' The adjective 'tough' unlike 'likely' cannot be used in the 'it is adjective that subject + verb' structure but in the 'it is adjective (for + NP) to infinitive' structure. Adjectives such as 'easy, difficult, dangerous, necessary, natural, clear' can be used in this structure. The sentence should be corrected to: I know that it is tough for other players to defeat her.

In sentences (1a) and (2a), the problem lies in where the relevant information is placed. In wh-questions, the answers must occur at the beginning of the sentence. In the question preceding sentence (1b), Tom asks Mary, "Who do you think is going to win?" Sentence (1b) provides the most natural response because it places the new information (corresponding answer to the question 'who') in the beginning of the sentence, in this case placing 'Susan' at the front of the sentence. Likewise in the question preceding (2b), Tom asks Mary, "Do you know where the final will be?" The most natural answer is to state 'Central Stadium' (corresponding answer to the question 'where') in the front of the sentence instead of structuring it in the back as seen in (2a). Answering in the manner of (2a) is very unnatural.

In a comparison of the two sentences (4a) and (4b), containing tag questions, the problem lies in the tag questions. Syntactically, according to a deep structure analysis view point, the 'here' in sentence (3b) and (4b) is not in a subject position but in an adverbial position. In tag questions, only a subject should come after an auxiliary verb. In the case of (4a), 'there' is a nonreferential expletive and is positioned in the subject position, which means that it can appear in a tag-question, as in (4a). Semantically, in a tag question, the subject which follows after the auxiliary verb should be a functional word (pronoun). 'here' in (4b) is a content word having a lexical meaning whereas 'there' in the tag question in (4a) is a functional word. Phonologically, nonreferential 'there' should not have a stress because it is a function word but the adverb 'here' can have a stress because it is a content word.

19   ③

20   The underlined adverb, 'rarely' in (i) belongs to a *usually* type and the adverb 'slowly' in (ii) belongs to a *carefully* type. 'rarely' can represent the two paraphrases as follows: It is rare that John talks with philosophers, and It is rarely the case that John talks with philosophers. However, 'slowly' cannot be paraphrased like the followings: *It is slow that the fish swims, and *It is slowly the case that the fish swims.

21   **Version 1** In <B>, (ia) is telic, while (ib) is atelic. With the accomplishment in (iib), the adverbial is ambiguous. On one reading, the sentence means that the task of eating the pizza will require five minutes from start to finish. On the other reading, the sentence means that the eating of the pizza is scheduled to begin five minutes after utterance time.

Version 2 In <B>, (ia) is telic, while (ib) is atelic. The sentence in (iib) is ambiguous and has two readings. The first reading is a (telic) event of duration interpretation, 'John will finish eating the pizza within five minutes.' And the second reading is an (atelic) event of delay interpretation: 'John will eat the pizza after five minutes.'

22　The associative use in <A> accounts for the use of the definite articles in the sentence <B>. The speaker assumes that the listener knows that a taxi must have a driver and that it usually has passengers; therefore, a definite article comes before both *driver* and *passengers*.

23　The two sentences of incorrect usages of the auxiliary will are as follows: *I'll be excited when the conference will begin* and *I'll help you until you will finish it*. This is because in adverbial time clauses the simple present tense should be used instead of the auxiliary *will* to express future time.

24　The two attributive-only adjectives in <B> are 'absolute' and 'urban'. The adjective 'absolute' belongs to Adjectives of Degree and the adjective 'urban' belongs to Associative Adjectives.

25　'married' in (i) is a verb, while 'married' in (ii) is an adjective. Sentence (ii) containing the adjective 'married' shows two properties of an adjective. First, since the adjective is a non-gradable adjective, it cannot be modified by a degree modifier as in '*They were very married until last Christmas'. Second, the verb 'be' can be replaced with the verb 'remain' followed by the adjective 'married' as in 'They remained married until last Christmas.'

26　Sentence (i) is grammatical. In (i) the intransitive verb 'came' can undergo 'locative inversion'. Sentence (ii) is ungrammatical. In (ii) the transitive verb 'lived' cannot undergo 'locative inversion'.

27　First, the phrasal coordination in (4b) shows different truth conditions from the clausal coordination. The appropriate clausal coordination is as follows: [The last objection concerned the cost] and [the most telling objection concerned the cost]. Second, under the condition where there are two different objections, the clausal coordination is true, but the phrasal coordination in (4b) is false. Sentence (4b) is true when there is only one objection. Therefore, they do not share the same truth conditions.

Part 03 Phonetics and Phonology

본문 p.245

Chapter 01 Phonemes and Their Allophones

01   minimal pairs (or minimal sets)

02   ① allophone
             ② onset

03   ⑤

04   ②

05   (1) phoneme
             (2) / p /

06   free variation

Chapter 02 Segmental Classification and Phonological Features

01 sonorant

---

02 affricate

---

03 /æ/

---

04 sonorant, obstruent

---

05 velars

---

06 [coronal]

---

07 **Version 1** Requirement 2 : The suffix -al must be added to the verb base having a [+anterior] consonant as a coda of the final syllable.

Requirement 3 : The suffix -al must be attached to the verb base ending in a [−sonorant] sound preceded by a [+sonorant] sound.

Version 2 Requirement 2 : If the final syllable of the verb it attaches to has a single coda segment, the segment has a [+anterior] feature.

Requirement 3 : If the final syllable of the verb it attaches to has two coda segments, the first segment has a [+sonorant] feature while the second has a [−sonorant] feature.

---

08 ③

---

09 The plural suffix '-s' is pronounced as [əz] after the stem-final sibilants.

Chapter 03 Phonological Rules

01   (a) [-sonorant] (b) [+consonantal]

The syllabic consonant [ŋ] is always homorganic with the preceding consonant because there are no instances of non-homorganicity so far as the syllabic [ŋ] is concerned; it only occurs after velar stops ([k] and [g]) when the syllabic [n] assimilates to the place of articulation of the preceding velar stops.

02   coronal

03   The two words where the underlined /oʊ/ is realized as [o] are 'soldier' in (b) and 'poultry' in (d). The revised generalization is as follows: /oʊ/ is realized as [o] when it is immediately followed by /l/ within the same morpheme (in the same stem).

04   The phonological process in (1) is assimilation, and that in (2) is dissimilation. The generalization is that the adjectival suffix '-al' is realized as the allomorph '-ar' when the final consonant of the base is [+lateral], whereas it is realized as the allomorph '-al' when the final consonant of the base is [−lateral].

05   The sound rule that changes the pronunciation of (i) is palatalization. The alveolar stop /d/ becomes the palatoalveolar [dʒ] when followed by a word that starts with the palatal glide /j/. The phenomenon that causes S1's confusion in (ii) is 'Spelling Pronunciation'. S1 mispronounces the plural form of 'fleas' as [flis] rather than [fliz] because of its spelling.

06   First, a dark 'l' appears before front vowels and a more velarized darker 'l' appears before back vowels. Second, the alveolar lateral becomes a high back lax vowel immediately after a vowel and it is deleted before a labial consonant.

07   ① stressed   ② unstressed

08   A glide is inserted between two vowels when the first is a high vowel or a diphthong. The palatal glide /j/ is inserted between the two vowels when the preceding vowel is a high front vowel or a diphthong with a final high front vowel, /aɪ/ or /ɔɪ/. The velar glide /w/ is inserted when the preceding vowel is a high back vowel or a diphthong with a final high back vowel, /aʊ/ or /oʊ/.

09   As shown in the data given in (1) and (3), schwa deletion occurs in fast speech when a schwa is preceded by a stressed vowel and followed by another schwa.

10   The words that do not belong to the underlined rule in <A> are 'riddle', 'saddle', 'battle', 'monitor', 'humanity', and 'comedy'. These words are divided into two groups: 'riddle, saddle, battle' and 'monitor, humanity, comedy'. The rule for the first group is that alveolar stops /t/ and /d/ are flapped when they occur between a stressed vowel and syllabic liquid /l/, and the rule for the second group is that flapping occurs between two unstressed vowels.

11   In American English, /j/ **cannot** follow alveolar obstruent consonants /t, d, s, z/, regardless of stress placement, as in (1b) and (2b). On the other hand, /j/ **cannot** follow alveolar sonorant consonants /n, l/ if it is in a stressed syllable, but /j/ **can** follow them if it is in an unstressed syllable, as in (1b) and (3).

12   ④

13   ④

14   ②

15   ③

16   (a) green car (1)   (b) send Susan (3)   (c) bit of (2)   (d) met Bob (1)

17   (1) Hi, would you do me a favor?
(2) Oh, did you?
(3) Why don't you come back tomorrow?

Chapter **04** Syllables and Phonotactics

01   First, in \<B> the two nonsense words are (b) rviss and (d) nkob. Second, the one phonological generalization is that in English the words with simple onset and complex onset (or onset clusters) have sonority increasing gradually towards the peak of the syllable (or the nucleus).

---

02   onset

---

03   rhyme (or rime)

---

04   ②

---

05   ②

---

06   (1) (b), (e)
        (2) (a), (c)

Chapter 05 Stress

01　① penultimate　② trochaic

The phonological generalization is that the noun-forming suffix '-al' can attach to the verb stem that has the ultimate stress (or has the primary stress on the ultimate syllable).

02　The two words are (b) disentangle and (c) accountability. Voiceless stops are aspirated only if they are the first segment in a trochaic foot (or occur in the initial position of a trochaic foot).

03　The two words where [ə] can be deleted in fast speech are 'chocolate' in (b) and 'nationalize' in (c). The foot structure that is most preferred in fast speech is a foot where a stressed syllable is followed by one stressless syllable.

04　① stress-shifting

　　② stress-neutral

05　⑤

06　(1)−① (b), (g)

　　(1)−② (d), (e)

　　(2)−① (a), (h)

　　(2)−② (c), (f)

07　① a long vowel

　　② a diphthong

　　③ multiple consonants

08　**Version 1**　(1) The word-initial consonants of function words are deleted.

　　　　　　　　(2) The vowels of function words are reduced to schwa.

　　　　　　　　(3) The word-final consonants of function words are deleted.

　　Version 2　(1) Consonants are deleted as in 'her' [ər].

　　　　　　　　(2) Vowels are weakened to [ə].

　　　　　　　　(3) Consonant cluster simplification occurs as in changing of [nd] to [n].

09　6 feet

Chapter 06 Intonation

01   ④

---

02   ① (3) | Tom | cooked | DINer?

이유: Kelly is reacting with surprise or disbelief to the information just received. In fact, Tom has never even boiled an egg before, but he cooked dinner for his mother. It was quite amazing to Kelly, so she is reacting to Tom's event with surprise or disbelief.

---

03   Peter as well as some other person met Jennifer in his office.

---

04   rude (or impolite)

Part 04 Morphology

Chapter 01 Morphology

01   ① conversion ② derivation

02   suffix (or suffixes)

03   ④

04   ③

05   ① semantic propeties   ② (b)   ③ (c)   ④ (a)

06   (1) 문법범주 : ① adjective   ② verb
           단어의 의미 : not able to be buttoned
       (2) 문법범주 : ③ verb   ④ verb
           단어의 의미 : able to be unbuttoned

07   (1) (d)   (2) (f)   (3) (c)

08   abstracten, greenen, bluen

09   (1) re-   (2) use   (3) -able   (4) reuse

10   (1) conversion (functional shift, zero derivation)
       (2) waters/watered the plants every day.

508   Answer Key

Part 05 Semantics and Pragmatics

Chapter **01** Semantics

01

Version 1

One interpretation of sentence (3) is that Mary visited none of the cities that Tom visited. In this case, *every city (that Tom visited)* can have a wide scope over the verb *refused*, having the negative meaning. The other interpretation is that Mary visited some of the cities that Tom visited, but not all of the cities. In terms of scope interaction, the verb *refused* can have a wide scope over *every city (that Tom visited)*.

Version 2

The first meaning that the sentence (3) can have is that Mary wanted to visit some, not all, cities that Tom visited. The second meaning is that Mary wanted to visit no cities that Tom visited. The negative meaning of *refused* can have a wide scope over *every city that Tom visited*, and *every city that Tom visited*, can have a wide scope over the negative meaning of *refused*.

02

The first sentence of (i) in <B> describes a telic event, but the second sentence describes an atelic event. The sentence (ii-b) *John will eat the pizza in five minutes* in <B> is ambiguous because, in the sentence, the *in* adverbial has the event duration interpretation or the event delay interpretation. According to the passage <B>, the *in* adverbial of sentences with future tense are ambiguous when they have the meaning of a telic event.

03

⑤

04

The situations described by the sentences of *for two weeks* in [A] are activities because they have no terminal point. On the other hand, the situations described by the sentences of *in two weeks* in [A] are accomplishments because they have an inherent terminal point. For the meaning of time duration, we use *for* adverbials in the case of activities, and *in* adverbials in the case of accomplishments.
If the type of situation described by the predicate in (3a) and (3b) is an activity, we cannot use the expression *in two weeks* for these sentences. In fact, the situation type of these sentences is an activity, and therefore the sentence in (3b) is ungrammatical.

On the other hand, if the type of situation described by the predicate in (3c) and (3d) is an accomplishment, we can use the adverbial expression *in two weeks*, but we cannot use the adverbial expression *for two weeks*. In the literal meaning of the predicate, we can use the adverbial *in two weeks* as in (3d), but we cannot use the adverbial *for two weeks* as in (3c). However, If the predicate in (3c) has a figurative meaning and the situation type of the sentence (3c) is accomplishment, we can use the expression *for two weeks*. The sentence (3c), therefore, does not have a literal meaning, but has a figurative meaning. The predicate *painted the wall* in (3c), for example, means 'described the wall' or 'talked about the wall'.

05   ④

06   The words long and short are gradable antonyms. The word long in (a) is used in an unmarked way, but the word short in (b) is used in a marked way. The word long represents the meaning of 'length,' but the word short represents the meaning of 'shortness.'

07
- 기호: (a), (d), (e)
- 전제를 암시해 주는 단어: angry, surprised, significant

08   (1) degradation   (2) reduction   (3) extension

09   The first clause *Laura managed to answer the question* implies the complement proposition 'Laura answered the question' is true. The second clause also says *Laura answered the question*. The two clauses are, therefore, redundant. In the same sentence, two clauses linked with a conjunction are tautological, and so the sentence is unnatural.

Chapter 02 Pragmatics

01

First, the word 'this' belongs to 'Cataphoric words' as shown in "Oh, wait, on her jacket, I found this. There is a letter P on it." Here, 'this' refers to 'a letter P (on it)' that is used later in the conversation. Second, the phrase 'sort of' belongs to 'Hedges' as shown in "He is in a blue coat. It is sort of neat." Here, 'sort of' is used not to express the truth of a statement categorically.

02

proxemics

03

① locutionary act (or speech act)
② socio-linguistic (or sociolinguistic)

04

④

05

④

06

①

07

②

08

① request
② hearer's
③ Would it be convenient for you to do this?

09   ① Do you know the land where the lemon trees bloom?
           ② he is a German officer

---

10   (1) coherent
           (2) lexical
           (3) cohesive
           (4) extratextual

---

11   ①

---

12   Arnold will infer from the Betty's answer depends upon the mutually known context.

---

13   getting someone to do something without saying anything at all

---

14   (1) invitation (request)
           (2) discourse
           (3) illocutionary
           (4) coherence

Part 06 Sociolinguistics

Chapter 01 Sociolinguistics

01
euphemism

02
(1) People have not taken their seat yet.

(2) You will agree that it is the best solution to use the plural forms *they*, *them* and *their* as singular unisex words because it is the most popular choice among speakers of English including Antonia Byatt and Bryan Magee.

Mentor Linguistics

멘토영어학
기출분석

초판인쇄 | 2023. 5. 10. **초판발행** | 2023. 5. 15.
편저자 | 앤드류채 **발행인** | 박 용 **발행처** | (주)박문각출판
표지디자인 | 박문각 디자인팀 **등록** | 2015년 4월 29일 제2015-000104호
주소 | 06654 서울특별시 서초구 효령로 283 서경 B/D **팩스** | (02)584-2927
전화 | 교재 문의 (02)6466-7202, 동영상 문의 (02)6466-7201

저자와의
협의하에
인지생략

ISBN 979-11-6987-255-3
정가 34,000원